ROUTLEDGE LIBRARY EDITIONS:
SOVIET POLITICS

Volume 21

SOVIET SUCCESS

SOVIET SUCCESS

An Account of
Soviet Russia Today

HEWLETT JOHNSON

Routledge
Taylor & Francis Group

LONDON AND NEW YORK

First published in 1947 by Hutchinson & Co. (Publishers) Ltd

This edition first published in 2024
by Routledge
4 Park Square, Milton Park, Abingdon, Oxon OX14 4RN

and by Routledge
605 Third Avenue, New York, NY 10158

Routledge is an imprint of the Taylor & Francis Group, an informa business

British Library Cataloguing in Publication Data
A catalogue record for this book is available from the British Library

ISBN: 978-1-032-67165-9 (Set)
ISBN: 978-1-032-67778-1 (Volume 21) (hbk)
ISBN: 978-1-032-67780-4 (Volume 21) (pbk)
ISBN: 978-1-032-67779-8 (Volume 21) (ebk)

DOI: 10.4324/9781032677798

Publisher's Note
The publisher has gone to great lengths to ensure the quality of this reprint but
points out that some imperfections in the original copies may be apparent.

Disclaimer
The publisher has made every effort to trace copyright holders and would
welcome correspondence from those they have been unable to trace.

SOVIET SUCCESS

by

The Very Reverend
HEWLETT JOHNSON,
M.A., B.Sc., D.D.,
DEAN OF CANTERBURY

With 16 Illustrations

HUTCHINSON & CO. (Publishers) LTD

London   New York   Melbourne   Sydney   Cape Town

To Nowell Mary my wife, to Mary Kezia and Helene Keren my daughters, to Inna Koulakofskaya and Tamara Solovieff my Soviet young friends and to progressive womanhood, past and present, everywhere, I dedicate this book.

Printed in Great Britain at
The Fleet Street Press
East Harding St., EC4

CONTENTS

LIST OF ILLUSTRATIONS

FOREWORD

THIS is the third of a trilogy of books. The first, *The Socialist Sixth of the World*, described, in its approaching maturity, a new experiment in corporate living. The second, *Soviet Strength*, was written whilst that same experiment, not yet completed, was subjected to the supreme test of war. This third book, *Soviet Success*, is written when the Soviet Union has emerged from the trial, bruised and wounded, but resilient, triumphant and confident and in spite of all hindrances, blunders and mistakes thrusts on, as it believes, to a still more hopeful future.

Soviet Russia is a new force in the world. This present book, springing from the experience of a prolonged and in some respects perhaps unique personal visit north, south, east and west in which no doors were shut and no interviews denied, and continued through close subsequent study of contemporary movements in Russia, aims at describing more fully and in greater detail the constitution and spirit of a new civilization which embraces many nationalities and groupings of peoples, studying the individuals which the Soviet Union produces; their nurture, and the moral, scientific and economic bases on which, on its material side, it all rests. The book deals with many and various aspects of Soviet civilian life and concludes with a description, based on first-hand investigation in Poland and Czechoslovakia in their earliest post-war moments, of Russia in relation to her immediate neighbours and to the outer world in general.

BOOK I

JOURNEY TO RUSSIA

ANOTHER book on Russia? Why?

Because Russia is a growing entity. Because Russia changes and develops from day to day. Because there is more to learn in Russia, and from Russia, than the West either knows or heeds.

Russia, consequent upon the war, stands forth with America as a twin world power greater than all the rest: "the new colossus," Marshal Smuts rightly calls her. Mutual understanding between Russia and the Western World is of prime importance in the interest of world peace and prosperity.

Also in the interest of wise social and economic action, for Russia, having achieved and practised socialism on a vast scale over a sixth of the world and among some 170 nationalities and groups, affords an example well worthy of study both by those who welcome socialist organisation of society and by those who dread it. Russia's example reveals lines of approach and danger points; what to pursue and what to shun. Mutual and widespread lack of knowledge—Russia of us and we of Russia—demands not less books but more if they are based upon wide extension of contacts.

My own claim to write another book, or indeed to write on Russia at all, rests upon opportunities and advantages which, coming my way, gave me what measure of equipment I may happen to possess. My mother inspired me with the curiosity which leads to travel, exploration and research.

Manchester University, which gave me my science degree, taught me to observe. Life in a Manchester workshop, with a straitened purse, taught me to experience industrial processes as the worker experiences them. At a later stage as practising engineer in businesses small and great, I learnt to view industrial life through the more favourable eyes of an industrial employer. To my parents, to Oxford, and to the Christian ministry I owe such sensitiveness as I possess to spiritual and moral forces, with an eye to all that fosters human welfare. The office of Dean, first in Manchester, then in Canterbury, provided entrances and opportunities denied to all but few. Books many and varied, hostile and friendly, together with the friendship of men with life-long study of world affairs in general and Russia in particular, places me under a debt impossible to repay and provides an equipment otherwise unobtainable.

Outstanding among these friendships is that of Mr. A. T. D'Eye
who, with an interesting Balliol career behind him, has been a close
student of world affairs since the days when he fought in world war
one and had, on recovery from the casualty of war, devoted himself ·
to the single-minded service of humanity as Oxford University
Extension Lecturer in Kent. At Mr. D'Eye's original suggestion we
jointly launched the Russian Medical Aid Fund, which not only sent
a million and a quarter pounds in goods and kind to medical relief
in Russia but, forging lasting links between British and Russian workers,
spreading broadcast, by means of literature and mass meetings in
town and country alike, knowledge of Russian people and Russian
ways, has awakened an admiration for Russian achievement in peace
and war which outlasts and will outlast all efforts now being made to
thrust a wedge between the Soviet peoples and ourselves.

Mr. D'Eye accompanied me to Post-War Russia, Poland and
Czechoslovakia. He himself wrote a vivid and interesting story of
the journey immediately upon our return, and has been kind enough
to read the manuscript of my story of journey and subsequent
investigations.

Twenty-five years of close and sympathetic study of Russia, first
as the scene of the "Great Experiment"—taking the chair as early as
1917 for Mr. Bertrand Russell at a Welcome-to-Soviet-Russia meeting
in Manchester—and subsequently as the home of what at length has
become the "Great Achievement", led to innumerable friendships
with the responsive and warm-hearted Soviet people, giving me contacts which enabled me during three months of wide travel and
research to see more of Post-War Russia itself than other men have
seen in as many or far more years.

Deep-rooted suspicions and radical misunderstandings on both
sides still persist and books such as this are aimed at removing them.
The same simple words mean different things to Russians and to us.
The word press, for example, means to our rulers primarily an organ
of information; to Russia's rulers an organ of education. Freedom
means to us primarily the right to express our preferences in speech
or print, freedom to choose our Parliamentary representatives;
freedom, that is, from oppressions by our brother man. To Russians
it means primarily the right to food, to work, to education, to medical
assistance and to a direct and responsible voice in the organisation
of daily industrial productive life and the conduct of local and social
affairs: freedom mainly against hardships of nature and inefficient
organisation of life.

Both peoples again, theirs and ours, are victims of past history.
Twenty-five years of foreign hostility, beginning with savage inter-

vention at the close of world war one; backwardness of the Tsarist heritage; enforced isolation from the whole outer world; and finally the German assault with appalling loss of Russian lives and destruction of Russian property reckoned at two-thirds of the fruit of her Five-Year Plans: these things and many more are items to be borne in mind in estimating Russia's present outlook and policy.

Nor must we forget the attacks, direct and indirect, through the whole chain of girdling countries contiguous to Russia, from Poland to Persia and on to Japan, that were launched after world war one against the Soviet Union by the armed forces of nine nations, Britain chiefest among them. The present rulers of Russia fought then in defence of the Soviet order. The crucial battles culminated then, as some two decades later, at Stalingrad, with Stalin himself, both then and now, as its defender.

The brief honeymoon during the war years had proved, as I predicted, all too short for real appreciation or radical removal of suspicion.

On the other hand, and again to turn to our own country, twenty-five years of misrepresentation of Russia had left deep marks on English thought which the same honeymoon has never wholly dispelled. Press, radio and a spate of books painting the picture of a Russia immoral, dragooned, blatantly irreligious, industrially inefficient and heading for inevitable disintegration and imminent disaster had raised a spectre not easily laid even when during the war, black suddenly became white and praises for Russia reached the skies.

To previous and long fostered misunderstanding of Russia and to an underestimate of Russia's strength, based on an initial dislike of Russian socialism, we owe in large measure that rejection of Russian collaboration and co-operation in the period prior to and after Munich which led along the perilous road of appeasement; which sacrificed Czechoslovakia and landed us at length in war.

"Russia is empty" were the words, as Stalin himself told me, that Gamelin had used to Churchill in reference to Russia's military ability—"words," he added, "based on reports from Poland's rulers."

Ill-founded propaganda had done its work so thoroughly, even with those who had designed and encouraged it, that the cry was raised in authoritative circles, as the Nazis invaded Russia: "The Germans will be in Baku within six weeks."

Stalingrad indeed wrought a decisive change. Russian morale and Russian industry had stood the ultimate stress of war: British and American press accepted the verdict and for the time at least joined in praise of Russia and Russians. A praise which slackened off when danger passed. Criticism then replaced laudation. Hostility raised its head and now spreads over a considerable section of the press. The hostile tide once more runs full spate. Not even during the brief honeymoon had there been any widespread knowledge of the real Russia among the great majority of the people, though knowledge formed a solid core in conscious working-class opinion. Still less to-day is there any real knowledge or deep understanding of Post-War Russia, of her social, civic, industrial, cultural or national life. And drifting from one misunderstanding to another East pairs off from West and war clouds threaten the horizon.

In spite of all, however, people still seek knowledge about Russia, and British people especially are more suspicious now than formerly of the "All-Black" tales. Everywhere, north, south, east and west, in converse and through the post, I am plied with questions which this book, crystallising the results of long study and wide travel through many thousands of miles of Soviet territory, backed up by subsequent, long-continued and close-up study of Russia's day to day life, writings and achievements, seeks to answer.

Here is a brief category of the questions asked:

(1) How much had Russia suffered in the war, and what steps at reconstruction is she taking?

(2) What prospects of speedy recovery and of resumption of those standards of life, material and moral, which gave her the guns, the will, the courage and unity which in Churchill's graphic phrase "tore the guts out of the German war machine" appear over the horizon of Russia's war-stricken landscape?

(3) Is Soviet economy moving away from the earlier socialism and communism and back again to a still earlier capitalism?

(4) What is the present state of Russia's agriculture, industry and trade?

(5) Where does post-war Russia stand with regard to science, to education, to culture? What steps is she taking to build up vigorous physical frames and free spontaneous human minds?

(6) Where does the Soviet Union stand with regard to religion in general and to various forms of institutional religion in particular within its wide domains?

(7) Has the boast "Lenin, the Liberator of the Peoples" been made good? What is Russia's attitude towards the 170 or more nationalities or national groups under the Hammer and Sickle flag?

(8) What is Russia's attitude towards her neighbours and towards us?

These questions and many more—questions as to Soviet trade unions, Legislative Assemblies and the Communist Party; questions as to sex and family; to art, drama, literature, painting and sculpture; to press; to wages, prices, distribution and property, to taxes, to liberty—have been asked and must be answered.

And then the supreme question of all: What type of individual has been produced and is being produced after twenty-nine years of Soviet rule? The ultimate test of any system is the individual it produces. Is Russia producing individuals spontaneous and enthusiastic; men and women of keen initiative, moral, likeable, lovable, ready to unite with others in establishing an integrated community of free and equal individuals?

The answer to these questions involved three months of long journeys, many contacts and hard work, and much subsequent study, reading and reflection. It involved three weeks' intensive study in Moscow at the heart of things as a start, followed by extensive travel northwards to Leningrad, southwards to Stalingrad, still farther southwards to the Republics of Armenia and Georgia and then still farther eastwards to Asiatic Tashkent and Samarkand. The study of Russia's relations to other lands involved preliminary journeys to Poland and Czechoslovakia, border states running along Russia's western frontiers.

Fortune favoured my quest. I travelled where I wished, saw what I wished, met whom I wished. I met Alexei, Patriarch of all Russia; Nicolai, Metropolitan of Kiev, and Gregory, Archbishop of Leningrad, amongst Russian ecclesiastics; I met the Patriarch of the Autonomous Church of Georgia, and the newly elected Catholicos of Armenia. I met Zhidkov, the Head of the newly united Baptist and Evangelical Christians. I met the Head of the Jewish communities and the Head of the Moscow Moslems, and in Tashkent I met and spent a whole day with the chief Imam of all Asiatic Moslems.

Every facility was afforded me for speedy travel. I expressed a wish to go to Leningrad: a plane took me there; to Armenia on a special date and for a special mission: a plane took me there. The same with Stalingrad and Asia: a special plane, manned by the men who flew Molotov to San Francisco, took me there too. Special planes took me to Warsaw, Cracow, and Danzig, now called Gdansk, and also to Prague.

I met educationalists, dramatists, artists, scientists, architects: Gerassimov and Korin the painters, Madame Mukina the sculptures, Kapitza the expert on nuclear energy; Tsitzin, who produces perennial wheat; Professor Alexandrov, who built the Dnieper Dam; Iofan, who planned the Palace of the Soviets, the world's largest building,

and Yudin, the world-famous Moscow surgeon. I met writers like
Ilya Ehrenberg and dancers like Ulanova. I met Academicians and
Governors in Armenia, Georgia and Uzbekistan. I met the scientists
who grow coloured cotton in Tashkent. I met peasants and artisans
of many nationalities. I met Shvernik, now chairman of the Presidium
of the Supreme Soviet. I met Molotov. I met Stalin. I am told that
few ever saw more or travelled farther than I in three months, and
that at a time when travel and contacts were eagerly sought and hard
to procure.

My first book, *The Socialist Sixth of the World*, was written in the
belief that we were witnessing in Russia the dawn of a new era in
world affairs. I was aware, and stated so in my preface, of dark
patches in Soviet past history; aware too that far outweighing the
evil was the great creative element which I attempted to describe.
Dark patches are the monopoly of no single land. The parliament
which gave us the liberties which we cherish to-day, as Trevelyan
says, cut off the head of its King.

This faith was justified. *Soviet Strength*, my second book, was written
when the Soviet Union had passed, and passed triumphantly, through
the stern task of totalitarian war. A message to America entitled
"Final victory can never be in doubt," written on 30th June, 1941,
eight days after Hitler's unprovoked attack, concluded with these
words: "I do not believe that the Nazi military machine, despite all
the ruthless efficiency and perfection it has shown, will sweep away
the Red Army as the French and British, Polish, Dutch, Yugo-Slav
and Greek armies were swept away. Arms and equipment were more
nearly equal.

"I believe eventually it will be the Nazi army that will be sent
reeling back, broken and defeated, to Germany. If so, then a new and
better chapter in the history of the human race opens. For Russia
stands for all that is progressive; for justice and equality between
classes and races; for the ending of exploitation of man by man; for
a juster and nobler economic social order. That is why she has been
so hated. That is why Hitler now attacks her."

That confidence, stated at a moment of almost universal pessimism,
and borne out by victory in war, has suffered no fundamental change
by anything I saw in Russia. The war has left its marks on them as
well as on us. All suffer spiritually as well as physically by war. Who
is not now less sensitive after it to human suffering and wrong? The
tone of our utterances has changed. And the tone of Russia's post-
war utterances also differs frequently from that of Lenin.

Russia's front-line troops naturally suffered spiritual degradation
most of all. Ninety per cent of the tales of ill-conduct in Austria, for

example, are doubtless untrue—as he discovers who tries to track them to source. Yet some are true. Stalin knew it would be so, reminding Benes that men passing to victory through years of hell across 2,000 miles of mutilated land and massacred lives cannot but suffer spiritually. Many men, he said, are bad. War makes bad men worse. In addition, Russia's best troops never set foot in Austria. Russia's losses, even before the last great push, which carried them to Berlin, exceeded ours by fourteen to one. The worst elements, not the best, met ours in Austria and Germany. It is misleading to judge Russia by those who had suffered psychologically most.

But Russia will recover, and recover the more quickly if working in unison with us. Our mutual contributions to the future well-being of the world are complementary. It will be a bad day for Russia, and for us, if her Western doors close. But to keep them open we must understand one another. It is Russia's responsibility to understand us. It is our responsibility to understand Russia, and that leads me to my story.

1 . TRANSPORT IN A FAR-FLUNG LAND

W E entered Russia from the south by way of Cairo, Baghdad and Teheran.

In Cairo we stayed with Bishop Brook-Gwyn, the finest type of Anglican Missionary Bishop. Outspoken too. To a fashionable and official congregation crowding Cairo Cathedral to the doors to celebrate the victory of Alamein he had said, scorning Cairo's war profiteers, "I had rather be a dead soldier in Alamein than a living millionaire in Cairo to-day." Bishop Gwyn spoke of General Wavell's astonishment when conveying to the Egyptian Prime Minister our British sympathy at the loss of 15,000 fellaheen in a disastrous epidemic, he heard the Minister say irritably, "Why do you trouble to come to me over that trifle? Why worry? We don't. There are too many of them anyway!" We had seen the fellaheen and their poverty. I remembered them and the Prime Minister's remark when three months later I saw other oriental towns—Tashkent, for example, or Samarkand.

In Baghdad, another Asiatic town, we moved freely amongst the people, penetrating their highways and byways. Beauty and squalor side by side. Poverty, filth and disease. Children's eyes swarming with flies: trachoma rife, blindness frequent.

I learned from the resident British Army Chaplain many stories of official corruption; of wheat cornered by the authorities in a distant town whilst people starved in Baghdad; and when released, on pressure, the wheat deliberately mixed with dirt to command a better price, though increasing weight and transport cost, and decreasing food value.

The following story illuminates the estimate of womanhood by Baghdad standards. A wealthy Baghdad merchant sought assistance, in his wife's difficult confinement, from a Canadian surgeon, a distinguished gynæcologist, who lived with the chaplain. The surgeon laboured long and successfully; wife and child survived. The bill of £20, sent after consultation with the chaplain, seemed not excessive.

The merchant exclaimed fiercely: "Twenty pounds! You joke! I could buy a better wife for ten."

I visited such oriental cities deliberately, seeking some standard of comparison with Soviet oriental cities.

At Teheran the British official attitude was definitely unfriendly to the Soviet Union, harking back continually to early Soviet excesses. A high British official said categorically; "We have nothing to learn from Russia."

At the British Embassy we saw the tablet recording the Churchill, Roosevelt and Stalin visit. At one formal banquet, we were told, a guest pointing to the British Admiral said to Molotov: "Our greatest English sailor since Nelson." Molotov inquired: "Was that the Nelson of the *Lady Hamilton* film?"

Learning that it was he said, "Stalin has seen it three times." Churchill, I was informed, had seen it some half a dozen times!

From Teheran to Moscow, 1,600 miles, as far as from Stockholm to Sicily, we flew in a single day, from early morning until late afternoon; one halt at Baku, another at Stalingrad.

An unconverted military plane with longitudinal benches was our craft. A mixed company our fellow-travellers. A loquacious Persian regaled all who wished it with an excellent liqueur to keep out the cold as we crossed the high mountains. Descending to warmer levels, Natasha, a Russian child, uncurled herself from a gorgeous orange-coloured muffler. She thawed, ate an orange, then a pomegranate, then some boiled sweets, the remainder of which she distributed to the company. My turn last. She emptied the bag itself into my lap and added, as a mark of peculiar favour, a green acid drop straight from her own mouth to mine.

Three fellow travellers were British; members of the staff of *British Ally*, the English counterpart of *Soviet War News*.

Huge and magnificent mountains guard Russia's southern approach; beyond them stretched the Caspian Sea, its vivid blue made bluer still by the contrasting ochre of the bordering hills.

(*Top*) No house remained intact in Sevastopol after the expulsion of the enemy.
(*Lower*) Restoration work on the Zaporozhstal Iron and Steel Works in the Ukrainian S.S.R.

(*Top*) The Kirov Works in Makeyevka have been restored and are
steadily increasing the output of high grade steel.

(*Lower*) At the Rasvet Collective Farm, farmers are restoring areas
devastated during the war.

Baku, where we refuelled, is modern, built on American rectangular lines. A Russian woman officer superintended the customs and searched our luggage for three hours with minutest care. English newspapers were removed. My diplomatic pass spared me personally much trouble and any search. The rate of exchange of twenty-six roubles to the pound represented no reality if one bought goods at ordinary shops, for the war had created internal inflation. A cup of tea costs five to six English shillings at the formal rate. Voks, our host in Russia, kindly provided ample Russian money for small current needs.

Re-embarking, we crossed the great Kalmuk swamps and plains. Leaving Baku at 11.30 a.m., hour by hour we flew at high speed and low altitude over monotonous grass-grown lands stretching on and on, far as the eye could reach, with no distinguishing features anywhere. Lonely as great oceans are these wide expanses. My diary reads: "11.30 onwards, grasslands . . . grasslands . . . grasslands . . . no trees, no mountains, not even mounds on the horizon; 3.30, first tree; 3.35, windmill and house built of unburnt bricks; 3.40, Volga below us; large island; factories and smelting works . . . Stalingrad." Round we swung, and dipping steeply landed without fuss on Stalingrad aerodrome, nothing visible but wreckage. Refuelling, we left at 4.30 p.m. The ensuing 650 miles to Moscow was rough and stormy. We descended in rain and gloom at Moscow aerodrome. Mr. Kolesnikov, Deputy Commissar of Health, Mr. Kemenov of Voks, Madame Maisky and others met us. Our hotel was the "National," with a peep of the Red Square, Lenin's tomb, and the rose pink Kremlin walls.

Flights from Teheran to Moscow; Moscow to Armenia; Moscow to Asia; Moscow to Leningrad; Moscow to Warsaw and Moscow to Prague made real the phrase: "Russia the land of vast distances." Even these flights are short for Russia. The Vladivostok-Moscow express from east to west takes nine days and nine nights. All climates range across this vast "World Island," as Mackinder calls it: on the Afghan frontier date palms whose "head loves the sun" thrive in tropical heat. Cape Chelyuskin with a winter of ten months sees icebergs drifting by on midsummer's day. Yakutia records the world's lowest temperature, minus 70 degrees centigrade: Kara-kum desert can register 70 degrees plus. Touching Czechoslovakia in the west, the Soviet Union reaches to within nine miles of India on the south, and its outer islands to within four miles of the territory of the United States of America in the east. The Russian group of Republics alone is as large as seventy Britains.

This huge and continuous land mass of Soviet territory, largest in the world, touches twelve seas, with outlets to three oceans: the land of the largest lake—the Caspian, eighty-five feet below ocean

B

level; the largest plain; the widest range of navigable waterways; the greatest forest lands with amplest wood supplies and the largest steppe. The Pamirs only yield by feet the palm of height to Everest. Vast rivers traverse these endless lands and possess high importance in Soviet economy. Transport rivers penetrate the heart of the fertile Russian plain. Irrigation rivers bring life to Central Asia and the deserts of the eastern Caucasus. Power abounds. Cheap hydro-electric potential in the Soviet Union exceeds that of Norway, Sweden, Switzerland, Brazil and the Argentine, China, Canada and the United States all lumped together.

Lake Sevan in Armenia holds the record as the world's highest great lake and Lake Baikal as the deepest, containing more water than the Baltic Sea. Lake Saraz in the Pamirs, the world's newest large natural lake, sixteen miles long and 1,600 feet deep, was created in 1911 when a landslide blocked the River Bartag in its narrow gorge. Artificial lakes appear annually upon the map as rivers are dammed for hydro-electric, irrigation or transport purposes; one of them, the "Moscow Sea," is 160 miles long. The reservoir created by the dammed Volga at Rybinsk, nearly half the size of Lake Onega, is another. Farmers become sailors, fishing fleets and ocean-going craft replace tractor and plough.

Russia's forests are endless, some endowed with a fascination all their own. Little known but intensely interesting is the "Ussurian Taiga," a mixed forest of unique character in the southern part of the far east. Escaping the glacial period, the Ussurian fauna and flora survived intact from still earlier periods, adapting themselves to a climate gradually cooling. Larch trees, elm, maple, oak, yew; Manchurian apple, Ussurian pear; African marigold with cork bark and a birch tree which when bent has iron-like resistance, all these jostle together, with cedars as high as church steeples. Reindeer mingle with wild boar; tigers six feet long roam the Ussurian forest.

The broad features of Soviet geography, easily mastered, consist of one huge low-lying plain, the Eastern European Plain, cut off from a second, almost as flat, called the Western Siberian Plain, by the Ural Mountains running north and south. Then comes the eastern part of the Soviet Union, cut almost in two by the Yenesei River, and containing the Central Siberian Plateau traversed by sundry mountain ranges. The huge central plains of the west are shielded on the south by mountain chains running east-west, which rise at times to great heights: in the Caucasus to 18,490 feet, in the Pamirs to 24,598 feet, in the Tien-shen to 22,975 feet.

Russia's distances provide problems for Russia's transport chiefs. Britain's far-flung empire has its own problems. We are apt to imagine our distances create the greater problems. It is not so. Easier routes traverse vast oceans than vast deserts and high mountain ranges. Accustomed to island distances we find it hard to grasp rail distances in Russia. A milestone on the Vladivostok railway reads 5,827 miles: Land's End to John o' Groat's is barely a tenth as long. Haulage is a constant and pressing problem. Vital, essential commodities grow or are produced long distances from where needed: southern areas rich in grain, northern areas in wood. Exchange means transport. Coal and oil for Moscow industry in the centre and Leningrad in the north is abundant in the Donetz basin, in Baku, or beyond the Urals, far to south and east. The Urals themselves abound in iron ore: Kuznetz, 750 miles east, provides the nearest coking coal for changing it to steel.

Rail, river and air transport thus assume supreme importance. The Soviet Union depends for its economic unity upon its wide transport network, rail, road, river and air. The railroad mileage of 56,250 miles in 1939, half as long again as mileage of Tsarist days, and able to girdle the earth twice at the Equator, is concentrated mainly in the west centre and in the Ukraine. Siberian railways, save for the main trunk line—the longest in the world—and Turksib still await the development already planned.

Soviet geography, under the impact of Socialist planning, changes, and the transport system changes with it. Industry drifts eastwards and 80 per cent of the new mileage was laid in eastern areas. The Turksib railway, a Soviet achievement, links Central Asia and Siberia. Another couples the Transiberian line with Lake Balkhash in the heart of Kazakhstan.

Russia's transport system has suffered devastating blows in the war. Destruction reached a scale hard to grasp: 40,000 miles of rail track was torn up—I saw the devilish machine devised by German ingenuity for the task—15,800 locomotives, 428,000 wagons, 4,100 stations, countless bridges and a whole telegraph and telephone installation.

Restoration proceeds apace. And fresh advance goes hand in hand with it. By 1st January, 1945, about 30,000 miles had been repaired and opened to traffic. Railway bridges totalling more than 180 miles—nearly the distance from London to Manchester—in length, requiring 550,000 tons of metal and 6,000,000 cubic metres of concrete, are scheduled to be restored or built anew during the next five years. That means 1,800 large and medium-sized bridges, besides 10,000 of smaller dimensions; 300 large bridges and 1,500 smaller ones were to be completed by the end of 1946.

Soviet repair crews restored bridges not only in Russia but in Poland, Yugoslavia and Czechoslovakia, as I perceived at first hand.

In the war 16,000 bridges, tunnels and other structures totalling some 240 miles in length were replaced. Many of the new bridges, as that projected for crossing the Dnieper at Zaporozhe, are of outstanding beauty.

Rolling stock is to be increased and still further modernised. Diesel engines with fourfold efficiency of steam and of especial service where, as in Asia, water is scarce, are replacing former steam locomotives. The use of woods, hardened under extreme pressure and with a durability approximating that of steel, together with plastics and alloy steel are estimated to save 30 per cent in empty weight. Experiments proceed with gas turbine locomotives, while streamlined high speed electric trains, such as I saw in Georgia, are to be developed wherever water power becomes available.

Telecontrol, where one man, seeing the set-up of all trains in a wide area on a screen before him, is enabled to control traffic and lessen the delay of freight-cars in sidings is an added aid to transport facility; railways become gigantic conveyors, part depending on part and the whole moving with rhythmical precision.

New routes have been developed in the war: the North Pechora Railway, for instance, which brings Arctic coal to central regions. Railways also link up the middle Volga with the Caucasus and other areas. Though the length of rails is only one and a half times that of Tsarist days, the loading capacity has increased 400 per cent between 1913 and 1938, due to improved tracks, larger wagons, automatic brakes, electric tractors and higher-powered locomotives. The Soviet rail system holds the world record for tonnage per mile of track; it stood the strain of war, maintaining unbroken the links between rear and front.

Water transport looms large in the Soviet Union, which holds first place in the world for riverways. The Volga has always linked forest belt and steppe zone. At Stalingrad I watched huge tug-drawn barges pass southwards down the Volga. The man in charge and his family lived in a house built on the deck. Sleeping beds stood in the open beneath mosquito curtains. The Volga provides water links between forest zone and steppe. Timber floats southwards, oil tankers plod northwards. The rivers Irtysh and Ob couple the Siberian trunk line with areas still farther to the north. River transport increases as Russia advances to maturity. New ports arise; old ports expand. Navigable mileage grows.

The wide flat lands of the Eastern Plain, with their massive slow-flowing rivers, permit canal systems to link together all the seas of the European U.S.S.R.—Baltic, White Sea, Caspian Sea and Azov Sea.

The Stalin Baltic-White Sea Canal, seventy-five miles long, com-

pletes the link-up of the White Sea and the Baltic. The sixty-two miles
of Moscow Canal provides, with the Volga, a deep waterway from
the capital to the ocean and yields an ample water supply for the city.
The Dnieper Dam renders navigable the Dnieper River far above
Kiev; with the rebuilding of the Dnieper-Bug Canal it links the
Black Sea and the Baltic. These works completed, five seas will be
coupled and a unified deep-waterway will permeate and vivify the
entire European U.S.S.R. The ice-free port of Murmansk on the
Barents Sea, giving Russia access on the north to the world's oceans,
grows daily in importance.

The Northern Maritime Route, amply supplied with ports,
coal, powerful ice-breakers, and air bases for reconnaissance, links
the west of the U.S.S.R. with the Far East through the Arctic Ocean.
Motor transport supplements rail and runs along several thousand
miles of great roads built in eastern regions.

Air transport, of special importance in this land of vast distances
and sparse populations, was already in 1938 running 78,750 miles of
airways.

We arrived in Moscow on 5th May. On Victory Day shortly
afterwards I was invited by our ambassador, Sir Mark Kerr, to speak
at the Thanksgiving Day Service in the Embassy. Quiet, formal,
sincere and impressive, the service was conducted by the resident
naval chaplain, a Baptist Minister.

Mrs. Churchill, concluding her journeys as I began mine, attended
the service. With her Russian Red Cross Fund Mrs. Churchill had
done magnificent work for Russia and Russian friendship whilst
in England. She crowned that work in Russia, winning the affection
of all by her sincerity and unaffected manner. With delightful abandon
she was demonstrably enjoying herself, impressed much by the love-
ableness of the Russian common people. Her speeches were short,
direct, well to the point and spoken with charming naïveté.

Victory Day dawned. Youth had been assembling in the Race
Course Square and the Red Square from an early hour, and on returning from service at the Embassy a dense crowd, enthusiastic and genial,
released at last from the long strain of war, blocked our road and
engulfed us, cheering every Englishman or American. They seized
General Younger, a British officer in full uniform, and tossing him in
the air, caught him as gently as if he were a babe. My turn came
next, and I saw a Moscow crowd from a considerable altitude.

In the afternoon, by invitation, we visited Alexei, Patriarch of
the Russian Orthodox Church, and highest ecclesiastic in Russia.
With him was Nicolai, Metropolitan of Kiev, and others. We met in
the Patriarch's private house, not palatial but spacious. Handsome old

furniture lent dignity to the quiet rooms, the outer one of which was a robing room, with beautiful vestments arrayed ready for use. It was Eastertide and we ate the pascal cake.

After friendly talk and customary toasts, the Patriarch, a noble figure with handsome face and long uncut hair and beard, welcoming me in a deep rich voice and with the kindly smile which is customary to him, presented me with a magnificent jewelled enamelled crucifix suspended by a massive gold chain. His own hands placed it round my neck, and he gave me the fraternal kiss.

I wore that crucifix throughout three months in Russia. I wear it still in Canterbury and otherwise in appropriate assemblies and on appropriate occasions. It always recalls Victory Day in Moscow.

After tea the Patriarch drove us in his own car to the cathedral, into which we had to force an entrance through crowds such as I seldom saw before. Russian churches are chairless. People stand, and on that day so tight was the wedge of humanity that movement was well-nigh impossible. At length we reached the enclosure which shuts the altar off from the congregation, and were given a place of honour between screen and people.

Near us sang the choir, men and women in everyday dress: the Cantor led the service with an immense voice which carried far down the huge building, and boomed out to the crowds in the street. Subsequently we drove thence to an evening entertainment at Voks.

One item in that entertainment stands vividly out in my memory. A short thick-set man with a broad, good-humoured, highly intelligent face stepped easily in front of the grand piano, and placing on his forefingers two india-rubber balls the size of tennis balls, painted to resemble human faces, he conducted a miniature pantomime. Fingers entirely unrobed magically assumed the rôle of bodies, arms and legs, as Mr. Andriyevich the magician, who had founded Moscow's famous puppet theatre, depicted love, passion, joy, despair, and "all lived happily ever afterwards."

On the veranda we witnessed the magnificent Victory firework display. The sky north, south, east and west blazed with coloured searchlight rays. A thousand feet overhead the searchlights played on a gigantic red banner held by invisible cords from invisible balloons.

BOOK II

DESTRUCTION AND RECONSTRUCTION

(A) *The Cost of War*

THE immediate object of my journey and subsequent study was to
estimate the damage caused by war and examine the Soviet steps at
reconstruction. My ultimate object to gain an impression of the kind
of human beings that the past two and half decades have produced
in the Soviet Union. After that a re-examination of the nature of
the various influences, physical, educational and cultural, which
mould human life in the Socialist sixth of the world. Then finally
a re-examination of the economic bases on which it all rests.

The impression of the immense extent of war damage in Russia
grew as one travelled far and wide. Impressive in Stalingrad, where
few habitable buildings remained of a modern town of some 600,000
souls; or in Rostov, or in . . . But it is impossible to enumerate further
cities or towns—1,700 of them, wholly or partially destroyed. The
extent of the damage was more impressive still as seen from the air
in long flights, as from Moscow to Warsaw.

My diary, written minute by minute during seven hours' flight
at tree-top level, reads with monotonous regularity: "trenches, more
trenches, tank trenches, shell holes, broken bridge, smashed cottage,
destroyed village." Seventy thousand villages were destroyed, 1,135
coal pits, 3,000 oil wells, 61 large power stations, 27 iron and steel
works, 749 engineering plants, 66 chemical factories, 40,000 miles
of railway track, 15,800 locomotives, 428,000 wagons, 4,100 railway
stations, 1,400 ships, 137,000 tractors, 4,000,000 ploughs, 49,000
combine harvesters, 1,500,000 homes, 9,000,000 head of cattle,
12,000,000 pigs, 13,000,000 sheep and goats. . . .

And what of human life? I once handled a poignant document,
the small leather diary of a Leningrad engineer with alphabetical
index at the end, the early entries in copperplate writing. Its owner
had been killed. The diary had passed to Tanya his daughter, aged
eight; the later entries continued in childish scrawls of blue pencil
under the alphabetical letters at the end. Curtly but exactly it stated:
"Grandmama died 25th January, 3 p.m., 1942." And so on, the
death roll of relations throughout 900 days of siege: "Uncle Vanya
2 a.m., 13th April, 1942"; Lexa (her brother); her mother, and then,
under the family name: "All dead." The final entry: "Left alone,
Tanya."

23

No unique story that. Twenty-five millions rendered homeless by the war: the loss of human life terrible. Seven millions was the total. Few families untouched. I met in Moscow a young married woman whom I knew in Yalta in 1937. Her small son was dead, husband dead, brother-in-law dead. . . . The civilian death roll in Leningrad alone, one city out of hundreds, exceeded the total British deaths, soldiers, sailors, airmen and civilians, by more than double. Military losses before the final push exceeded ours by fourteen to one.

Losses like these have a profound bearing on Russia's attitude to post-war problems. Russians believe that they are the most innocent of all participants in the war. They feel that the inter-war years were marked by lost opportunities and worse, successive Governments in Britain and France permitting German rearmament in hopes that Hitler would turn eastwards.

To this same attitude they attribute the breakdown of the 1939 British-Soviet conversations in Moscow, and the snub at their suggestion of a conference after the Germans had occupied Prague.

In their view the instability of the pre-war years was due to Russia's exclusion from the Versailles Treaty, with German rearmament permitted through dread of the Bolshevik Bogey.

Russian policy is determined to prevent a recurrence of errors which cost her so dear.

If an examination of the damage Russia had suffered in un-provoked warfare was one side of the immediate object of my inquiry, Russian efforts at recovery was the other. Stalingrad afforded an appalling picture of the one and an illustration of the other. Therefore to Stalingrad we flew. Approaching the city from the air, one gains a vivid bird's-eye view of one of the sorriest battlegrounds of history: fields—far into the distance and on every side—torn to shreds by trench and crater holes. Alighting, we drove amongst gaunt walls and empty shells of a one-time prosperous town.

Stalingrad is a symbol, the city of imperishable soul. Stalingrad marked the turning point of world war two. Stalingrad struck the final blow which swept to limbo the myth of German invincibility. At Stalingrad the tide of war reversed. From Stalingrad began the march which ended only when the red flag flew on the ruined Reichstag in Berlin.

None enters Stalingrad unmoved; it is sacred ground. In silence we drove through ruined streets to one of the few buildings left even partially intact, a small hostelry in a quiet tree-lined avenue. Our welcome was moving. My bedroom, a well-windowed chamber, glowed with fragrant summer blooms, roses, snapdragons, blue corn-flowers, arranged with skill in a great bowl on one table; scents, scented soap and cigarettes on a table near by. Fresh towels, fresh sheets and soft white pillows piled up in Ukrainian fashion—Stalingrad is Ukrainian—into a picturesque pyramid.

Even whilst washing my hands in the only room where fresh water ran from a tap—precious commodity here—an elderly Stalingrad matron, despite all protestations, knelt and blacked my boots as I stood.

The afternoon was hot and Stalingrad hotter than Armenia, Georgia, Asia, or any other land we visited. But the windows of my room stood open, and a light breeze blew in from the Volga, which flowed near by, a deep blue streak beyond the wreckage, with green wooded banks rising on its farther shore. Enjoying our meal, I made closer acquaintance with Mr. Karaganov, the incredibly young vice-president of Voks, our companion here, and later on in Asia.

Karaganov had recently returned from Rumania, his first visit to a capitalist land, where he had delivered a course of lectures on Russian life. He told amusing tales. Faced once, for example, with a charge of 10,000 roubles for a boot-shine, he had reduced it by bar-gaining to 1,000, the current price being only ten to Rumanians, the grounds for supercharge being: "We use English blacking."

Dinner conversation was vivid and wide-ranging as usual with Soviet youth. We discussed all topics from *The Times* newspaper, commended by us in general as informative, to estimating which was the greater religious force in the Europe of his day, Luther or Huss. After dinner we walked with leading citizens around the ruined city, visiting first a small basement room in a large gutted store, where Paulus had established his headquarters and where finally he had capitulated. The little room remains precisely as Paulus had left it, after, as they said, haughtily demanding a superior officer to be sent to take him and after he had craved food for himself, regardless of his comrades' needs.

A couple of hundred yards westwards we descended to a basement room forty-five feet deep in the Central Park, where the Central Defence Council had made its heroic stand and whence, with doctor, nurse, the colonel and nine soldiers the little company had fought its way out with hand grenades, finding refuge a few hundred yards eastwards on the river's bank, there to hold on till, on 15th September, the German resistance collapsed and the end of Nazi Fascist dominance began.

Every yard of this steep river bank records its own heroisms: caves for quarters, drain culverts for roadways. Only at one point did the Germans reach the river, nor were they suffered to stay beside it long: every yard of territory was bitterly contested.

From the landing stage, an old two-storied ship anchored in the river, we entered a launch in which we crossed the wide Volga to bathe on a sandy beach in the dusk. The water was warm and delicious. Bathing at noon the next day the sand was too hot to traverse with bare feet; hot enough, I think, to cook eggs, as in Asia.

Arising at 4 a.m., I wandered in the cool around the central ruins. By 4.45 Germans were at work in demolition gangs. Stripped to the waist, they looked strong and fit. Restoration proceeds with a will. All share in it. A notable block of flats, made memorable by the thirty days' defence of nine men and a sergeant against terrific odds, had been rendered habitable by the labours of women teachers from the children's kindergarten school. Clerks, factory workers, scientists and housewives use pick, saw, trowel or spade. A volunteer hairdresser offered to cut hair. "No time yet for haircuts, learn to make bricks," they said. He did.

The zest of reconstruction was exhilarating, beginning at once with the tractor plant, with the Krasny Octyabr Iron and Steel Works and the Barrikady Engineering Works. Essential machinery was a first priority. If the Ukraine was to be cleared of Germans and send grain back for Soviet use Stalingrad must supply tanks and tractors for the job, and within two and a half months of the German departure, 23rd April, 1943, the first machines rolled off the tractor plant. Buildings followed: 56 schools, 118 children's institutes, already operated in the summer of 1945, and 20 hospitals, the first two of which were equipped by the Joint Committee for Soviet Aid, the organisation which grew from the First-Aid to Russia Fund founded by D'Eye and myself, at D'Eye's suggestion, soon after Hitler's attack. The Joint Committee's work grew to great proportions. A magnificent volume of 600 octavo pages, enriched by the arms of 100 cities, commemorating the 600 towns and many thousands of individuals of Great Britain who sent a quarter of a million pounds, has already been taken by Mrs. Pritt, the vice-chairman, to Stalingrad, a gift to the heroic city and a memorial to British craftsmanship in printing, heraldry and binding, worthy to rest beside King George's sword which they proudly exhibited to us in the Civic Hall.

We visited one of these hospitals, part of which is used as a maternity ward. During our visit a baby born the previous day was, at the request of the staff, photographed in my arms.

(B) *The New Stalingrad*

Stalingrad is to be rebuilt, courage for defence matched by courage for reconstruction. A daunting task of clearance awaits the workers. Forty thousand buildings were destroyed. Massive and useless walls, mountains of rubble and the torn roads of a city which sprawls for thirty miles along the Volga present innumerable problems heroically tackled. Rebuilding takes place to a new magnificent plan.

With a map spread out on the deck of a launch the city architect explained to us designs for a riverside city as noble as any in the world.

Little has remained from the old Stalingrad of material value; a network of sewage drains, water mains, telephone cables, walls and wrecked buildings, that is all. Nothing else, save opportunity to plan anew and correct numerous old faults.

For Stalingrad had grave defects. Its rectangular chess-board outlay ignored the terrain of hills, gullies and ravines. The city, spreading out along the Volga side, was cut off from a grand water frontage by freight railway lines, its single main street making inter-urban communication difficult. The town lacked green areas and parks for recreation. Ill arranged gullies marred natural features of great beauty. Disproportionately high buildings, badly placed, blocked excellent views.

The new plan eliminates these blemishes. Designed to make Stalingrad an efficient industrial centre, it also utilises to the full the natural æsthetic advantages of slopes and hills and the glorious Volga River.

Railway tracks are to disappear from the river front. Freight moorings will be confined to the southern area of the city, the great metal factories to the northern area. The central strip of the river, with its steep banks, rolling slopes and intersecting ravines, will be laid out as one vast pleasure promenade running lengthwise by the city's side, easily accessible to every city dweller.

Stalingrad is long and narrow, thirty miles in length and nowhere more than three miles in depth; rebuilt it will take full advantage of its riverside situation. Three trunk roads will run its full length. The lower road, nearest the river, served by a trolly-bus line, which, avoiding the whole central area of parks, squares and monuments, will link the metal town on the north with Krasnoarmeist on the south. The middle road, higher up and farther inland, will link the residential districts. Intersected by limited crossings this Middle Road will aid speedy traffic. The upper road, running along the city's perimeter, will serve as by-pass for high-speed transit.

The spiritual significance of a city which twice within a quarter of a century has proved the turning point of vital struggles must never be forgotten. The centre of Stalingrad is devoted to great squares, public parks and monumental buildings, linked together by a Victory Avenue leading down to the passenger landing-stage and the Volga— their names, Pavlov Square, etc., and the character of the buildings themselves, e.g., the Museum of War Relics and the monumental groups, all designed to recall the epic of Stalingrad. The Central Boulevard, Square of Fallen Heroes, Victory Avenue, and New Square will form one single coherent and spacious design dominated by a thousand feet high monumental column.

Full advantage will be taken of valleys and slopes to provide amenities for residential areas sufficiently removed from noisy traffic. The Great Ravine, cutting the city in half and traversed by the River Tsaritsa, is to be laid out as landscape parkland over which the main streets will pass by means of viaducts. Transport freight will be excluded, Stalingrad Central station being reserved for passengers alone. Station II, three kilometres distant, will be expanded to meet the needs of freight distribution. Railways will be hidden from sight, passing beneath the city by means of tunnels. River freight likewise will be dealt with at Krasnoarmeist, river passengers only embarking in the centre.

The city's silhouette as seen from river or bank of ravine has been studied with conspicuous care, blocks of buildings along the embankment limited in the main to two stories and skyscrapers disallowed. Parks, still waters and trees will enrich the interior of the city, and extended green belts add to its outer amenities.

Stalingrad, however, is only one, though an outstanding example of a civic reconstruction which is to be nation-wide. Some Soviet towns like Stalingrad are planned for radical change, others less so, others again devoted to wholly fresh uses. Istra, for instance, forty miles from Moscow, formerly a small sleepy cathedral country town, almost levelled to the ground by the war and now to be restored as a lovely recreational town wholly devoted to health, rest and culture.

The Soviet Government speeds on, as specially symbolic, the reconstruction of Leningrad. Its acreage of city parks will increase. Numerous sites will be cleared and planted with trees. Two new districts will arise with model administrative centres. A waterfront boulevard on Vasilievsky Island will fill a long felt want. Architectural treasures, such as the mansion of Count Laval, will be restored in exactly original form.

In Moscow also, which has suffered from war damage and war-time neglect, big architectural changes take place overnight. The new Five-Year Plan calls for complete reconstruction of all main traffic arteries, with augmentation of a host of additional municipal services. Trams before my hotel disappeared in a day, replaced by the silent trolly-bus. By 1950 buses of all kinds will be increased four times, taxis ten times, gas consumption ten times. In 1946 140,000 trees and over a million bushes were planted. Dmitri Chechulin, Moscow's City Architect, plans to make Moscow one of the most beautiful cities in the world; his superb Tchaikovsky Concert Hall, modern, restrained and superb in its simple lines and graceful curves, augurs well for the future.

Russia is quick at the start. Exactly forty-eight hours after the last German soldier left Kharkov, experts from the Commission for Heavy Machine Building had arrived to plan the construction of the big turbo-generator plant. Five days after the liberation of Smolensk it was announced that the city would have 22,000 new agricultural cottages by winter. A gigantic plan, covering the whole U.S.S.R., aims at the construction of 25,000,000 houses in ten years. Stalingrad families were already, by the end of 1946, moving into new flats at the rate of forty a day.

Reconstruction of great industrial units like the Dnieper Dam are a natural priority. This vast undertaking, producing annually 3,000 million kilowatt hours of cheap power and crystallising around it one of the largest industrial centres in the land, had been ruined by the war. The dam was blown up. The power station completely wrecked. The water level reduced by seventy feet. Rapids reappeared. Navigation ceased. Only the torn dam itself and twisted installations remained as evidence of former gigantic works.

Undaunted, work began in 1941: rail tracks, power lines, concrete factories, saw mills appeared; 300,000 tons of exploded concrete and 100,000 tons of structural iron disappeared. During 1945 50,000 young men and women gave voluntary labour, working to the accompany-ing roar of seventy foot cascades of falling waters as the level rose once more. Work in 1945 exceeded 1944 by 30 per cent. "Start the Dnieper Station in 1946" ran the slogan. And it has been done. Two massive turbines made in Leningrad's reconstructed factory are now installed. Lights on the countryside go up. Nine turbines are scheduled for operation within two years. The output of power of the new installations will shortly exceed the old by 90,000 kilowatt units.

Coal is another priority. Reconstructional scaffolding arises in the Donbas where 90 per cent of the mines had been flooded and wrecked. Two thousand powerful electric pumps are needed to drain the 600,000,000 cubic feet of flood waters; one of the many tasks which will demand—quite apart from housing and other external work—an army of 100,000 men and engineers for three and a half years' time.

There has been no delay in the start here as elsewhere. Two hundred million cubic metres of water have already gone. Mines are operating. Forty per cent of pre-war output is achieved. Miners did not wait on bricksetters to restore the pithead buildings. They learned brickcraft themselves and laid bricks before hewing coal, violating no trade union rules and dooming no other men to unemployment.

"Bedsteads to aircraft; aircraft to bedsteads" is the order, as factory after factory swung from peace to war and now swings back from war to peace. The Kirov Works at Chelyabinsk in the Urals produced 18,000 tanks and 48,000 Diesel engines in the war: re-jigged and re-tooled, it now produces tractors. The switch-over took four months and a half.

Speed is achieved by team spirit and willingness of workers. Everything is designed for the welfare of the people. They know it and work the team spirit with a will. Men work and women work—women were plastering, repairing and painting on every landing in my Leningrad hotel with stimulating dash. A hoarding-poster showed women plasterers working on a high-up cornice against a background of the Neva; the caption ran: "We defended you, Leningrad; we shall restore you."

Bricklaying champions perform incredible feats. The record for a shift of straightforward work in 1945 was 10,000 bricks. Mortar, warmed in winter, was poured on the brickwork by one girl, bricks handed to the bricklayer by another. The bricklayer evened out the mortar, dressed the brick, cleaned the face, and required fifteen seconds per brick. Kulikov during an exceptional test far exceeded this rate. Shavlyugin, the Moscow champion, claims to have laid 3,000,000 bricks in fifteen years.

(c) *Town Planning in Soviet Life*

Russia after a quarter of a century of intensive study and wide experience has much to teach in the art of planning—industrial planning, agricultural planning or civic planning. The task has been simplified by the fact that land, mineral deposits, waters, forests, mines, mills and factories, with the bulk of dwelling houses in cities, all belong to the whole community of people.

Furthermore, the entire resources of the nation stand behind the planners, and astronomical sums have already been spent on the execution of their designs. In 1939, the capital to be expended on the Five-Year Plan was 193,000 million roubles, designed amongst other things to supply dwellings for 5,000,000 people, besides providing 500 machine and tractor stations, with elevators and storehouses capable of holding 10,000,000 tons of grain.

And here again, planning in general wins the willing co-operation of the whole people, who have in very truth a vital share in plan-formulation and thus feel responsible and eager for its execution. This is a matter of such high importance if we would appreciate the Soviet's claim to be the most democratic people in the world that I have devoted later a whole chapter to its consideration.

It took ten years to prepare the ground work for planning. By 1928, at the beginning of the first Five-Year Plan, ninety-six towns and cities in the R.S.F.S.R. were planned, thirty-six in the Ukraine, thirty-five in Georgia, Armenia and Azerbaijan, apart from new towns and towns of less than 50,000 population. By 1940 plans were drawn up for 225 towns in the R.S.F.S.R. alone, and 145 of these had already been completed.

State planning institutes, with regional planning and design institutes for great towns like Moscow, were supplemented by architectural planning bureaux, with responsibility for details.

The largest organisation, charged with the biggest problems and known as Giprogor, planned the north sea route and towns in the Arctic and the far east. When the hydro-electric power stations on the Volga resulted in the inundation of twenty-six towns, these were removed and rebuilt by Giprogor. Of individual town plans the biggest, of course, is that of the Moscow Soviet, which is responsible for a ring of four and a half million acres, containing 200 inhabited centres within its circle.

Innumerable planning principles were proposed and needed sifting: lineal cities, garden cities, super-colossal cities, cities of gigantic blocks of flats, or cities of small cottage homes. I saw great flats and small villas in Kiev; and in Stalingrad a new estate of small houses, prefabricated and timber built—some from Russia and some as reparations from Finland—laid out alongside the tractor factory.

Plans are prepared and executed in three stages:

(1) Local and regional surveys are made, collecting all available material information concerning existing railways, roads, industries, minerals, climate, prevailing winds, rainfall, etc., etc., together with an estimate of civic needs as to fuel, light, heat, food or raw materials for industry.

(2)   A conference of experts—hygienists careful for health, engineers with an eye to transport, architects with an eye to balance and beauty, economists with an eye to financial circumspection and the like—meet to deliberate what form the plan shall take.

(3)   The third and final stage is the working plan itself, and the provision of a time schedule.

To specially selected bodies—Government departments, factory trusts, co-operative organisations—is entrusted the task of carrying out the actual building programme. Local architectural and planning bureaux supervise the actual work.

(*Top*) Alexii, Patriarch of Moscow and All Russia, with his retinue at the pulpit during services on Christmas Day.

(*Lower*) The Author with Inna Koulakovskaya at the exhibition of Armenian artists in Erevan.

(*Top*) A new apartment house in Moscow, occupied by workers of the shipbuilding industry.

(*Lower*) A Moscow family at breakfast.

BOOK III

NEW PEOPLE OF A NEW ERA

1. A YOUNG WOMAN OF THE INTELLIGENTSIA

WHAT now, to come to my most fundamental quest, can be said of the type of individual the Soviet society is producing as one sees it in post-war years? Let me answer that question by describing several individuals intimately known to me and typical of the many more whom I met. Young people most of them, born within the new order.

Opportunities for studying the nature and character of Soviet citizens, especially of Soviet youth, were extensive: in Soviet farms and factories, in Soviet studios, theatres, surgeries, laboratories and homes I met them. Wide travels with youth of various nationalities in the distant Caucasus or in Asia—lands as new to my companions as to me—in joyous abandonment and merriment, or in danger and difficulty and fatigue; in joint first hand study of ancient civilisations, strange religions, modern achievements, revealed many sides of Soviet personal life. Youth unbends to youth, and I saw Russian youth mingling with Caucasian youth, with Georgian, Jewish or Uzbekian youth; I saw Ukrainian youth with youth of Leningrad. Not only saw them, but shared their life, their festivities, and even their secrets. I saw them in laughter and tears. I saw their passionate devotions, and heard of their aspirations and troubles.

My first picture shall be of one I know the best, Inna Koulakofskaya, our chief guide and companion throughout three months of journeyings.

Inna Koulakofskaya was born in Zhitomir, not far from Kiev in the Ukraine, in 1917, a real child of the Revolution, daughter of a medical man who died through the effects of the war and of a mother who is a graduate and teacher and who now shares Inna's home in Moscow. Inna's husband was killed in the war; she has two children, four and six, to whom she is devoted.

Inna afforded me an opportunity for study which few can possess. I saw her in every conceivable light: in festivity, in danger, in difficulty, in toil, in perplexities. Through her conscious or unconscious guidance I learned much of Russian womanhood. In her experience as child, daughter, student, wife or mother I could trace, as it were, the stages, motives and impelling powers which have marked womanhood's

33

C

emancipation and enlargement in the Soviet Union during the past
three decades.

Much of this I learned incidentally; then as we grew more intimate
Inna unfolded her earlier experiences. She permits me to record them.

Her father was a radical of the middle-class intelligentsia, serving
as doctor of the Red Army under Budyenny during the Polish campaign
of the first world war. Although he never became a Communist until
1922, he was elected as their representative by the soldiers, the only
officer of his division thus chosen. He was wounded. His sickness
continued throughout the civil war.

Anxious that Inna should be strong, agile, and skilled as a boy,
he taught her early to climb trees, swim, ride . . . habits which never
forsook her; every available tree and every wayside brook or river
in Asia or the Caucasus on our travels called to her. I rode a bicycle
race with her round the Great Square in Leningrad one summer's
afternoon on racing machines lent by contestants whilst awaiting the
arrival of the long distance road race competitors.

Inna's mother worked as the first woman barrister after world
war one. Inna, though then an only child, was sent to a kindergarten
school: home affected her more profoundly than school.

Witty and kindly, her father was a man of honour and character,
skilled at converse with small children. The fairy tale he composed
of the elf who explored the mystery of a journey across a child's
face—traced stage by stage with eagerly awaited finger—the blue
lakes (the eyes), the great plain (the brow), the dark forest (the hair),
the mysterious caverns (nostrils and ears), ending at the dreadful yawn-
ing cavern (the mouth), from whose shuddering depths the elf fled in
terror—keeps a small child rooted with the spell.

Honourable and truthful himself, he sought truthfulness in his child.
"Inna," he said, after detecting a childish deceit, and looking stead-
fastly into her eyes. "Inna, I see a dark spot in your eye: you have not
told the truth." She never lied again and her father had cause to say,
"I can always trust Inna."

A wide reader, Dr. Koulakofskaya had built up an interesting
library, in which Inna browsed freely; that and the eager discussion
of newspapers and of every political and social question at home
doubtless contributed the major part of her education. No books
were forbidden, though her father's "I would not advise you to read
that" steered her away from books like Ehrenberg's *Free Love*, which
she picked up casually at thirteen years of age.

Obviously a capable child, Inna had small need of help with her
studies. In the sixth grade, at the age of thirteen, she joined the school
literary circle and read a paper on Tolstoi. She was familiar with the

Bible: had read it in French and learned its stories from her parents. Tolstoi's *War and Peace*, devoured when ten or eleven, was eagerly discussed with her father, to whom later she read her Tolstoi essay for criticism.

Her childish memory was good, her handwriting bad. Her Tolstoi essay, though excellent in composition and idea, was atrocious in spelling and punctuation. Of the handwriting Dr. Koulakofskaya said "To write so that others read your letters with difficulty is abominably egotistical, deserving the rebuke administered with a returned ill-written letter: 'I did not read your letter. I could not read your letter. Please re-write your letter.' "

Inna suffered from a complication of illnesses in her seventh year —measles, scarlet fever, pneumonia—hovering for two months between life and death. Her father never left her. The hospital administration permitted him, on reduced salary, to work only three hours a day, the rest of his time he spent with his child, sleeping in those rough days on a wooden bench by her side. She has suffered no severe illness since then.

At fourteen, her school possessing no fourth grade, she went to the technical school. For the curriculum there of metal-work, sewing and embroidery she had no aptitude, her eyesight being below standard. She entered the language school, where she studied mathematics, chemistry, literature in general, English in particular, and at seventeen qualified as interpreter and translator.

Dr. Koulakofskaya had rejected religion as he had seen it presented, but possessed a profound belief that good would triumph over evil, that nothing is simple in life, that duty to family and country are of paramount importance, demanding hard work and providing infinite joy.

As a student Inna was taught to take nothing for granted, never to be contented with any achievement, to seek a background for every branch of study, to read around a subject, to understand its hinterland. At sixteen she joined the young Communists and took her membership seriously. It was a solemn occasion for her, akin to what she felt on entering the university, akin to an English girl's feelings on Confirmation day, and like that celebrated at home by a ceremonial cake.

With an outstanding capacity for making casual friends, Inna has one real deep friendship which began twenty-two years ago and still endures. It began with a childish dispute over a lilac tree in the common garden when her parents first came to Moscow. Inna begged for the better tree and was refused. She scratched the other girl. A week later there began a lasting friendship.

Though not prudishly brought up, Inna learned from her parents decency and restraint and showed distaste for unpleasant stories told by a relative of hers in order to make girls blush. Like most Russian girls she neither smokes nor "makes up."

At sixteen she fell in love with a boy who in his turn fell in love with her girl friend, a passing adolescent infatuation which continued for two years. Seeing it was hopeless, Inna parted from the boy. When too late the boy fell in love with her. Later he married a specialist in physics, the girl he first loved having in the meantime married another handsome youth. There were no children by either marriage and the man is now devoted to Inna's children.

Inna met her husband at a friend's house when she was nineteen and he twenty-four. It was love at first sight. Though trained as a geologist he had entered the philological school, being transferred thence on account of his abilities to Moscow, where he and Inna met and after five months married. The happiness of the marriage was marred and they separated because, as she said, she was too young physically and disliked physical contact. They remained friends and he adored her child. At length they were reunited and lived in complete happiness until he was killed in the war.

Inna, like many more students, had not yet graduated when she was married. She continued her studies as a married woman. The examination was in June. She was delivered of her child in May. She was granted two months' leave of absence prior to the birth of the child, and having studied intensively at home, was permitted to take the examination at the end of April.

At the history test, the examiner; seeing her condition, said: "I had better not question you in the normal way; show me your books and your notes." Refusing his kindly offer and taking the examination in the normal way she added "distinction" to her three excellents.

Her husband took Inna to the maternity home when she was expecting her child; her friends showered roses upon her; later her husband took her and the child home. The next six months were the happiest period of her life. Then followed military war duties with another spell at home, when her husband was appointed chief editor of *Voks*. The child was three years old. When the Germans advanced on Moscow her husband volunteered for the workers' battalion. He was not a party member.

Moscow grew dangerous and, being again pregnant, Inna and her sister were sent at the end of October to Christopol in New Kazan on the Volga after she had worked with her husband at the Moscow defence trenches. She was given work at a butter factory in Christopol and after three weeks' paid training was allotted her task and received her ration cards. At four months' pregnancy the standing in the bitter cold was difficult to bear, worse than digging with numbed fingers in Moscow.

Then came news that her husband had two months' leave. She returned to Moscow; a dangerous journey, largely on horse sledges. Meeting two strangers in the market place, bound for Kazan, she joined them, promising as high a fare as they wished. To make matters worse she had mumps. The rough men, Bashkiris of forty-eight or fifty, who spoke Russian and swore vigorously at their horses, tended her as a child, wrapping her in furs and carrying her to and fro to the best seat in the rest houses on the way, where she snatched some sleep in the warmth. One of the men was a returned invalid—the other in a reserved profession. At times they teased her, saying: "Why take her farther: why not kill her now and seize her money; she must be rich."

Inna's father, meeting her at the Kazan station, urged her return. To her brief plea, "Father, should he never come back could you ever forgive yourself?" he replied shortly, "Go." So she went. Reaching Moscow she entered their room. It was empty. Rushing to a neighbour, however, she discovered he was still in town. Supremely happy, she bought jam and rare fried nuts—the result of much denial of food—and had a feast to celebrate the meeting.

Moscow by this time was suffering severely. But by the light of an amateur lamp they worked together for one blissful month in a small but tolerably warm room. Inna taught her husband English. He was recalled and they had a parting feast of candies, cakes and wine. He knew Inna had wanted a black velvet frock and said she should have it when she was twenty-five. He gave her a book on Balzac, writing in it: "Not as a substitute for the velvet frock, which will come in due time." It never came.

Seeing her husband off, Inna faced the growing difficulties alone—scanty food, blackout, no electricity, no ration card, one meal at the printing house dining-room eked out with small parcels from her father: she was always hungry. In April a letter came. "Is it your husband's handwriting?" said a good neighbour. "I gave her no answer, I only cried."

That was the end. Inna telegraphed to her father. He returned, able to resume his work at the Institute of Hygiene. They were happy. They read and studied English together. They planned to write a book about Soviet doctors and nurses at the front. Then he had a stroke. After two days he died. Shortly before the end he said: "**Don't** weep, child; it will spoil the milk for the babe." She and the **babe** were left alone again.

Inna's university career was successful. She achieved thirty-seven distinctions in three years. She missed her final examination by a misfortune, being much upset at the death of a friend in the house. She had already achieved three of the necessary four excellents. For the fourth paper there were three questions. The third was from a book she had not read, but she answered well. The examiner asked: "Did you read that book." "No," she said. Her honesty cost her the excellent. She could have demanded a second sitting but refused. And now she has no need; but her studies continue.

Her memory is astonishing. At one banquet upwards of twenty speeches were made proposing toasts to my health. One of the speakers, Ilya Ehrenberg, spoke in rapid French, and was far removed from me. I asked Inna afterwards, "Can you recollect Ehrenberg's speech?"

"I remember every speech," she said.

On another occasion, spending the whole morning at the Cotton Agricultural Scientific Institute in Tashkent, I was writing careful notes on scientific data. "You may write them if you like, Dean," said Inna, "but if you would avoid the trouble I can remember all."

At Leningrad, desiring a record of Tanya's little diary, I suggested our return to make a copy. Inna, though never asked to memorise it, remembered every entry and wrote it out in full.

English she knew perfectly, reading Chaucer in the original, and translating in five days, with a friend, Priestley's latest play *The Inspector Calls;* together we attended the "first night" in Moscow. She could discuss literature of any period, or philosophy, or theology. She read French as she read English. A charming companion, she was sincere, modest, witty; she supplied me with a treasure house of Russian proverbs. She was helpful and kindly to everyone. She did as all are supposed to do, valuable voluntary public work. Always thoughtful, always cheerful, and though at times she must have been tired to death with the tremendous strain of organising our tours and expeditions, she never flagged, never shirked a single task and never made a mistake. The staunchest patriot, Inna believed in the rightness and wisdom of the new Soviet Socialist order, and felt she and others were working within it for a mighty purpose. She venerated Stalin as the engineer of Soviet Socialism. To have produced an Inna Koulakofskaya was no mean achievement for any regime.

2. A YOUNG WOMAN OF ARISTOCRATIC BIRTH

Tamara Solovieff introduced us to Moscow's world of theatre, opera, ballet or puppet show. Under her guidance—she is a student of art criticism at the University—I learned to understand Russia's post-war cultural activities. I learnt even more of and from Tamara herself, her personal history, her character and spirit. She joined us one Saturday, after an exacting week, on a picnic into the far reaches of the Moscow waterway.

Returning from my visit to Generalissimo Stalin at the Kremlin on the previous evening, I had written out the story of my interview with every detail fresh. Retiring late and rising early I wrote the article on Stalin for this book, and another for the press. A friendly journalist burst in on me at breakfast and exclaiming "You are bang in the news to-day!" handed me a copy of *Pravda*. He took my MS. and I was free to enjoy an unfettered holiday, though echoes of the interview pursued me, even to the waterway, in blaring wireless as we drove up to the imposing stairway of the Port.

The commandant of the fleet of pleasure steamers, a smart girl in naval uniform who yet contrived to be as feminine as her beauty demanded, took us to the large diesel-engined launch commissioned for our use. We enjoyed the cool shade of the wide, low, open windows throughout a lovely Saturday forenoon and afternoon.

Two Englishmen; Mr. Go-Mo-Dzo, a distinguished Chinese scholar and publicist, destined to be our companion on long subsequent journeys and, like most of the Chinese, gentle, courteous and considerate; an Irak Professor of Art and Archæology, speaking French but neither Russian nor English, together with our young Russian companions from various republics, made up a mixed international party. Inna was there and Tamara. This was Tamara's day.

Sliding slowly down the wide waterway past docks and building yards we entered a canal almost as wide as the Thames at Westminster, save where it narrows through hilly country. Frequently it broadened out to great lakes with wooded banks and farm buildings and rest homes for children; or with yachting pavilions where spoon-billed craft, shooting their taper masts far into the blue sky, swung smoothly at anchor. Muscovites love yachting and large collectives like the Dynamo works provide clubhouses and craft at a trifling fee for the use of their members. Artists, writers and others also own private yachting craft.

The banks swarmed with bathers of all ages and depth of tan, basking in hot summer sunshine—mainly night workers spending the day with their children. No resumption yet of Saturday holidays.

Small boys swam out to meet the swell of our craft. One mischievous youngster with a deft shot deluged the Persian professor who, arrayed in blue shirt, leaned far out of the window.

The smooth river gave me the opportunity I sought, and Tamara related much of her family history and the impact on it of the new order. Her large dark eyes, outstanding beauty, her carriage and bearing had already told me of the aristocratic and southern strands in her ancestry.

Tamara had been thrilled with the visit to the Kremlin and, like Russian youth in general, asked eager, anxious and affectionate questions about Stalin. Did he look well? Had he grown old?

She had still further grounds for interest. She had been at school with Vassily, Stalin's son, and Svetlana, Stalin's daughter. Their mother, a lovely woman with auburn hair—"the type of beauty Leonardo loved to paint"—was dead.

Vassily, inheriting his mother's blue eyes and red hair, had disliked academic studies. "We shall tell your father" was the only threat that made him work. But he was no fool and quickly found his feet in the Air Force during the war, rising rapidly in rank. At twenty-four he became a colonel. Military authority wished to appoint him to a generalship. Stalin protested: "He is too young yet."

Svetlana was cast in another mould. Clever and studious, at twenty-one years of age, though already a mother, she pursued distinguished historical studies at the University. Not particularly good-looking as a child, said Tamara, at sixteen her schoolmate developed into a beautiful woman. At eighteen she married a brilliant youth who on demobilisation, after passing through the Institute of International Affairs, had entered upon a diplomatic career.

Tamara's grandmother, a beautiful and high-born girl, had studied at the Smolny, the Petrograd school for daughters of the nobility. In early youth she had married a nobleman. Later she married a professor at the Academy of Agriculture who devoted his life to forestry. Both joined the revolutionary intelligentsia, and at length lost their liberty thereby. Tamara's father was born in prison. When Tamara as a child did anything particularly outrageous, her mother would say jokingly, "What can I expect: your father was born in prison!"

The revolution brought the professor into his own. Sent to Baku by Lenin, he organised the socialisation of the oil industry, coming into conflict with the English proprietors of the oilfield. He was one of the first three recipients of the Order of the Red Banner.

As army engineer, George Soloviev, Tamara's father, has risen

to high rank as a general. In an excited whisper at the theatre one
night Tamara said, "My father has been awarded the Order of
Lenin."

Criticism of art is Tamara's choice of subject at the Institute of
History and Philosophy, now incorporated in the University.

Whilst we were talking the others had prepared a picnic lunch:
sandwiches of caviar, sausage or sardines with local mineral waters.
Needing a tin opener, they sought the captain's help. After a while
the saloon carpet stirred, rose, and revealed a hatch from which
emerged the tousled head of the girl engineer, with a hatchet for
the tin! Facetiously the Russians call these tins "the Second Front"—
so difficult to open. After lunch, entering a broad lake, we ran the
launch against a low bank and landed across a plank to bathe—the
men in one creek, the girls in another, mingling only in deep water.
It was an exquisite day, with the water well warmed by the blistering
July sunshine. We sunbathed on flower-strewn grass in birch wood
shrubberies, idly gathering wild strawberries.

The Irak professor, unused to Western ways, appeared among
the girls as they were dressing, himself almost unclothed because he
had mudied his shirt, and wished helplessly to know what he should
do. Tamara, in broken but emphatic French, bade him depart. That
sort of thing, she said, was not done in Russia. At length she called
for our help, and we withdrew the professor.

The unfortunate man then lost his wrist-watch, for which we
searched in vain. At length I sought the precise spot at which he had
entered the water. Our grimy engineer girl donned big wellingtons,
entered the water, dived her hand downwards and extracted the
watch from the mud as if she were a silver diviner.

Re-embarking, we turned homewards in the cool afternoon. The
Chinese gentleman, displaying thin legs and socks as he rested his
feet on the bulkhead, suggested Chinese art and we plunged into a
discussion on Tang, my favourite, and Sung, Tamara's favourite;
she preferring Sung for its spatial quality, its suggestion of completeness, everlastingness; something whole, without beginning or end.

Others joined in the discussion, which roamed from this to that
with eager vivacity. Young Russia to-day moves in a wider environment than a dozen years ago. The day finished with a banquet, where
I met some forty representatives of the arts. Tamara had introduced
us to a very goodly company. She will reappear a few pages later when
I write of Madame Mukhina, the sculptress, and her son, Vesavolod,
one of Tamara's friends.

3. A YOUNG MAN OF PEASANT ORIGIN

ALEXANDER KARAGANOV was born of peasant parentage in 1915. I met him on his return from lecturing in Rumania, in which language he was fluent.

Rumania, he said, lacked discipline. It had no plan. Its people were feckless. The Soviet plane at Sofia had circled twice round the aerodrome to avoid two sheep on the landing ground. A typical occurrence. The same careless, happy-go-lucky spirit prevailed everywhere as in the summoning, organisation and leading of meetings, which would be fixed for 7 o'clock and not begin until 7.45.

Worse experiences of a friend in Italy had shocked him. The U.S.A. authorities, in supervisory control of the South Italian mines, do not encourage, as he felt Russia would have encouraged, the use of pit machinery. Mere boys worked the mines, receiving inadequate food, descending and ascending the mines for great distances on rope ladders: eighteen journeys a day with coal on their backs. To young Karaganov such conditions were intolerable. But the Western allies made no protest and sought no change, nor showed sympathy with those who did so. Rumania to Karaganov and Italy to his friend were the first and only countries where they had seen capitalism at work or in control. They were shocked. They are young.

Unlike Inna, born in professional circles, and Tamara with aristocratic blood, Karaganov's parents were poor peasants from Martenovo, a small village in Moldavia, buried deep in forests, far from railway routes, where life was rudely rural and culture at a minimum. Not till 1926 did education reach Martenovo. With effort and sacrifice Karaganov's father, mother and aunts scraped together money needed for his food, clothing and lodging and Alexander passed through early school with distinction and entered the office of a small district newspaper. He became a journalist. With intimate knowledge of village life, handling a spade before handling anything else, he was ambitious for continued education.

In June, 1934, the local council selected him for the University. The qualifying examination began on 2nd August, and demanded work done in the ten year school. His education had stopped at the seventh year. Three years' work demanded in thirty-five days. His friends helped him. Working night and day he passed and became a student at the Western Institute, choosing Western literature as his subject. In those difficult years his student's stipend of 115 roubles per annum was scarcely adequate. Special dining-rooms and shops helped him:

and in the second year things improved. From the third year onwards he was qualified to lecture at the middle school and able to send money to his parents. "My mother," he said, "is simple and proud."

In 1939 Karaganov graduated. Owing to the army call-up and the dearth of teachers he had to sandwich an advanced course on teaching into his own scientific study of the history of literature: the youngest member of his class was a year his senior. The progress of the war interrupted further scientific work. He was asked to lecture on Fascism as the enemy of culture, its origin and development. He issued a series of booklets.

The situation becoming yet more perilous he joined the army and after a month's training at Stalingrad shared the defence of Moscow. He was wounded at the front. A second and more serious wound detained him eight months in Shandrinsk, where he lectured on Shakespeare, Balzac and Tolstoi. He returned to the army as a military journalist.

At the request of the civilian authorities, he was released for urgent cultural work with the Young Communist League. He trained youth in history and other cultural subjects, organising circles for the boys and girls working at a large military industrial plant. His success put him in charge of all cultural work for youth in the Southern Urals, important work amongst battalions of young workers engaged in mass production of tanks and other military equipment. Repercussions from the front met instant response in the Urals. Tigers and a new type of machine-gun appearing, Russian types to meet them were in mass production within twenty days.

Constructional tasks were colossal but enthusiasm ran high. With a staff of 300 skilled workers and 3,000 unskilled youths a blast furnace was built in seven months in place of the normal thirty. Newspapers resounded with praise. Yet these boys and girls were little more than children, shooting darts across the dinner table, crying at times at their own small troubles. Karaganov's task was to teach them the art of living. He organised brigades and classes and special schools for instruction where youth continued cultural studies. Industrial proficiency, which Karaganov had found in Rumania to take four years, in the Southern Urals took three months, the more difficult processes in four.

Impressed by his work, and perceiving his gift in teaching and foreign literature, he was recalled by the authorities to become one of the four editors of the *Komsomolskaya Pravda* and then appointed to the vice-presidency of Voks, in which capacity I met him.

Karaganov is a handsome youth who enjoys life to the full, eager to swim in the Volga and eat a merry lunch beneath the trees.

Eager for argument or discussion on any matter social or literary, and affording many sidelights on the young Soviet mind. Discussing labour efficiency and output of work with him, I once urged that though Russia's total Plan, preventing useless and unsocial work, free from boom, depression and unemployment, was admirable, yet in minor matters our efficiency often exceeded theirs: our universal use, for example, of pickaxes instead of crowbars; or of barrows wheeled by one instead of boxes with poles carried by two.

"You are right," said Karaganov, "but there are reasons. First, we lack deep roots of industrial culture; we are young, you are old; but we learn. Secondly this is but the first stage in a lightning-quick process. Doubtless somewhat one-sided, and often like the poet whose vision, focussed far ahead, fails to see things on the table before him. We, too, are looking forward. A big goal lies before us. We press on towards that. We often neglect lesser immediate things. But we learn."

Karaganov spoke of lack of specialists and described the efforts to train skilled leaders and skilled organisers, a difficult and slow task. He was also entirely aware of the temporary and inevitable weaknesses of the Soviet Order. "You, in a capitalist country," he argued, "have an early advantage over us. You have the immediate pull of the pocket, with your profit motive. Millions of our people," he admitted, "are unable even yet to think beyond this. It has not been easy to create the ideal of socialism in the mass mind." But Socialist competition, he added, "appealing directly to the immediate profit motive of higher earnings and fostering also the wider, grander motive of aiding the whole community," was tilting the balance in the right direction.

That led to discussion on good people and bad in the Soviet Union, and Karaganov repeated the words—wise words he called them— of Generalissimo Stalin to President Benes when he gave the toast to the army: "The army is composed of many millions of men and they are not all angels. Some behave less well than we desire. But remember that they have travelled through death and struggle for thousands of miles. They feel that they are conquerors and those who are not good think that as conquerors they may do as they like; they may behave as others may not behave. Please understand this and let your judgment be merciful."

Passing one day along a wrecked street in Stalingrad, Karaganov paused and looking at the rubble around said: "Here is the spot." It was the spot where once his lodgings had stood; all gone now, together with his fine collection of upwards of a thousand or more volumes, mainly English classics.

At the early age of thirty Karaganov, whose boyish looks suggest twenty, was appointed to his present post. With a keen and honest mind, he can discuss Soviet feelings and Soviet problems and has a sympathetic undestanding of ours. He is devoted to English literature and culture in general and eager to understand English points of view.

4. A SCULPTRESS AND HER SON

A T a banquet given to us in May many guests made speeches: Borodin, Kolesnikof, Kapitza, Ehrenberg . . . At my side sat a lady, middle-aged, short, firmly built, with cultivated face and genial, assured manner—counterpart of a Cheltenham or Bedford head-mistress. In her brief and formal speech she said she would like to create and give as a permanent memorial to her country a bust of the Dean of Canterbury, her country's friend, if he would permit it and attend her studio. It was Vera Ignatievna, the widow of Dr. Zamkov, better known by her professional name of Madame Mukhina, Russia's noted sculptress. Cordially accepting the invitation, I entered a charming home. Madame Mukhina lives with her son, Vesavolod Zamkov, and the faithful and competent maid who had been with her since her youth and is deeply attached to the family.

My first of many visits was on a summer's evening. The house stands at one corner of a large traffic-ridden pentagon on the outskirts of Moscow. The exterior was as shabby as the neighbourhood in which it stands—a derelict yard giving entrance to a fine old house fallen on evil days. Huge blocks of timber cumbered the hall ready for Mukhina's chisel. The lofty dwelling-room bears signs of former greatness and contains now in a quiet way many lovely things; china and silver on the coffee table, meadowsweet from the Zamkov country cottage; pictures and books, strewn in the haphazard and slightly disorganised way common in the homes of great artists— the ante-room to a studio rather than the drawing-room of a formal home. Signs of culture everywhere. No trace of wealth or luxury, and artists are among the best paid of Soviet workers.

The old serving maid, learning that I was a priest, and seeing my cross, seized it eagerly and kissed it. "She is a believer," said Madame Mukhina, looking with affection at the old lady, and using the term employed for those who practise their orthodox religion.

Drinking excellent coffee in interludes of work we enjoyed the liveliest of conversation. Voyla, as we called Vesavolod for short, is twenty-six, a youth with the thoughtful, charming manner one often finds in boys cut off in their early youth by ill-health from normal activities: he has suffered from various forms of tuberculosis.

With intensive training in his youth Voyla learned at an early age to read, and rambles far through the realms of literature. He speaks fastidious English. Professionally he works on the optical side of physics and my visits coincided with his final examinations at the University. Discussion with him and Tamara, a close friend, took lively and kaleidoscopic turns, punctuated with merry laughter. Madame Mukhina looks up, smiles and works on. They had just been and admired the film *Henry V*. They found it less realistic than most films, giving greater scope for artistic eliminations and concentration.

Tamara, dark frock, dark eyes, green necklace; Voyla in a short-sleeved blue shirt with deep collar and open neck, made a charming pair. I found Voyla a fascinating youth. If ever I had had a son he would have been the son of my choice. He shall form the last of the "close-ups" of Soviet youth; as his mother, whose story is of necessity bound up with his, shall form the first "close-up" of men and women reaching early maturity when the revolution overtook them.

Voyla and Tamara conversed with vivacity, understanding and wit on every conceivable subject: sometimes artistic, sometimes archæological, sometimes theological and philosophical, sometimes scientific. Artistically and archæologically Voyla is interested in the Madonna and Child as seen in all civilisations. He hopes some day to produce a thesis upon it. I recalled Nehru's rapt musing over the ancient, pre-Christian Madonna and Child when I took him to the Chinese Exhibition in pre-war days.

Voyla has a passion for English life, literature and culture, and hopes at length to study at Oxford. One day he produced a large seventeenth-century English MS. discovered in an old shop. He read of the description of a remedy for eczema—pansy leaves. His friend, suffering from eczema in Paris, consulted a French specialist, who recommended a concoction made from pansy leaves which he described as the latest and most efficacious remedy.

For philosophical problems Voyla had an eager and untramelled mind. Like many other Russians he agreed that death is the end of a chapter, rather than the end of a book, but found it hard to think of the ego, as we know it, proceeding in continuity there; ready, however, to admit the force of the argument from the scientific fact of the ever-increasing individuality within an ever-increasing integration as the rule of life in its evolution; suggesting that the same differentiation and integration may not unreasonably be characteristic of continued life hereafter. Voyla has an intensely practical side, helping his mother in every conceivable way. The Zamkovs, for instance, are building a new house and studio in Moscow. Voyla carries through all the plans, a difficult matter at the present moment there as here. In the studio he helps his mother, whom he loves devotedly and admires highly. He prepares the clay, arranges the stands and chairs and photographs the sitter from every angle. His photography is brilliant.

The studio contains beautiful objects, and shelves of sculptured heads—some obviously mere portraits, others interpretations. Madame Mukhina carves as well as models, her medium being a brown hard knotted wood. The monumental head of a professor stands in the studio. Of my own bust I would say two things. First I saw in it what I never saw in my mirror—an uncanny likeness to my mother. I amused her in the second place by saying, as the work neared completion, that she had depicted the kind of man God meant me to be rather than the kind of man I am. Her work is monumental.

Our last morning was memorable with talk and humour. Madame Mukhina had just returned from France, where she had attended a conference of 3,000 women, some English, some Italian, but mostly French; one delegate came from Spain and, to her astonishment, only one from Belgium, where women still lack the vote. For Madame Mukhina there is no freedom in a land where women have no vote.

Madame Mukhina's carefully prepared paper on art was read by mistake at Marseilles, where it was not understood, instead of at Paris, where it would have been understood. She had prepared a criticism of French art as being too abstract and lacking in content. Asked what precisely she meant by content, she pointed to a bronze figure of a robust young peasant woman with full breasts and rounded figure standing with folded arms four square and head erect, suggestive of confidence in honest work and the plenty that accrues from an ordered economy.

"That is content," she said.

The figure had attracted Mussolini, who ordered a replica of it for his lakeside villa.

Like Gerassimov, Madame Mukhina cannot appreciate the work of Picasso. Alex Exter's work she prefers as possessing at least some content in addition to exquisite colour sensibility. The talk was curiously frank as well as interesting and witty.

Russia, the least prurient country that I know, and the most sanely moral, is also, at times and on occasion, the most outspoken. In an entirely natural way and without a touch of nastiness Russians speak of things which find no utterance in English drawing-rooms.

Tamara, for instance, had just returned from conducting an

Australian scientist round a stud farm where he had insisted on a full
explanation of artificial insemination as practised there. The family
were amused at her dilemma. We discussed again the work of Voyla's
father, Alexander Zamkov, the story of whose life and death I had
just learned from Madame Mukhina herself. Madame Mukhina
and Voyla had explained in perfectly natural terms Dr. Zamkov's
discoveries and experiments in injections of sterilised urine from
pregnant women, which possessed, he maintained, for the safety of
the babe, an overplus of creative energies; and which he had used
for cure of many diseases, his object thereby being not to conquer
disease but to fortify those elements in the human body which resist
disease attacks. The statistics of Dr. Zamkov's cures were impressive.
Madame Mukhina said, having used the injections herself consistently,
she had never suffered from any sickness for eighteen years. More
interesting, however, to me was the fact that the whole discussion
could be carried on by a young man and young woman in the presence
of the young man's mother with complete detachment, without a
suspicion of awkwardness or touch of pruriency. Carried on, too, by
the same Tamara so recently indignant and almost hysterically upset
at the Irakian professor's intrusion on the girls' privacy as they dressed
after bathing. Madame Mukhina, jealous for her husband's discoveries,
was disappointed to learn from the Pasteur Institute in Paris that no
further experiments had been made with the urine of pregnant
women. We discussed artistic matters. Madame Mukhina agreed
with Tamara in the wish that it had fallen also to the lot of Korin to
paint my portrait, though agreeing with the excellence of Gerassimov's
work: "It would have been spiritually more interpretive." Madame
Mukhina is making new experiments in the casting of my bust.
It is to be in bronze, the garments dark, the hair whitened by a special
process and the face left dull red bronze.

Madame Mukhina told me her life story. Her father was a rope
manufacturer; a rich man who had lost two million roubles of fortune
at the revolution. Russians, she was careful to explain, take these
losses less seriously than Western people, accustomed as they had
long been to Tartar and Polish attacks.

Her mother, from whom she had inherited foreign blood, German
or French, perhaps through the Napoleonic invasion, died at Tar-
brucken in 1891, when she was twenty-nine and Mukhina one and a
half, and her father, afraid for the children, had removed to the
Crimea, where he had set up a hemp oil factory at Feodosia.

Madame Mukhina had a passion for drawing from her earliest
youth. I studied an old photograph of her: a beautiful child with
broad brow bending down intent on her drawing.

Her father died when she was fourteen and she was taken by her guardians to Gorsk, where she matriculated, and whence she passed on to Moscow to study drawing in the same school as Tamara's mother, taking her first lessons in painting from Maskof, a well-known contemporary artist. The year 1912 marked a turning point in her life.

Sledging down a precipitous road, the horse shied and the sledge crashed down the mountainside. Her face struck a rock. Recovering consciousness she knew that she was badly hurt. She felt her forehead first. It was whole, but her nose was severed and hung by a thread. Happily a doctor who was immediately summoned was expert and joined the broken and severed parts in so skilful a manner that it was only when Madame Mukhina stood quite close that I discovered the widespread scar which still remains.

At the time, however, her face was badly disfigured. She had been beautiful. She was a sensitive girl. She feared she would be forced, in the manner of that day, to enter a convent and finish her life in seclusion. She was utterly depressed. Then she was seized with a sudden desire to go abroad where, unknown, she could continue her art and her studies. Her guardians, though at first resisting because it was deemed improper in those days for a young girl of twenty to go abroad alone, being at their wits' end, at length yielded and she went to Paris. To her marred face Madame Mukhina attributes her artistic success: "That mountain crash did much to enrich my life."

In Paris she joined the painting academy of Bourdel, a pupil of Rodin. She remained two winters and left: "That was all the teaching I ever had," she said. "I am but an amateur."

Bourdel, however, taught her a lesson she never forgot: "Bourdel taught me to see monumentally. Rodin, Bourdel's master, was never monumental. His 'Burghers of Calais' is not monumental. His 'Victor Hugo' is not monumental. I have learned more from Egypt and India than from Rodin," she said.

She spoke of Rodin's "boulevard" eyes. He saw things as the man in the street would see them; saw them thus and depicts them thus. She could mention twenty-eight instances, she said, of this kind of vulgarity. She also saw in Rodin elements of sex appeal which were equally distasteful to her.

Her two years in Paris worked a vital change. She had seen many people and studied intensively. She had attended a cubist school. She wished to learn all that could be learned. She wished to understand all. She found herself working in two worlds, utterly different worlds. With Bourdel she was in the school of nature. With the Cubists

D

she was in the school of the abstract. The cubist abstractionists had
to work from nature but strove to avoid the sense of nature.

She had been obliged to master the cubist theme and understand
its technique: "I cannot neglect anything I do not understand until
I have mastered it," she said. Master it she did, but only to discard
it: "Abstract art leads away from the reality of things," she said. She
remembered the cubist art school with a certain gratitude: "It was
a kind of laboratory, where we tested things." It played a good rôle
in her art life. Before she left Paris she had discovered her own line
of work: she must seek and depict the inner soul and content of
things, and express it monumentally. She left Paris with a passion for
realistic art; for something which starts with things as they are but
does not end there; which steps on from the what is to the what may
be and might be and must be. Her art is monumental, exalting,
inspiring.

I thought of my own bust and of my remark: "That is the kind
of man God meant me to be," not the man, alas, that I am, but
starting from the man I am. That was why I saw the family likeness
to my mother. There was nothing merely abstract there, but something
real and realistic. That, too, is why that peasant girl, four square, who
stood akimbo before me was no photograph of any actual peasant girl,
but the ideal of all peasant girls. That, too, was why the magnificent
youths on the Soviet Pavilion at Paris are not photographs of any
Soviet youths you will ever see in Soviet towns and yet express the
inner spirit which inspires all Soviet youth.

Madame Mukhina returned when the war of 1914 broke out. Duty
called. She had left Russia as an unhappy young girl in the misery of
spoiled beauty; she returned two years later a matured and purposeful
young woman eager to serve her country as a Red Cross nurse. She
worked on during the civil war in a hospital which was situated in
Moscow between the lines of the Whites and the Reds; aristocrats
and proletarians and bourgeois alike came to her wards. She tended
all. Her hospital struggled on through difficulties, shortage of supplies,
shortage of food. At length she removed her worst patients to a military
hospital, recalling the date, 17th December, 1917, for there she had
met Alexei Zamkov, whom a year later, in 1918, she married.

Mukhina had been happy in her married life. Her husband had
great qualities, was good and exercised a powerful influence over her
character. He respected her artistic gifts. He set her free for her art.

Throughout the civil war life was hard. She made a living by
poster work, but passed on later to sculpture and at length received
an appointment at the central school in Moscow.

In 1920 Voyla was born, and though at first Mukhina's hands were tied by domestic household duties, she was soon back at work again and in 1927 won the school Jubilee prize and went to Italy. At length she received the coveted commission to design the sculpture which was to adorn and complete the famous Soviet Pavilion at the Paris Exhibition where, for the first time, I saw her work. It was large scale work and a staff of 200 workers, including thirty engineers, assisted her. The tremendous arch of the scarf floating in the air, though an arc thirty metres in length and weighing five tons and a half, only touched the group at two points. The whole task was difficult and only possible owing to the full help she received from the government. It was educative and gave the workers a new understanding also. Many still seek to join her team. Her prize she shared with the workers.

Voyla and Tamara love English culture. Looking to the U.S.A. for engineering, for mass production and technique, they look, they say, to England for culture. America, they add, is too prosperous and materialistic. American culture will come later. Culture in a country is at its best when that country is like a ripe cherry, slightly overripe, indeed; when wealth is adequate and its quest no longer absorbs the cream of national energy, when life provides leisure for things of the spirit: and at that stage England has already arrived.

In her finer, more private inner boudoir, where Madame Mukhina writes and reads and rests, I had seen on a small table the photograph of a strikingly handsome man with strong, kindly face. In front of it fresh flowers always stood. It was the portrait of Dr. Zamkov, Madame Mukhina's husband, and on that final day she told me the story of his life, and of the struggles by which he became a doctor and of his creative activities in scientific medicine. He died as he had lived, in utter unselfishness; arranging with care all business matters, never revealing until the last the fatal malady which killed him.

I was sad to leave the studio, the bronze peasant girl, the professor's head, the bust of a powerful bare-armed youth—a relative, tortured to death by Nazi brutality—the great blue vase, the massive crystal, the old china, the old serving maid and Voyla and Tamara and Madame Mukhina and the merry, witty, homely, purposeful, serious Soviet family I had grown to love so well.

5. TWO PAINTERS

WALKING one night with Tamara in the foyer of the Bolshoi Theatre during an interval in a musical ensemble, we met a stoutish man of middle age dressed in pepper and salt tweeds, loose, bluish-grey waistcoat and gold chain, with a frenchified coloured tie drawn loosely into a bow under the coloured collar of a soft shirt.

"That," said Tamara, "is Gerassimov, the artist. May I introduce him?" We spoke. He accepted my invitation to join us in our box. At the close of the performance he asked that we might meet again and in his own home. He wished to paint my portrait.

Gerassimov's house was a typical small Moscow villa. It lay in a little settlement off the great high-road that leads to Leningrad. The approaching lane was atrocious, as are most lanes in the outskirts of this overgrown city. Bumping over it, we came to a neat suburban road with trees and grassy sidewalks, and found a small house with a large studio standing in its own rough garden where Gerassimov lives and paints.

The studio itself is a large outhouse of plain bricks and exposed beams, whitewashed throughout even to the brick stove crowned with a magnificent horse's head in plaster-cast. A wide settee of yellow maple wood with a Persian rug spread across it, a fine old table littered with magazines beneath one window, and trestles strewn with paints beneath the other, together with a chair of yellow wood and fine design in which the "subject" usually sat, formed the sole furniture. The floor had once been waxed.

The magazines came from every country: England, France, America and Spain. Gerassimov kept abreast of artistic movements the whole world over. He had his preferences, his likes and dislikes, as all artists have. Picasso raised his reasoned scorn. Turning over leaf after leaf of Picasso's book he explained his dislikes: "Picasso lacks contact with the objective world. Picasso paints subjective things, things done in his own mind, things bizarre and fantastic."

The walls of Gerassimov's studio were a blaze of magnificent form and colour: a Rubenesque room. Immense canvases and smaller canvases. On one large easel stretched an unfinished painting of the Big Three meeting in Teheran, and the various life studies for it. Far more striking and arresting, however, were the other pictures: a village street gay with painted wooden houses under springtime birches, where the artist himself was born; a large portrait of an Uzbek dancer. Most striking of all was a group of women in a Russian bath-house: a huge canvas showing Gerassimov's technique at its best, with superb painting of water-soaked flesh glowing amidst the steam of the bath tubs: a masterly piece of work, worthy of exhibition in any gallery in the world.

In painting my own portrait Gerassimov's penetrating eyes would search me from head to foot, glancing intently for several seconds and then, moving swiftly to the big easel which stood beside me,

thrust on splashes of colour here and there to catch some fleeting
lights or quick expression. After a spell he would stop, light his pipe,
and calling for his man-of-all-trades, who apparently, besides cooking
and cleaning and rendering all other services, was always available
for critical study of the artist's progress. Together they would discuss
hands or head and so forth. Gerassimov welcomed criticism. When
Inna said that something was missing in my expression, he studied
it again and again, and at last with a swift stroke would catch and
express what she had suggested and he had begun to see.

His touch and rapidity of work were masterly. I can never forget
how in two or three minutes my jewelled crucifix, my wrist-watch
or ring came to glittering life. Absolute sureness of touch everywhere;
supremely so when he painted face and eyes and mouth.

I walked in the intervals in the sunshine round his small rough
garden, which resembles the gardens I knew in my youth in northern
Scotland even to the little shed tucked unobtrusively in a corner of
the garden to serve as toilet. There is no luxury in a Soviet artist's
home.

"I like Gerassimov's portrait," Tamara said one day, "yet I
could wish that Korin had painted you. Gerassimov paints a portrait
in the traditional manner and paints it superbly. Korin paints the
soul. People seldom see Korin, still less his work; Korin is a recluse;
Korin is religious. I wish you could meet Korin."

Sharing the wish, one day we met. Tamara engineered it.

We met in the Korin home, a small house tucked quietly away
in a crowded quarter. A house with a garden in the very heart of
Moscow, with great flats and blocks rising gaunt around it: a real
retreat with Korin and his wife as the recluses, living like Nesterov
in a world apart, but only in order to see life steadily and miss no
aspect that others might ignore.

Paul Korin is fifty-four; he looks thirty-four. Close cut hair, open
shirt, grey suit, quiet and unassuming, no hint of the artist. We met in
his dining-room, a prim nineteenth-century chamber. We examined
the pictures whilst awaiting our host: rare twelfth-century miniatures
painted on boards in rich colours—gold, crimson, black. Exquisite
delicate paintings of his own hand, landscapes and towns; long panels
three feet by ten feet in the minute style; one, a panorama of Venice,
each detail exact, a Canaletto.

Paul Korin was born in Palekh, where for 300 years his family has
maintained unbroken the tradition of what is now called Palekh
miniature craftsmanship. His wife's training, temperament and
character accord admirably with his own. Brought up in Moscow
at a convent by a descendant of Queen Victoria, she is quiet and

efficient, with the calm remoteness one connects with ancient Chinese lineage. Madame Korin played for us with taste and feeling on a large American organ; all from ear. She plays church music, particularly from the Christmas Mass, with which she had been familiar in her convent days. After tea in the garden we entered the huge studio. Gorky, early in the revolution, in which he took a leading part, recognised the worth of this religious painter and the supreme value of his work. Giving Korin every encouragement, he procured for his use this studio where he has worked ever since, and where at present he is busy, amongst other tasks, in painting Conference portraits.

The next two hours live vividly in my memory. First we saw a large canvas of Nesterov, painted during the last war, and entitled "A little child shall lead them." Against a lovely background of fields and wooded hills, nuns with blinded soldiers—followed by a great crowd of workers with Tolstoi in their midst—one old man in the front holding an ikon, another a candle—advance across the flowered meadows down to the banks of the Volga; a peasant child, simple, innocent and beautiful, leads them.

After that sympathetic introduction came Korin's superb master-pieces. Some fifteen or twenty individual portraits, completed studies for a vast canvas he projects, in which he will assemble the leading ecclesiastical personalities during the tremendous events which shook Church and State from 1917 and onwards. Figures of heroic size but realistic and intensely individual. We confront real persons: patriarchs, bishops, monks, nuns, abbesses, beggars, cantors . . . particular persons, the patriarch Sergius, not a patriarch in general. Portraits, but more than portraits. It was the spirit which Korin wished first, foremost and all the time to portray. It was this that overcame and mastered realism greater than anything I ever saw before. The technique is superb. Black pigment predominates, acting as a foil to the delicate tints of face or the gorgeous riot of colour in the robes.

The figures simply step from the canvas to meet you; noble, long-haired figures. Now it is Sergius, Metropolitan of Moscow; now the young priest who gave up a medical career in answer to the call of conscience and was ordained in 1931. The stately procession moves on, one by one: Trikon, an actor; the Archbishop of Yaroslav, who had worked as an architect until 1923; the Dean of a convent, who in Alexei Tolstoi's opinion was the greatest tenor since Chaliapin; Princess Goldestena with two nuns; a dignified abbess who refused to sit for her portrait until told that religious duty demanded this record of a great period that future generations might be inspired. Here was the Church's own story in living flesh and blood, outward and visible signs of something inward and spiritual—expressing for the day of reconciliation the very soul of religious Russia. For such is Korin's motive and aim in painting the masterpiece he projects and for which these studies took eight years to complete. Here is institutional religious Russia portrayed in paint, as Tolstoi had portrayed it in words, a massive heroic conception. Personally Korin is likeable and lovable. He gave me a beautiful miniature, in the true Palekh tradition, of the scene from his upper studio windows of mysterious Moscow, with grand old golden cupolas dominant in front.

6. A SCIENTIST

OUTSTANDING in Russian scientific circles is Pyotr Kapitza, a former pupil of Lord Rutherford in Cambridge. In 1923 at the age of twenty-nine Kapitza received his Doctor of Philosophy degree, winning many honours and working as Professor appointed by the Royal Society in a laboratory equipped specially for him at their expense and at a cost of £15,000. Recalled home in 1935, he received in the Soviet Union unstinted help and encouragement and has continued to make contributions to science and industry of world-wide significance. Anxious to know a man whose work on the ultimate problems of matter was of so high repute and who knew both worlds east and west from intimate personal experience, I met Kapitza in 1937, when he told me how happily he was working in and for his country.

In 1945 I met him more frequently and learnt more of his present work and of the facilities which he enjoys for its pursuit. In a speech of welcome which he kindly made at a ceremonial dinner given to me on my last visit he emphasised the need for truth—truth in mutual understanding and truth in scientific research. In his search for truth Kapitza seeks advance in the orthodox scientific way by finding out where a fact upsets a theory. Such facts are generally carefully hidden: they must be extracted. Kapitza seeks for them ruthlessly: "The incomprehensible should brook inquiry," is his favourite saying and his rule in life. Kapitza selects super-low temperatures as his special implements. He knows what he is doing thereby. He has compared his work as scientific researcher to a geological traveller in an unknown land who may return empty or full but has been guided throughout by known laws and not by luck.

There was nothing fortuitous, therefore, in his use of low temperatures. For temperature registers the speed of atoms: the higher the temperature the greater the speed and vice versa. Lower the temperature and the motion slows down, like slow-motion pictures of

tennis players. Slow the atoms down and you may learn how matter
works, as the tennis player seeks for slow-motion pictures of the expert.
At exceedingly low temperatures matter revealed wholly new qualities.
Helium, for example, at a temperature thousands of times lower than
the temperature of a room loses viscosity or stickiness. Water is less
viscous than treacle. Yet water takes long to flow through a glass
tube with exceedingly fine bore. Helium liquefied at a temperature
of —273 degrees centigrade, flows through almost instantaneously.
It is super-fluid. Kapitza gained a Stalin prize for that discovery.
No one knows yet where such knowledge may not lead.

We do, however, know where some of Kapitza's work leads,
especially his achievement in cheap liquidation of oxygen. Oxygen
is obtained most cheaply from air, whose two major parts are nitrogen
and oxygen. The process of extraction is simple in theory: Liquefy
air. The nitrogen in it evaporates more quickly than the oxygen and
can be distilled off by gently raising the temperature, leaving pure
liquid oxygen behind.

Liquid oxygen has high value, as we know, for welding, for cutting
metals or aiding respiration at high altitudes. Oxygen is a vital agent
in life and a basic fact in combustion. Abundant in nature, forming
one-fifth of the air around us, if produced cheaply in bulk oxygen
would speed indefinitely industrial processes such as reduction of
iron ore in blast furnaces and clean our smoky skies through more
efficient use of solid fuel. But oxygen, produced hitherto by the com-
pression of the piston thrust, was dear and the process slow. Kapitza
made it cheap. Realising, as a practical engineer—he is proud to be
such as well as a scientist—he experimented, with Rayleigh's suggestion
of a cooling turbine and succeeded where all others had failed. His
refrigerating turbine becomes a prime tool for scientific research
and industrial usage: it won for him a second Stalin prize.

From first to last the Soviet Government had given Kapitza
encouragement and magnificent equipment: his refrigerating turbine
has no need to fight against private interests, or await tardy development, slowly working its way from one industry to another. The new
method becomes a matter of State interest, the State ordering its
employment wherever cheap oxygen is needed. A State Technical
Council for the utilisation of oxygen, empowered to supervise the
execution of this order, has been created. Pyotr Kapitza has been
appointed as its head.

Integration is an idea with deep roots in Kapitza's thinking;
Integration, or the contact in thought and imagination of this
scientific worker with that, and integration or tying up, or contact,
of all scientists with the public at large and the world at large.

Scientific achievement, Kapitza urges, must be popularised, though not necessarily by the scientist. It must also be spread by propagation. A scientist must make known his achievement to his colleagues and influence thought, philosophical outlook and technical processes thereby.

Integration of age and youth with mutual needs is also much in his thought. He recalls Rutherford: " Kapitza, you know it is only thanks to my pupils that I feel young myself." "And now," comments Kapitza, "that I am approaching old age"—he is but fifty-three, counted old where all are so young—"I feel that only the society of young people can prevent me from withering away. Whilst passing on my own experience to youth I keep myself alive and interested in all that is new and progressive in science: conservatism is worse in a scientist than premature death, for it holds back the development of science."

7. A SURGEON

I n the Tretiakhov gallery, outstanding amongst Nesterov's competent pictures is the portrait of a youngish man whose Roman face, painted in profile, comes sharply to a point. The head is thrust forward, in burning eagerness. The man wears glasses, a skull cap, and the white overalls of an operating theatre. Long supple fingers pointing forward have the same thrust as the face. Clusters of bottles on the table complete the picture of George Yudin, a world-famed surgeon and Moscow's pride. I met Yudin more than once, and spent one memorable day with him in the Central Emergency Hospital where he works as surgeon-in-chief.

Taking me through the wards, Yudin greeted, and was greeted by, innumerable patients. He had a word for each and moved like a father amongst children in rooms sadly overcrowded through the exigencies of war.

We met a young girl. He called her to him. She placed her head against his shoulder as he stroked her hair. He had given her new life and new hope. She was one of his œsophagus patients, rescued from living death by a unique operation. We came to the bed of a recent arrival. The cast of features seemed familiar. Thin, dark, delicate—of course, she was Armenian. Actually she came from Echmiadzin, 1,400 miles distant, whence I had returned myself a few days previously. Patients in this hospital came from many lands, another instance of the far-flung nature of Soviet Health Services.

Yudin explained with a sketch his famous operation, whereby

he replaces the destroyed œsophagus, or tube extending from the mouth to the stomach, by another tube composed of a severed length of the patient's own bowel, delicately severed, then threaded outside the ribs and beneath the thick pad of flesh and skin which covers them, forming thus a new channel betwixt stomach and throat.

"But will not the patient subsequently be vulnerable and need guards for the chest?" I asked.

Yudin beckoned a passing girl and bade her drink. We could see the movement of the liquid in its passage from throat to stomach. He slapped her soundly along the new channel way. She never winced, only smiled.

I said: "How did the girl come by her sickness?"

"Perhaps a mistake," he said. "Children sometimes drink the strong chemical resembling water placed by the window in winter to prevent frost. Soldiers often make similar mistakes.

"Sometimes," he added, "it is attempted suicide." A recent patient had drunk carbolic acid after an unhappy love affair. Her œsophagus was destroyed. If she was to live it must be by feeding her through a silver tube direct into the stomach, or by Yudin's operation. Friends and officials had hurried the patient to the emergency hospital 1,400 miles away. The operation was successful. Recovering quickly, the girl returned to her parents, who never knew and never needed to know of her attempted suicide, or of her recovery at Yudin's hands: he saved that woman body and soul.

We passed through the out-patients' wards and visited the yard where stood a line of cars, with medical attendants always near by in readiness for emergency calls. A car must be on the road within two minutes of the call, the radio in the car continuing directions, warning the doctor what he must expect to find. Operators in the surgery stand ready for instant work. Lives are saved by prompt attention.

Farther along the corridor we stepped into a room flanked by flasks and bottles: blood for transfusion. Yudin with a questioning look asked: "Do you think it wrong to take blood from a corpse to save human life?"

"Could my dead body serve the living I would gladly donate it," was my reply.

Yudin was pleased. Some protested on religious grounds. Italy refused the publication of Yudin's books on blood transfusion.

Use of cadaver blood had begun with experiments on animals; Yudin's assistants, Doctors M. G. Skudina and S. I. Barenboim, proving that cadaver blood when transfused into an animal dying of acute anæmia was capable of reviving it.

Dr. Yudin frequently needed blood speedily and in large quantities. Blood from living subjects was too slow and sometimes insufficient in quantity: it is dangerous to mix blood from different living subjects. Bodies killed in accident were frequently available at the Emergency Hospital. Yudin made his first experiment on a human subject in the case of a young engineer who had slashed both wrists in a suicide attempt. He came to the hospital pulseless. Transfusion with blood from the cadaver of a man, aged sixty, killed in an automobile accident six hours before revived him.

Cadaver blood remains sterile, preserving its living properties for long periods, if obtained within six or eight hours after death.

"To-day I am about to perform for the one hundred and twenty-seventh time an œsophagus operation," Yudin said, as we walked towards his own private room. "Would you care to see it?"

I was eager. So we drank tea, donned overalls and, adjourning to the operating theatre, I sat a few feet distant and watched a master-piece of manipulative skill: this was the Yudin of the Nesterov portrait. The patient, a young girl, was conscious throughout the operation: spinal injections were made for the work below the diaphragm; sub-cutaneous injections for work above it. Skilled nurses aided Yudin; the leading nurse, the wife of the Minister of Health, anticipated his every want. Even laymen could see the intricacy of an operation which exposed and drew forth a stretch of bowel long enough to form a new passage from throat to stomach, slowly severing it from innumerable arteries running to feed it through the connecting membrane that spread out fan-like in Yudin's hands.

"A delicate and dangerous moment this," Yudin said in a low voice as he began to sever the arteries and then, measuring the length of bowel, said with satisfaction, "Yes, long enough."

Yudin then thrust with great force and resounding noise a spade-like tool, followed by one larger still, under the thick pad of outer flesh and skin which covers the bones on the chest and, making a passage up to the neck wide enough to receive it, threaded in the new tube, which was subsequently to couple throat and stomach.

The task finished, Yudin gave the girl a final pat with a pleasant "How are you?" The girl replied cheerfully, "All right, thank you." During the operation he had several times made the same inquiry. "*Nichevo*": "Go on, it is nothing . . ." had been the reply.

Here was craftsmanship at its highest: no flurry, no hesitation, no impatience; speedy, deft, and sure action, accompanied by conversation that we might understand what we saw.

Yudin had lived an interesting life. Born in 1891, his father had owned a caviar factory at Tsaritsin. He met his wife in hospital. She was suffering from paralysis. "A happy paralysis," he said, with a pleasant smile at her, as we drank tea in his study. His wife, heiress to a large fortune, which she had lost at the revolution, is devoted to her husband and to her country: they served together at the front line in the war. On 14th July, 1916, in the last war Yudin was wounded. On 14th July, 1943, in this war Yudin was made Fellow of our Royal College of Surgeons. Appointed surgeon-in-chief of the Emergency Hospital at thirty-seven years of age, he has published sixty-eight books and monographs and has visited England and America.

Yudin is passionately devoted to his hospital with its noble architecture of 1803 and draws inspiration from the tale of its origin. A count, rich and respected, had married a serf who became an actress. His angered relatives accused the wife of infidelity. The count and his steward following her one dark night saw her enter an old building to apply bandages and dressings for sick aged folk. He removed her to Italy. Expecting a child, they returned to Moscow.

"Do you," he asked, "still wish to help old sick people?"

"Indeed, yes," she replied.

"Then it shall be a place worthy of you and your work," said the count, and built this vast palace for her. A boy was born and the countess died seventeen days later. That is the tale.

From the large entrance hall, which had formerly been the chapel, Yudin took me to a gallery where the friezes had been blocked up with boarding. These boards are to be removed and the friezes—of Jesus healing the sick—will be exposed once more to view.

In a laboratory where glass jars containing cancer growths crowded the shelves, Yudin, handling one with conspicuous care, gravely said: "That cancer grew in my mother's body. I removed it." He paused and turning to me said more gravely still: "God helped me. My mother lived after its removal thirteen years. She only passed away seven days ago. There had been no return of the cancer."

My last sight of Yudin was after a tour together of the old buildings in various parts of the Moscow he loves so well. We visited a patient at a hospital where he was consultant. He returned to find some small city boys gathered with longing eyes around the car. Crowding them on to the step, with an arm through the window to support them, he said: "Hold tight," and to their immeasurable delight drove them round the great hospital oval.

8. QUALITY OF SOVIET YOUTH

I T has been difficult, once started, to stay the story of Russia's
personal life as I learned to know it. One individual leads on to another.
Of necessity I have been selective. Inclination would lead me indefinitely on to sketch the airmen who flew us, the chauffeurs who drove
us, the men and maids who served us; to sketch the great healthy
smiling agronomist, Tsitzin, who urged us to stay longer and examine
more closely and under his own guidance his work on perennial
wheat; to sketch the young but brilliant Odessan Jew, Bonderevsky,
an evacuee in Tashkent whose command of English, whose historical
knowledge and grasp of events on the world scale would grace the
long-matured professor, politician or diplomat; or the driver at
Yerevan who met timidity at hair-pin bends with the merry cry
"Quite safe, quite safe; I drove a tank at Stalingrad," and who tended
me through two weeks of service as a son a father, and wept at our
parting. . . .

They crowd in upon me, the memory of those human lives, so
attractive, so approachable, so eager for contact, so willing to talk
of their own daily life and hopes and troubles and so anxious to hear
about life in England. As willing to share *life* as to share property.
So courageous too, picking up the threads again, as at Stalingrad,
of a devastated life, and yet so unembittered and unhostile to the
Germans working beside them on a tractor belt.

Running through all this personal life, particularly through young
Soviet personal life, are certain general characteristics, chief of which
perhaps is quiet enthusiasm and earnestness of purpose. Russian
youth has unbounded capacity for fun and merriment and a vast sense
of humour; they have neither time nor taste for frivolity. Russian
youth does not drift, is not aimless, knows what it wants, sees a clear
road ahead and is eager for responsibility.

There is nothing to thwart or balk Soviet youth from pursuing
any purpose which attracts them, or for which they feel aptitude.
Nothing at least outside themselves. Do they feel the urge to be a singer,
an agronomist, a doctor or an expert in atomic energy, an open door
awaits them at the start leading on to other doors admitting anyone
of proved ability and purposeful desire to the goal they seek.

Soviet youth knows no major frustration outside himself. A boy
ambitious to be a scientist may lack essential mental quality or a child
desiring Arctic exploration the necessary physique. They never lack
the opportunity which awaits quality, application and desire.

Encouraged by these open doors and seeing other youth enter this profession or that and pass from one achievement to another, Soviet youth is eager for responsibility. In Parks of Culture you may see youth queuing for a parachute leap. Boys and girls like themselves try and succeed, so they press forward, eager to don the harness and take the plunge. Precisely so the would-be engineer is eager for the responsibility of difficult jobs. No disheartening barriers await him at the start: every branch of profession and every industrial activity calls aloud for men and women willing to equip themselves and eager for responsibility. Youth responds, mass youth responds, not just youth of this class or that. Those who plan Soviet economy know that they can draw on the widest areas of youth to man it. And youth knows that the ever-expanding plan has room for them and a responsible job in whatever branch of activity they choose and will never let them down.

Soviet planners therefore have no fears that the cream of Soviet youth, killed off by the war, will rob them of to-morrow's leaders: whole battalions of youth, competent and equipped, line up for the responsibility which now devolves upon them.

And Soviet youth in general knows that a big task awaits them. A task primarily of reconstruction at home but with ultimate repercussions on the world at large. First to make good the ravages of war. Next to carry their civilisation and their standard of life on from the point where war interrupted it. Finally to produce a civilisation and a standard of life higher than any other in the world. They believe in this possibility and accept it as a mission. No military conquests are sought—nothing is further from the mind of Soviet youth than militarism—only the conquest of idea and example.

This essential earnestness of clearly defined objective produces great simplicity and strength of character. Young Russia is single-minded, with life unified by dominant purpose. And this involves no fanaticism or narrowness of outlook. Indeed, part of the purpose is the development of a wide culture and an eagerness to examine and master culture in all its ranges as exemplified in their own and other lands, thus adding beauty to simplicity and encouraging the frankness which recognises good where they see it and lacks reservation through eagerness to share.

Another marked feature of Soviet youth is love of roaming and adventure. Encouragement meets them here from authority of every kind—government, trade unions, collectives, co-operatives. Children roam to camps in summer time; youths roam from republic to republic in great companies or privately for sport and pleasure. The flat monotony of Russian landscape may contribute to the passion for roaming. Variety is sought and books of adventure and scientific quest are as eagerly read to-day as when young Stalin surreptitiously devoured the adventure stories of Jules Verne in his seminary at Tbilisi.

Faults they doubtless possess and these are rightly lashed at in the press, which is more educative, as I have already said, in its tendency than informative. The Stakanovite movement and the movement for Socialist competition aim at defeat of inherited laziness and the "it-does-not-matter" attitude to life and work. A fault combated may lead to super-emphasis of the contrasted virtue and Russia's gigantic feats of work and endurance, as in the defence of Stalingrad or the reconstruction of the Dnieper Dam are the modern counterpart of the ancient *Nichevo* (it does not matter).

Russia has emerged as a great power. The old submissiveness has gone, a new audaciousness takes its place. Not, I would urge again, military arrogance. Only a desire no longer to be treated as inferior people. And an inferior people they certainly are not.

With this brief suggestion of prevailing elements in the quality of Soviet citizens we pass on shortly to examine the lines of training which produced Soviet youth and the economic organisation on which these rest. But first a word about the engineers responsible for the training and the organisation.

ENGINEERS OF SOVIET SUCCESS

1. A PILGRIMAGE TO GORI

I MET Schvernik. I met Molotov. Finally I met Generalissimo Stalin himself, who, with other comrades and under the guidance and inspiration of Lenin as master architect, has fashioned a new civilisation dominant over a sixth of the world.

Three weeks before our meeting, I had made a pilgrimage to Georgia, the scene of Stalin's boyhood and youth. In Gori, his birth-place, my mind instinctively ran back to the domed church, rising high in a hot Italian plain, within which stands another and smaller church—a shrine linked with the memory of Francis of Assisi. Within its panoply of marble, in this highland village street of Gori in Georgia, stands the miniature room where Stalin was born of pious parentage.

For seven centuries Assisi has drawn its pilgrims. Maybe for seven centuries Gori will draw pilgrims of a later day, as will Lenin's mausoleum in Moscow, for Lenin and Stalin are bound to leave deep and lasting impress on the course of human history, and the world honours the humble beginnings of its benefactors. Simplicity of origin is high adornment to greatness.

Stalin's early home contains two rooms. The landlord occupied one, Joseph's father and mother the other. Thirteen feet by twelve, this small but not uncomely room, lit by two casement windows and opening on to a small veranda and the cobbled street where the small boy could play under his mother's eye as she worked, was Joseph Djngashvili's home during his early years.

Neat, clean and orderly, every article of furniture presented by his mother to the nation and arranged by her precisely as it was when the child lay in the handsome old oak bed with turned corkscrew rails at head and foot. The bedclothes were rolled up by day and stored in one of the two built-in cupboards with moulded doors; the other cupboard contained the crockery and cooking ware. A chest with vermilion peasant design stood by one wall, a small cupboard side-board holding a lamp and a circular swivel mirror with side-brackets for candles stood beside another. A table and stools completed the furniture of the room where Joseph learned to walk and received from a simple pious mother his first instruction.

Stalin's birth certificate with various pictures of his youth hang

64

on the walls of the landlord's room. And now to-day like a mighty awning, sheltering the wee home from the weather and supported on marble columns so delicate that they leave the whole house free to view, rests glazed and fretted roof. The dark shafts with white roof above in no sense clash with the house they enshrine, neither do the squared black and white paving stones which connect formal canopy with formal garden of Italian design, framing itself in clipped ever-green hedges waist high against a background of taller shrubs and trees.

It was an entrancing picture as we entered from the dusty village street, the fluted columns of the shrine reflected in the still waters of the formal pool, the garden bursting with flowers and filling the hot July air with sweet and varied scents.

Gori is grandly placed at the foot of an escarpment where the high hills drop steeply down beside an emerging river into the orchard-covered plain. A grim and ruined castle perched high on the hillside dominated the town. In the village street we met an old lady in traditional Georgian dress, her gown reaching to her heels, her dark blue velvet cap, two inches high, sitting squarely on her head, pressed halfway down her forehead and covered, save for the face, with a blueish veil dropping to the shoulders on either side, precisely like the portraits of Stalin's mother in the landlord's room. The mother was pious and the child learned from her lips those simple lessons of Christian charity and morality which were destined to bear high fruit in the man who lived to integrate many nationalities into one and raise all from poverty to reasonable standards of living. That it bore early fruit, even in his schoolboy days, I learned from an old school-teacher, a contemporary friend of Stalin at school who in the next door house still lives on where he had lived as a boy; a frail old man now, needing support as he rose to meet me. His eyes glittered as he spoke of Stalin.

"I see him still, just as if yesterday, entering the school. He led us all. Once," he added, when I had asked him for stories of Stalin's boyhood, "there had been a robbery in Gori. Three thieves were caught and hanged. Deeply moved, the boys discussed among themselves whether the thieves would be punished in hell. 'No, no; certainly not,' cried Joseph; 'that would be intolerably unjust: they suffered punishment here. It would be monstrous should they suffer there as well.'"

Justice and fearless pursuit of truth were keynotes of this competent boy. Before he was fifteen—at which age he went on, owing to his ability, to the seminary at Tbilisi—he had secured books or pamphlets and studied the physical evolution theories of Darwin and the social evolution theories of Karl Marx.

His passion for knowledge grew and when he went to Tbilisi,

E

despite all hindrances from his tutors, he studied Mendeleyev's chemistry and kindred books, and because Tbilisi possessed only one copy of Marx's *Das Kapital* he and his friends pooled their pennies to procure a transcript copy. Fond of fiction, he read Jules Verne, Gogol, Thackeray and many more writers of fiction. He knew Shakespeare. He wrote poems. He sang. The seminary authorities, detecting by spies the literature he read, and perceiving his influence in the college, inflicted severe punishment and condemned him to long hours in the solitary cell. Finally he was expelled.

In 1903 Stalin became acquainted with Lenin by correspondence. They had long been moving on parallel lines and Stalin was a ready pupil and ardent devotee of "the mountain eagle" as he called Lenin. In his lesser sphere in the Caucasus Stalin had become a noted and courageous leader. He trusted largely to argument and logic and in debate was noted for his quiet restraint and rational force against the noisy vehemence of his opponents. The quality he admired most in Lenin was that same irresistible logic which overpowered and at length completely won his audience.

Not until 1905 did the two men meet, and Stalin's impressions and observations of the meeting are interesting. "I was hoping," he said, "to see the mountain eagle of our Party, the great man, great not only politically but physically, because in my imagination I pictured Lenin as a giant, stately and imposing. What then was my disappointment to see a most ordinary looking man, below the average height, literally in no way distinguishable from ordinary men."

Stalin felt the same disappointment at Lenin's bearing at conferences, sitting in obscure corners, talking with most ordinary men. He quickly learned, however, that this avoidance of conspicuousness or lack of emphasis on his high position in the movement, which was no mere pose, was of inestimable value in a leader of the masses. The workers felt in very truth that he was one of themselves.

Stalin and Lenin did not meet frequently at first but kept in constant touch with one another: Stalin fighting grimly on in his sphere and Lenin in his. Many times was Stalin seized by the police. Six times was he exiled to Siberia. Once, "to teach him a lesson," he and other political offenders were brought into the prison courtyard and compelled to "run the gauntlet" of blows from the butts of soldiers' rifles. Stalin walked through the blows with head erect and a copy of Marx in his hand.

Stalin with his scholastic mind perceived the value of the written word and organised a series of secret presses, one of which I saw in Tbilisi, built by a relative and operating under the nose of the police of his own student town.

The thing was skilfully done. A kinswoman of Stalin built herself a little villa in what became a commonplace suburban street. It had a basement kitchen and below that a deep cellar, built by relays of workmen to avoid suspicion. The lower chamber was entered through a deep dry well in the garden, along a horizontal passage and up through a trapdoor. In that lower kitchen Stalin worked at the printing press, aided by others who lived under the semblance of lodgers in the innocent villa. When danger approached the lady pushed a warning bell and the press stopped.

Joining Lenin at Cracow in 1912 Stalin produced in his article *Marxism and the National Question* one of his many classics. Lenin wrote to Gorky. The letter began: "A wonderful Georgian here. . . ."

In 1917 Stalin returned from Siberia, assuming leadership of the revolutionary movement until Lenin's arrival, when they shared the October conflict under Lenin's leadership. Lenin remained at the centre, Stalin travelled. It was Stalin who solved the food problem in the early and critical days. Stalin who visited and superintended operations on the several fronts in the civil war, and Stalin who created the Red Army as an organised force, revealing the military leader and strategist he was.

Never for a moment, however, even in the heat of conflict did Stalin forget the written word, and in the famous *Pravda* article *The October Revolution and the National Question* we find him still hammering away while the iron was hot at his favourite theme.

After the death of Lenin in 1924 Stalin assumed supreme control. Backed by the Party and through agency of the Five-Year Plans he has lived to see Soviet Russia emerge as a powerful industrial society served by a highly efficient mechanised agriculture.

Stalin's numerous writings reveal the penetrating theorist, the clear-headed thinker and the brilliant interpreter, able to grasp and unravel complex problems and explain their nature and suggest their solution in clear language to the masses. Of the Stakhanovite movement for instance he writes: "The Stakhanovite movement is a movement of the working men and women which sets itself the aim of surpassing the present technical standards . . . and demands the creation of new and higher technical standards, designed capacities and production plans. . . . Its significance lies in the fact that it is preparing the conditions for the transition from socialism to communism." Communism, being a higher stage than socialism, demands a higher level of production, a higher culture and technique, capable of raising productivity to such a level as to ensure abundance of articles of consumption, making it possible to distribute them according to the needs of the members of the Communist society.

Of Stalin, Henry Barbusse writes: "His life story is a series of victories over a series of colossal difficulties. He is a man of iron. His name describes him: Stalin—steel. He is as inflexible and as flexible as steel. His power lies in his profound common sense, his extensive range of knowledge, his astonishing internal concentration, his passion for precision, his inexorable consistency and the rapidity, certainty and intensity of his decisions."

That is the not unreliable picture of Stalin as the Russians see him, and any Western estimate into which other factors are bound to enter must take this at least into account. From the Russian angle it is small wonder that the mass of common people contrasting their position to-day in regard to health, education, culture, wealth and world respect with their position three decades ago should revere the man to whom, together with Lenin and beyond all others, they owe it. Full well they know, as foreigners can never know, the strenuous activities, the courage, the sacrifices, the love and understanding of the man born as a babe in the one-roomed house in Gori and feel towards him as Americans feel towards Abraham Lincoln born in a log hut in Kentucky. "What does he look like? Does he look well? Does he look old?" were the eager, anxious questions as of children concerning their parents which assailed me, as I said, especially by intelligent youth, after my visit to the Kremlin. Nor can I ever forget the shocked look and voice of the young woman of whom I innocently and not unnaturally had asked who was likely to succeed Stalin on his death, or the deep pain with which she exclaimed: "Oh, don't talk like that; don't talk like that!" My question, I suddenly realised, was as indecent in Russia as if I should ask any child in any home, "Who will succeed your father on his death?" Stalin is father to Soviet youth. They love him. Naturally I was anxious to see Stalin and glad when an invitation came to do so. Here are some of my impressions, just as I wrote them down immediately on my return from the Kremlin.

2. STALIN IN THE KREMLIN

At 6 p.m. on 12th July I was informed that Generalissimo Stalin wished to see me at 8 o'clock on the same evening. Tabulating various questions for discussion in my mind—the institutional religious question; interchange of visits and personal contacts of peoples with peoples; whether Russia still needed medical aid, not forgetting also the problem of the Russian girls married to English youths and hindered from accompanying their husbands to England—I made preparations for the visit.

Arriving promptly—indeed ten minutes too soon—at the western entrance, I motored at a leisurely pace through the grounds facing the river-side. A lovely evening showed the Kremlin terrace at its best. The river swept in graceful curves below the rose-pink walls. Nestling with quiet dignity on the opposite shore was the British Embassy, small, sedate, eighteenth-century in character. Beyond the river spread the great suburban growth of the city.

Past the tall and many-domed church, past the great bell, largest of its kind in the world and standing, minus the cracked segment, unhung upon the ground, past the great cannon familiar from our childish history books, we made our way at length to the section adjacent to Lenin's tomb. There I was received at a private entrance immediately behind the great wall which faced my own hotel veranda.

Entering by a simple porch and leaving my hat with the attendant, I was carried silently by a slow moving lift to an upper story. Thence along a corridor, clean, neat, newly painted and newly carpeted in severe official style, I was led to an ante-room with its thirteen chairs arranged around a large table. Soft drinks stood on a side-board, and an officer entertained me till the electric clock reached 7.58, when we moved promptly through three or four rather large office rooms with officials working at official desks, and at last entered a second large plain workmanlike room, furnished mainly with one long baize-covered table. A board-room obviously. The Generalissimo and Mr. Molotov were awaiting me there.

We greeted and shook hands.

Stalin was dressed in uniform with a single star at his breast, his epaulets denoting his rank, Molotov in a plain grey suit.

Stalin is short, his face small. His features are regular and finely chiselled as is frequent with Georgians. His strong dark hair, now turning slightly grey, comes down low on his forehead—again a typical Georgian.

I saw at a glance that rumours that the Generalissimo's health was seriously threatened were quite ill-founded. He looked a well man.

Stalin is calm, composed, simple. Not lacking in humour. Direct in speech, untouched by the slightest suspicion of pomposity. There is nothing cruel or dramatic nor any attempt to look forceful about Stalin's face. Just steady purpose and a kindly geniality. Nothing could be more unlike the face of Mussolini or Hitler. I cannot help recalling Stalin's own description of his first meeting with Lenin and his comment on Lenin's looks and manner: "Only later did I realise that this simplicity and modesty, this striving to remain unobserved, or, at least, not to make himself conspicuous and not to emphasise his high position—that this feature was one of Lenin's strongest points as new leader of the new masses, of the simple and ordinary masses, the rank and file of humanity."

Here then was a man who had helped to plan a new order and a square deal for the masses, and who had been determined from first to last to let nothing hinder the execution of the plan; the man who would see that justice was done on the broad scale though it meant drastic action against any opposition or any individual opponent. The man who had been calm when the massed forces of the allied armies had hammered at the gates of Stalingrad in 1917, and also again when the powerful forces of Hitler hammered at the same gates in 1942. The man whom no assault could terrify and no atom bomb intimidate or deflect.

In short, and in the calm of advancing years, this was the same person who as a boy fifty years earlier had revolted against "intolerable injustice"; or the quick-witted revolutionary youth who perceived the need for printed propaganda, and had audacity and courage to use a secret press in a very stronghold of Tsarist policedom: Joseph Vissarionovich Stalin, the man who through fifty years' tenacity of purpose has earned and won the name by which he is now exclusively known—Stalin, or steel.

We sat down. I sat opposite Stalin. Molotov was on his right. The interpreter, a young man in the grey uniform and with the epaulets of the diplomatic service upon his shoulders, whom I had seen at the reception given two days previously to T. V. Soong, and had acted as interpreter when Molotov spoke to me on that occasion, sat at the head of the table between us and wrote down rapidly in longhand every word I said; he then translated it carefully to Stalin.

When seated Stalin said: "Did you enjoy your trip?" I had just returned from Armenia and the Caucasus.

"Immensely," I replied, "and was deeply impressed by what I saw."

"Had you been there before?"

"Never, it was my first visit, but I quickly discovered ample means to gauge the progress. Erivan, for example, twenty-five years ago was a large straggling village of 27,000 inhabitants: it has grown to-day to a fine modern city of a quarter of a million.

"Even more impressive to me, however, were the children, physically so fit and culturally so advanced."

We talked on Georgia. "I went to Gori," I said, "and visited the cottage where your Excellency was born. The new setting of marble which protects your old home in no way clashes with the little house it shelters. The gardens were full of bloom. I was presented with an armful of roses. Next I visited the seminary in Tbilisi where you were taught and the small suburban house in whose deep and hidden cellar you operated your illegal press. It was clever work." And I then demonstrated with my hands the nature of the scheme and how it appealed to my engineering instincts.

Here Molotov smiled and looked intently as I explained the mechanism of the approach and exit.

Stalin was amused at the reminiscence.

"Finally," I said, "I stood bareheaded before the tomb of your mother in the church up the steep hillside above Tbilisi."

"My mother was a simple woman."

"A good woman," I added.

"A simple woman," he repeated, with a friendly smile, which broadened as I added: "One often sees the portrait of the mother in the disposition of the child."

When my turn came to direct the conversation I inquired, "May I ask one or two questions?" Stalin nodded assent.

Mostly as we spoke Stalin gazed down at the pad before him, drawing designs upon it with coloured pencils, blue and red.

From time to time he would throw back his head and gaze at me whilst listening. He looked intently when I asked:

"Can you suggest methods by which we can further the task of creating good understanding and unity betwixt our countries in the post-war years?"

"It will not be easy," Stalin replied, after a pause for reflection. "We were friends in the war. That was natural enough, confronted as we were by a common and terrible foe. Now the Germans are beaten the tension will lessen, it will be less easy now to avoid friction. But we desire it, and we want to keep firm the unity already achieved not only by words but by deeds. We have no wish whatsoever to hurt England or to hinder England. We would act towards England as friends in deed as well as word. Whether we succeed or not will depend largely on your politicians. If they have the will, we have the will."

Stalin proceeded with some warmth: "The main obstacle is the press, which too often gives false and biased news. The press creates prejudice. The press never before the war gave accurate accounts of the Soviet Union."

Recollecting the history of the past two decades I dare not deny the charge and explained to Stalin, what obviously he knew better

than I, that the British and U.S.A. press in general was owned by
millionaires, largely reflecting their attitude and directing public
opinion into the channels which the wealthy class desired. But, I added,
"England possessed one paper, at least, the *Daily Worker*, on whose
editorial board I sit, which is supported by the pennies of the workers,
which already has a daily circulation of 100,000 and which might be
500,000 were paper available."

Stalin turned to exchange glances with Molotov as I said this.

I related several incidents concerning the press and passed on to
observe with pleasure that Russia had always in the past kept her word
and that this amongst other things had encouraged a more general
belief in my statements about the Soviet Union. It had not always
been so: few had credited Russia's strength until the war revealed
it. General Montgomery, for example, had expressed astonishment at
the Russian achievement at Stalingrad and sought the ground of my
own confidence in her strength.

Stalin proceeded to explain how England had got her false estimate
of Russia's military strength. The responsibility lay with the French
and behind the French the Poles.

"Mr. Churchill asked General Gamelin what was Russia's strength.
'Russia is empty,' said Gamelin. 'Russia has *no* strength.' Gamelin and
the French relied for this information on the Poles, who were and had
long been hostile to Russia."

In this connexion I recalled and related the false estimate held
by the English military chiefs as to Russia's achievements during the
Russo-Finnish war, an estimate corrected by a post-war article by *The
Times* military critic, but overlooked when Russia's military victory
had caused interest to subside.

I then proceeded, and with his encouragement, to speak of the
religious question.

"Much distrust of Russia and hostility to Russia had been caused
among English people in the past by charges of persecution of the
Church, which I had reason to believe were not unbiased and were
certainly exaggerated. But for various reasons the religious question
had always loomed large in England, for English people are very
religious."

Stalin replied:

"The Church and the State each has its own history of the post-
revolutionary period. The then Patriarch of the Russian Orthodox
Church pronounced an anathema on the Soviet Government and urged
non-payment of taxes. The State must defend itself. The State must
act.

"Doubtless," he said, with a half smile, perhaps at his own understatement, "in time of war and tension there were excesses on both sides.

"But all that is gone now," he added, "and the war has created a new and different situation. The war has revealed to the Church the patriotism of the State and to the State the patriotism of the Church. The Church," he added in parentheses, "had been very closely tied up with the Tsarist regime."

"Yes," I interposed, "perhaps sometimes closer to the Tsar than to the true head of the Church, Jesus Christ. Personally," I said, pursuing the point, "I observe in many actions of the Soviet Government things done for the mass of common humanity by the Soviet authorities in closer accord with Christian teaching and morality than elsewhere. There is some ground at least for the trite exaggeration that those who profess belief in a God of justice and love act as if they did not, whilst those who deny it act as if they held it."

Stalin and Molotov smiled.

"Naturally," I continued, returning to the immediate point, "the increasingly helpful relations between Church and State gave me great pleasure. I had spoken to high ecclesiastical authorities in many Churches. To the Patriarch who gave me this," pointing to my crucifix, "to the Archbishop of Leningrad, to the Catholicos of Armenia and to the Archbishop of Georgia and others. What I heard and what I overheard had encouraged me. Especially was this true of Armenia, where I found the visiting Armenians from many countries rejoicing at the physical fitness of the children and at their high cultural and educational level."

"Religion," said the Generalissimo, "is a matter of conscience. Conscience cannot be ignored. Conscience is free. Worship and religion are free."

We next discussed the work of the Soviet medical service. "Do you desire," I inquired, "that we continue our work of medical aid for your country? We have seen the ravages of war and the depletion of all essential stocks and apparatus."

"I thank you and we desire it," he said.

We spoke of the forthcoming British elections and I assured him that if not at this election certainly at its successor the Labour Party would be returned to power.

I glanced at my watch. Already we had spoken for three-quarters of an hour.

"The hour is late," I said, "but may I make one or two further remarks?"

He bowed assent.

"We attach great importance," I continued, "to personal contacts

between individuals of our respective peoples. We are anxious to see
a wide extension of exchange visits. Thousands of my countrymen
seek, with every possible good will, to visit your country. I am especially
anxious that the young should meet."

"It is most desirable," he said with emphasis and instanced several
cases of false information as to the situation in Russia through depending on second or third hand information.

Before proceeding to my special request I assured the Generalissimo
that the great mass of workers of my country possessed a lively and
friendly feeling towards the Soviet Union. This was increasingly true
also of the intelligentsia and particularly of the technicians. As an
instance I related my experience in a factory employing possibly
45,000 persons and producing the world's finest aero engine. After
a speech concerning Russia to the workers in the shops, the managers
and experts kept me nearly two hours discussing the achievements and
methods of Russia.

Stalin was pleased and said, "Technicians are by nature realistic,"
looking at Molotov as I added that though in the past technicians
had tended to neglect politics as outside their technical range, this
rapidly ceases to be the case, and technicians as well as workers begin
to recognise the importance of both these activities of life.

My second remark was a request concerning the young married
couples. English young men despite strongly expressed advice of their
superior officers, had married Russian girls who were forbidden by
Soviet authorities to leave the country.

"I speak with diffidence and hesitation, for I would avoid all appear-
ance of meddling with your internal affairs; but one matter, small in
comparison with greater affairs, but apt to cause ill-feeling out of all
proportion to its magnitude troubles us, and we are anxious to remove
any and every unnecessary cause of friction between our peoples. . . ."

Stalin beckoned me to proceed.

"Some thirty young Englishmen having married Russian girls,
are now ordered home. Soviet regulations prevent their wives from
accompanying them. Could this hardship be remedied?"

Stalin looked at Molotov with a quick questioning glance, inquiring
if it was so.

Mr. Molotov smiled and nodded an equally quick assent, adding
something I did not understand. I proceeded to point out that though
the number affected was small, the friction, magnified by a hostile
press, was great: "It has been a constant charge in the past that
Russian Communism aims at the disintegration of family life. This
enforced separation might easily be construed to prove a false point."

Stalin inquired again the number of couples affected.

"About thirty."

"Something will be done," he said spontaneously and cordially. And then with slight correction he added. "Something will probably be done: it is a matter for decision by the Supreme Soviet."

Molotov nodded assent.

Thanking Stalin for his courtesy in seeing me, I ended the interview by assuring him that we recognised how much workers and others in my own country and indeed in all the world owed to him and his people for their mighty share in smashing fascism and introducing a new planned order into the world.

Stalin bowed. We all rose and shook hands.

The interview began at 8 and ended at 8.50. It was my first and will probably be my last visit to the Kremlin. But the imposing pile of cream-coloured official buildings, encircled and guarded by the massive pink-coloured Chinese-like wall with its seven spired towers will wear now for me at least a less coldly remote and austere aspect. They will recall the red-carpeted corridors, the plain, clean, businesslike room with its upright brown leather chairs, orderly desks and telephones. A fitter background than all the splendour and the plush and gold of the great State buildings for the small, easy man with his utterly unselfconscious manner, listening intently, thinking quietly whilst stroking the pad before him attractively with coloured pencils as other men flick ash off their cigarettes, ready when occasion arose for a solid observation or wise advice. No man of mystery dominates the Kremlin. Stalin is the embodiment of good-humoured common sense, as much a man of the people to-day as when he plied the secret printing press in the commonplace villa in Tbilisi, just as direct, as knowledgeable and practical as when he used the Marxian Socialism he had mastered not as a philosophical theory but as a plan of action for common men. Stalin I found exactly like the speeches he had uttered through a quarter of a century as mouthpiece of the new Soviet Order, as interpreter of its attitude to the outer world: unstrained, unposed, unmelodramatic; honest, direct, sincere. A man, furthermore, who sincerely seeks friendship with Britain and believes in its possibility.

3. MOLOTOV

MOLOTOV had interested me from the first. His dress—white collar, necktie, cuffs, "like a schoolmaster on prize-giving day"— contrasted vividly with Stalin's simple uniform of khaki before he was made Field Marshal. His face, too, differed from Stalin's. Large, square-faced, chubby, grey-haired now, with rimless pincenez glasses always before his twinkling, amiable, smiling eyes. You could see his prototype in the self-assured school-teacher who has risen by his own efforts to an assured position where he now exercises easy sway. A man who knows his world and his job, and the power of the authority which places him where he is, and trusts him and will back him up.

I had seen Mr. Molotov on many occasions and spoken to him on three. He was always the same. He stands back, looks and listens with smiling face, and then says directly and pleasantly all that is necessary for that occasion.

There is no mystery about Mr. Molotov, as there is no mystery about Stalin. Both men had been revolutionaries, and of neither would you think it. Both had mounted to positions of immense power. Neither had been broken by the strain. Neither were embittered. Neither had swelled heads. Both were ready still to fight when occasion demanded it, but both recognised that they stood now with immense forces behind them. Hence their air of easy but not arrogant assurance. Molotov has now probably the more difficult task of the two men. Stalin's task is to aid by his wisdom, by his knowledge, by his common sense, by his pertinacity and by his personal prestige the running of the great Soviet organisation at home.

Molotov's task is to struggle for his country's hand at the council chamber abroad, and behind that easy smiling face lies the stubborn negotiator. He knows what he wants, and he thinks he knows how to get it. He has been likened, and there is point in the likeness, to a local bank manager, affable and helpful with the customer whose dealings are sound by the standards of the banking organisation which he represents, awkward and firm with those whose standards differ and of whose past transactions he has reason to be highly suspicious. A man unmoved by the hauteur of the *ancien régime* or by the bluster of pushful adventurers.

Molotov has his standards. They are the standards of the mighty movement of which he is both child and creator. They are not the same standards as those of the world with which he must negotiate. He is willing to treat with these other men, as a bank manager is willing to treat with men of other standards than his own, but determined to take no risks, ready to conclude his bargain on his own terms. He knows he can rely upon the great power and purpose of the whole organisation of which he is the immediate representative and executant. He knows what they want, he knows that they trust him and he knows he must never yield an inch to the powerful men he deals with when the stakes are high. He knows also when to refer a question back and to play for time.

And after all Molotov's methods of diplomacy are not widely different from those of any other country. Russia has a Socialist economy at home. Abroad she negotiates as any other country negotiates: she makes bargains. Molotov, for example, disliked the entry of the Argentine into the U.N.O. at San Francisco, but was ready to yield on condition that the Polish Provisional Government was recognised by the other allies. He will pay highly for what he wants, and if he drives a hard bargain for what others want he knows when reason and wisdom bid him yield.

BOOK V

DEVELOPMENT OF THE SOVIET INDIVIDUAL

1. PHYSICAL LIFE AND POSITIVE HEALTH

BY what steps, methods and organisation has the Soviet Union fostered, developed and stimulated human life, physical, psychological and cultural?

We shall start where human life starts, with the body, and its healthy growth. And note that from first to last Russia's health services are free of charge. Not a penny to pay for doctor, nurse, hospital or convalescent home from birth to death.

A Russian woman enters a tramcar. She is pregnant. All make room for her. Russia alone reserves special seats in tramcars for pregnant women.

With a Russian doctor I visited a drab room in a drab house. On chairs round the walls Russian women, straight from factory or home, were donating human milk for human babes. Abundance of human milk, the child's essential food, is always available for every Moscow babe. What other city makes like provision?

Outstanding from the Soviet point of view then—and these illustrations underline it—in their quest for physical well-being is the specialised care for women and children in country and town. The first decree on mother and child protection was signed by Lenin in December, 1917.

Each district in town and country alike has its own consultative centre and maternity clinic, providing specialist advice concerning child and mother and rendering where necessary specialist aid.

A pregnant woman receives peculiar care. Factory and home conditions are under constant observation. Where defective, a remedy is sought. The mother is freed from toil both before and after childbirth and adequate food and medical aid are assured for her and her child from the first.

Sanitary instruction of every kind is given, and much is needed, for Russia has lingered far behind the rest of Europe.

Abortion is permitted, and officially performed when occasion demands it. Never permitted, however, save where the mother's life is in danger, when a first child is concerned. Certain rare social conditions are an exception, but even in these cases there is no abortion in the case of a first child. Every effort is made to avoid abortion, and to bring home to women the harm of its practice.

Practically all births now take place in maternity homes.

Wonderful recoveries are made possible through extreme care in pregnancy. Mrs. Churchill, for instance, was shown a baby which at birth weighed 1½ lbs. It was well and thriving at sixteen days old.

Births are registered, and a district nurse visits the home and keeps the new born child and mother under constant observation, providing aid where needed. The supervision continues till the child is three years old.

The first year after birth is the critical year calling for skilled attention and careful feeding. Doctor and nurse visit the home intensively during the first year, especially in the case of the first child, where the mother is usually young and inexperienced, the nurse giving demonstration of correct procedure and examining the schedule carefully to make sure that her instructions have been observed. At times the nurse will spend a whole day with the inexperienced mother.

Infantile intestinal troubles being serious at present in Russia demand and receive special attention to milk and curative foods. Milk kitchens are associated with health centres and mothers in need can there obtain special foods. Russian mortality rate has decreased, even during the war.

The same thought-out care pursues the growing child through all its early years. For instance, I would often enter a large building, sadly the worse outside for wartime wear. Inside, however, there is always light, air and activity. It is a school, and at a desk in a small room off the corridor sits a woman in a white overall; a stethoscope lies on the desk before her and bottles on the shelves behind her. That room is a school dispensary and the woman the resident school doctor. Resident doctors, rather than visiting doctors, are the rule in the Soviet Union.

The doctor's room may be roughish, easy to criticise. Often it is roughish, but it is there, and the resident doctor is there too—a rare sight in England, a common sight in Russia.

Obviously from the outset Russia approaches health in infant life and onwards in a scientific manner, and as a scientific whole it should be studied and for that study we had exceptional opportunities. Mr. Kolesnikov himself, the Deputy Commissar for Health and the Head of the Russian Red Cross, gave us an exhaustive description of the scientific structure and logical method of medical work in the U.S.S.R.

Mr. Kolesnikov, a big, smooth-faced man with quiet voice and quiet manner, met us at the Ministry of Health in Moscow, and gave us—happily punctuated on two occasions with tea, cakes and sandwiches—three hours of formulated talk. Interesting, illuminating and stimulating, that talk provided a bird's-eye view of a health service as wide in its scope as it was closely knit in its parts, which enabled us to approach with intelligence and understanding each contributory department of the Soviet Health Service.

Faraday, prince of experimenters, was wont to stop when shown a new experiment, put his hand on the operator's arm and say, "Tell me first what to look for." Kolesnikov told us first what to look for. And that spring morning in his room at the Health Centre symbolised the right method of approach to all of Russia's many-sided but closely knit aims, activities and achievements.

The splendour of the picture as a whole in contrast to present achievements in various parts is salutary. For Russia has not yet achieved in anything like full measure the thing aimed at or described in Kolesnikov's talk, and he was the first to admit it; but his masterly outline of aim and intention enabled us to detect everywhere progressive and continuous steps to the goal. It is here, as in all activities of Soviet life, the movement and its direction which counts.

It is indeed of supreme importance, in any study of Russian activity, no matter what it is, to examine on the one hand the steps in relation to the goal, and on the other to measure present achievements against past backgrounds. Russia at no stage or in no department should, in the first instance, be compared with similar things in the Western world. All should be studied in relation to Russia's own plan and compared with Russia's preceding achievements.

Thus it was more than the mere scope and method of Soviet Health Services that I learned in Kolesnikov's room and in the equally important subsequent and orderly examination of the various departments of Russia's Health Services.

I learned the only correct method of approach to each Russian activity; how to say of each, "Tell me first what to look for."

Nothing is more futile than to scurry round Russia, as so many foreign visitors, journalists and writers do, and inspect this item of detail or that out of relation to the plan as a whole and out of its Russian time context, and then compare that detail with a better kindred detail at home. That is the way of illusion.

It was precisely that which, before the war, led to widespread misjudgment of Russia's strength and achievement in industry, transport or agriculture. Close and patient prior study is always needed, otherwise the picture will be dangerously false however technically accurate as to details.

*   *   *   *   *

The salient features, then, as outlined by Kolesnikov are these:
(1) First and foremost, the Soviet Medical Health Service forms one co-ordinated and closely knit whole, with a common plan of action and a budget which meets the cost. Health Service in the Soviet Union is State Service. Russian medicine in all its branches is a State affair. All organs of medical service being under State control, with the manifold advantages of unified administration, the fruits of invention and discovery or the practice of new and approved methods of treatment can thus be immediately and of set purpose made available for all.

This State responsibility for the health of the whole community has been Russia's intention from the first. Following the revolution of 1917 the Soviet Government decreed that beneficent health treatment should be universal. It insured as early as July, 1918, by the appointment of a People's Commissariat for Health, that a single State plan should guarantee the better utilisation of the funds and the more efficient allocation of medical and sanitary institutions in conformity with local conditions.

(2) Secondly, positive health rather than mere cure was henceforth to be the quest of the new State Health Service. Prevention of disease and promotion of health were from now on the keynotes. Cure is indeed essential. It is, for example, important to seek a cure for intestinal disease when it breaks out in a factory. It is much more important to prevent the outbreak of intestinal disease and more important still to surround the factory worker, not only with sanitary conditions which ward off attack of intestinal disease, but with conditions which shall enrich him with new strength and new vigour to add positive joy and enrichment to life. All three things are in their due proportion and in full measure the care of the Soviet Health Services.

Again, to take another example, tuberculosis must be cured when it occurs. But outbreaks of tuberculosis must be prevented when possible. And since tuberculosis is a social disease and depends on housing and living conditions, the prevention of tuberculosis and positive health are linked up with the entire social structure of the State. Laws on the shortened working day, on wages, on labour protection, on social insurance, and on grants to mothers were all seen to be powerful aids in the prevention of tuberculosis and soon bore fruit. Social legislation is the Russian doctor's right hand.

Overcrowding—to take an interesting illustration—predisposes to tubercular disease. Normally the better paid worker can procure the better rooms: not necessarily so in Russia. The Apartment-rent Law was framed to overrule this disability. Rent is charged not only according to cubic capacity of house-room, but also in a sliding ratio to the

F

wages of the tenant. Hence a low-salaried man has equal chance with a high-salaried man of moving into healthier apartments.

(3) Thirdly, the Soviet doctor does not stand, as it were, over against the Soviet worker in a caste apart; a caste whose job consists merely of curing disease. Physicians, surgeons and scientists form officers' cadres—bodies of officers, that is, to train, instruct, encourage and guide an army which is nation-wide, whose aim is positive health, with cure of disease as but a technical department of a greater whole.

Workers everywhere are enlisted in the warfare against disease, urged to attack insanitary conditions wherever they occur, encouraged in conducting voluntary search for centres of infection, specially qualified inspectors merely directing but not usurping these tasks. Lavatories are cleaned. First aid is given. Each house is on a visiting list. Doctors alone never could undertake so great a task, less qualified also than the neighbour is to do it. Doctors can instruct the workers.

Turn to definite warfare against disease.

The incidence of preventable disease must be discovered as soon as possible: once discovered, the State is willing to provide the means, if necessary, for its elimination.

Cretinism has been conquered in the Caucasus by the provision and use of iodised salt, a matter not left to the patients' own responsibility or knowledge or purse.

Similarly scabies, affecting 30 per cent of the population in Belo-Russia, has been abolished. Every individual of its six million inhabitants has been examined and where infected cured. Similarly again trachoma and syphilis have been eliminated in Middle Asia: the Red Army and Red Navy are singularly free from venereal disease, only those areas of Russia contaminated by the Germans remaining infected. Medical corps were sent to deal with these districts, where sometimes 50 per cent of the population suffered from the disease.

The whole power of the State can now be marshalled against specific disease as its armed might was marshalled against the fascist menace.

Turning next to sickness in home or factory, Mr. Kolesnikov described the various methods of attack, which differ somewhat in country and town.

In both cases medical service is free of charge.

In the cities, polyclinics and dispensaries are provided according to the need of the population as to treatment and prevention of special or prevalent disease.

Dispensaries will concentrate upon the cure and prevention of any particular disease, say tuberculosis. Every consumptive in the district must be catalogued and induced if possible to seek hospital treatment, special cases being given special treatment with necessary standards of living supplied free of cost.

In polyclinics the main general assistance is given. Any person can visit a polyclinic, where special and competent members of the staff attend to special diseases, the common man having thus access to specialist advice. Where necessary the patient receives hospital treatment.

Treatment by a private doctor at the patient's own expense is, of course, permissible. A pregnant woman, if she desires it, can have her confinement in her own home, treatment sometimes sought by those who are elderly or ultra-sensitive. The two services, public and private, can and do exist side by side, but the private doctor is rare, the majority preferring free public services.

The overwhelming mass of doctors also prefer working in State institutions, where their personal welfare is fully ensured and where, in co-operation with their colleagues, they have all means and equipment at their service and can make the fullest use of modern achievements in medical science. A physician's work ceases to be individual artisanship: it becomes organised social effort.

Patients too ill to visit the polyclinic can summon help by telephone, stating temperature and recording their address.

Special doctors have charge of special districts, bound to acquaint themselves with their allotted group of houses; it is their business to know their patients, to know their sanitary conditions and to estimate their standard of living that they may judge whether or not it will enable the treatment they prescribe to be successful. If insufficient they ensure that help is given.

In 1931 the number of home visits in the town was 391,000: in 1941 it was 29,370,000.

Emergencies happen and receive emergency first aid. In case of accident, sudden illness or difficult delivery, for instance, a telephone call will bring an ambulance, doctor and male nurse attendant.

Since, however, industrial workers spend a large part of their lives in factories, where men and women pay a special price in giving themselves up to factory life, they have the right to special benefits.

The upsurge of industrial life which began in 1921, when the Soviets switched over to the peace-time upbuilding of economy and culture, had a twofold consequence on the Health Services. First, by increasing wealth it made possible the extension of medical-prophylactic and sanitary institutions for the protection of mother and child and for the warfare against tuberculosis, syphilis, trachoma and other diseases. It also increased leisure and extended health-giving amenities, athletic clubs and the like: it ministered to positive health. Secondly, it increased the number of factories and with them the need of first-aid posts.

Every large constructive works is equipped with its own medical centre. In 1941, in addition to the local factory clinics, factory points at various enterprises numbered 10,000, each shop possessing its first-aid point with doctor and nurse in constant attendance, charged with a wide range of duties and responsible for all that pertains to the health of the workers. They supervise the cleanliness of the shop, its ventilation, its special precautions against accident, against skin disease or any form of industrial poisoning or disability.

In addition to local points, every large factory is equipped with a medical centre for specialised treatment. Local points save precious time and facilitate detailed inspection of particular problems arising in specialised processes. Each factory medical centre is required to make monthly returns of incidence of disease, absence due to disease, of skin troubles due to dirty overalls or other causes, with special reference at the present moment to intestinal diseases, due maybe to bad sanitary or dining conditions. Such information equips the head of the organisation to wage intelligent warfare against disease in the factory.

Village medical work differs from that in towns owing to differing modes of life. The principle, however, is the same, immediate help, specialised help and healthy conditions for all. Villages are grouped into districts for convenience, 80,000 to 100,000 being the normal unit. Each district will embrace several medical points—one to every 15,000 of population—each point controlled by a doctor and equipped with a laboratory, a small polyclinic or even a hospital with ten to fifteen beds. Patients from surrounding villages attend this local point or are sent for specialised hospital treatment to some larger centre.

Peasants whose sickness prevents attendance at the centre can summon a doctor, while doctors on their part can, where necessary, apply for Government help to meet specialised needs or secure for their patients specialised treatment. The rural medical points are empowered to organise crèches, or even to provide their own maternity and medical centres with their own chemist's store. The remotest areas must come into the network of health organisation.

Government decisions of 23rd April, 1938, "On Reinforcing Rural Doctors' Stations," contributed to the wide improvement of outpatient hospital service in the countryside, and otherwise caused progress in rural medical service by setting it on an entirely new and scientific base. Young doctors poured into rural districts in considerable numbers, forming a medical corps, stiffened from time to time with the skill and experience of thousands of older and abler men from large university centres on advisory visits. Rural doctors in these Soviet medical village outposts supervise anti-epidemic and other sanitary measures of the countryside in addition to giving medical assistance to the peasants.

The Soviet doctor, with the few exceptions of those who for some reason or other prefer private practice, is a State servant, set free from financial care and financial temptation. His income is secure. His future secure. He can devote himself wholly to his proper task, the promotion of health and the cure of disease. He is given ample scope and as the country prospers his equipment grows.

A Soviet doctor's hours—six in peacetime—are strictly limited. Work in polyclinics proceeds in shifts. Doctors are not called up in the middle of the night after a long and tiring day, nor are they overworked.

Doctors, however, are expected to be competent, well informed and up to date in method. For this they are required once in every three years to spend six months at cost-free refresher courses at full pay, and when back at work free provision of medical journals keeps them in touch with modern medical science.

Russia has every right to be proud of her Health Service and its achievements. Right to be proud, too, of her hospitals despite shortcomings—of which Kolesnikov was thoroughly well aware—as the result of German occupation and destruction and the immense strain of war. Essentials are frequently in short supply. The system and aim is good. The attainment often, and as yet necessarily so, leaves much to be desired. Dr. Kolesnikov spoke with great candour of deficiency in hospital equipment. The standard in many departments naturally falls far behind English and American standards. We see hospitals to-day after years of devastating war which would have been vastly different had war never come.

The Soviet Health Service in general studied over the whole field, studied as Kolesnikov had outlined it, and as one discovers from innumerable scientific monographs, has achievement to its credit as colossal in bulk as wide in aim.

War supplied the proof. War, the acid test of every sphere of

activity, of industrial front as well as military front, morality as well
as guns, found the Soviet Health Services ready for the test. The appalling mortality which darkened world war one was absent from world
war two, when 73 per cent of hospital cases returned to the fighting
fronts. And this despite the difficult and rapid movement of world
war two with consequent strain on transport and hospital mobility.
Only in comparison with the past can we gauge the magnitude of
Soviet present achievement. In 1941, for instance, hospital beds
were provided for 500,000 urban patients and 170,000 rural patients,
a fivefold increase in little over two decades. Practically all hospitals
in rural areas possess pharmacies, where medicines are dispensed,
many equipped with laboratories, disinfectant chambers, Röntgen
installations and physio-therapeutic appliances. Furthermore, and
most significantly, medical establishments have grown most rapidly
in the national republics, practically devoid of hospitals prior to 1917.
Uzbekistan, for instance, with 0.9 beds per 1,000 inhabitants in 1913,
had 8.6 beds for 1,000 in 1941.

An important factor, to be noted in comparing Soviet Health
Services with that of other lands, is the fact, already hinted at, that
while Soviet health owes much directly to Soviet medical science
and Soviet medical practice, to clinic and to hospital, it owes no less
to the increase of wealth consequent upon a planned economy and to
legislation which directs that wealth into channels which enhance
life, physical, mental and spiritual, to the general increase of foodstuffs
and the distribution of special foods for special needs, to the increase
of wages, to the shortening of working hours, to the provision of paid
holidays in healthy pleasure resorts and to adequate insurance in
sickness and old age.

Soviet Health Service cannnot in short be understood apart from
the whole complex in which it is set. In Russia more than in any other
land is this true, because the whole of Russian economy is planned.
Health is supported by a nation-wide plan, not negated by deleterious
elements in an unco-ordinated whole.

The current Five-Year Plan projects ten hospital beds for every
1,000 urban dwellers, with a trained midwife gynœcologist for every
10,000 in the towns: 95,000 medical workers are to be trained within
five years. The hospital system destroyed by the war is not only to be
restored: it is to be expanded by over a third. Every hospital of over
fifty beds will possess X-ray apparatus; those over seventy-five will
have a physio-therapeutic department; over 200 a department for
corrective physical education.

2. SOVIET FAMILY LIFE

THE family is an association of profound importance to the State. In the family we see the initial fellowship of life, where contacts are first made and friendships first formed. Life is essentially mutual, there is no such thing as an isolated person, and the family is the earliest home of mutuality and personality.

Plato, in his most impossible, most fantastic of all Utopias, allows no place for the family nor for the artist, the one being too spontaneous, upsetting the applecart, the other too social, possessing initial loyalties which act as rivals to the State. Plato therefore finds no use for the family. The Soviet Union does. No country in the world indeed, quite contrary to common belief, welcomes the family more cordially or guards it more jealously than Soviet Russia.

Christianity, by its insistence on monogamy as the ideal form of marriage, emphasises the supreme importance of the family, regarding father, mother and child as the real unit of society, the mutual love of man to woman shedding its warm light across the home. Love creates community. The family, the home of love, is the breeding ground of fellowship and community.

Precisely for the same reason the Soviet Union buttresses the family with much understanding. The Soviet Union insists that the family is the basis for the normal and healthy upbringing of children, for developing qualities of solidarity, mutual aid and responsibility which are essential to the well-being of the community.

The attitude of the State to the family has been dramatically shown in the severe discouragement during the past twenty-six years of "factual marriage," that is cohabitation or living together without legal marriage.

In the first code of laws on marriage and family, published in 1918, where the basic principles of family relations were laid down, no legal protection was given to unregistered marriages; if the man she lived with died the woman had no claim to his property. This was intentional. Such unlegalised marriages tended towards undesirable results, to plurality of partners, to irresponsibility, to promiscuity and to instability of the family, and as such was condemned and penalised. This law was reversed later, but only as an accommodation to a period of stress and strain. In 1925, a period of economic difficulty, in which womanhood often lacked the chance to maintain herself, when economic equality did not always operate, and when women if they must live with a man at all had to live with him, if he so insisted, out of wedlock, the woman of such "factual marriage" had the right to alimony, a share of property acquired during "marriage" and to inheritance on the death of the other partner.

When, however, industry again advanced and planned production gave women scope to gainful work—eleven million in industry and nineteen million in agriculture—the whole position changed. Now women were independent, both economically and socially, and therefore the State could again by its legislation offer a new basis for the relations between man and woman. In these new circumstances the State refused to protect factual marriage, and condemned it because no conditions either social or economic now compelled women to enter into marital relations not regulated by law.

Such unregulated marriage would only be the result of thoughtless and flippant attitudes towards marriage and towards the family. It must therefore be sternly discouraged. The same principle may be observed beneath the changing regulations in regard to divorce. Law changes in Russia when conditions change. The principle behind the law remains constant. The principle here being respect for family life. Divorce is possible and has been possible ever since 1917, when it was granted by petition from either party without motive being stated. This enabled the breaking of artificial and unnatural marriage ties which were a hangover from the past. But when those early days were gone, when in 1936 marriage had largely become what it should be, a mutual love partnership, then the laws on divorce were revised. To prevent frivolous use of the right to divorce changes were introduced and more onerous conditions attached to it.

In 1944 further steps were taken to prevent frivolous attitudes to marriage. Divorces must be made public, and only granted through decision of court. Motives must be investigated, reconciliation sought, and if unsuccessful the petition must pass to a higher court. Divorce involves regulations as to control and maintenance of children and as to distribution of property. Divorce costs 100 roubles on application and from 500-2,000 roubles when granted. If marriage is sought an application must be made to a registrar, accompanied by a statement that no legal obstacles hinder it, that each has been informed of the other's health, etc. When the couple make their signatures, and when the witnesses add theirs, then the registrar hands to them a certificate carrying evidence of marriage.

The legal age for marriage in most states is eighteen; in some southern states sixteen. Monogamy is the law. A woman may take the name of her husband or retain her own. Property possessed by either party before marriage remains their own, that acquired since marriage is shared; the woman's work in the home and with the family being regarded as equivalent to man's work in the factory. Members of a family are obliged to provide mutual support for one another, none may live at the expense of others.

The relations between children and parents also are strictly regulated by law. Father and mother have equal rights in relation to the child and equal responsibility for its maintenance. The State protects the interests of the child. The State also aids the family as a whole, promoting its well-being as well as guarding its integrity. When the registrar hands over the certificate it is more than mere evidence of marriage. It is a token that the State recognises, approves and supports their new married life. The State takes them under its protection. The establishment of strong bonds between parent and child is the guiding motive of the State. The Soviet Union makes every effort to provide conditions for the development of the family as a closely knit unity, but a unity intimately connected with the community. Within two months of the October Revolution in 1917 the protection of mother and child was declared to be a direct duty of the State. Whatever hardships befell the young Soviet Union—civil war, harvest failure or famine—mother and child always received the lion's share of available goods.

So it was through the stringencies of the last world war. Even when one-third of Russia's food-bearing lands were overrun the expectant mother received extra rations of butter, sugar and cereals. In 1944 the ration was doubled and each expectant mother from the sixth to the eighth month of pregnancy was entitled to $1\frac{3}{4}$ lbs. of butter, $1\frac{3}{4}$ lbs. of sugar, $2\frac{3}{4}$ lbs. of cereals and 21 pints of milk monthly in addition to her ordinary ration; nursing mothers receiving the same for four months. Pregnancy leave has been extended to eleven weeks.

No expectant mother waits in a queue for a bus and it is exceptional in a town for a woman to give birth to her child other than in a lying-in hospital. No nursing mother works at night. It is illegal to work over-time for six months after the confinement. One half hour each three and a half hours is allowed in a factory for a mother to feed her child, with no diminution of pay. If a nursing child is ill the mother is granted leave of absence with incapacity pay. Mothers with large families enjoy special amenities and payments to meet their extra liabilities and receive in addition medals and honours. The unmarried mother receives equal consideration. The child at any rate must not suffer. No longer need such mother apply to the courts for an alimony or maintenance order against the reputed father; she receives forthwith a State allowance of 100 roubles a month for one child, 150 for two and 200 for three until the children are twelve years of age.

It is a far cry now from the days when prostitution was rife in the

Soviet Union. Prostitution was not abolished by preaching or punishment but by re-education and prophylactic treatment side by side with increased facilities for employment under satisfactory conditions, there to learn that discipline, responsibility and morality offer greater rewards than licence and immorality. The principle is always the same —the expulsive power of a new affection.

Women, as I seek to show in the next chapter, enter now side by side with men into endless forms of activity external to the home. Nor has the family suffered through this external activity. Far from it. The family has benefited. For side by side with the outside work which enlarges her life, the mother has been relieved of many narrowing but essential tasks: public laundry and public restaurant lessen kitchen drudgery and the nursery school and crèche, together with the kindergarten, give to the masses of women what every woman who can afford it in other lands eagerly seeks, skilled and trained assistance in the upbringing of her children. Experience has shown, and increasingly shows, that the woman concerned with other interests outside her own home is not the less interesting as a wife or as a mother, or less happy in her own personal life than the woman who remains exclusively in the house and with the children.

Viewed externally Russia is the most moral land I know. During many months in Russia, in great towns and small, in country places and seaside resorts, in back streets and front streets, at all hours of day and night, in bookshops and railway stalls, in theatre and picture house, I never saw a sight I would screen from the eyes of a young girl. And the secret? A possible purpose in life and a creative job for all; no economic necessity for a girl to sell her honour; no economic drive to harness pruriency for profit; ability for all to marry at the biologically appropriate age—such I suspect are the main reasons for the undoubted fact.

3. SOVIET WOMEN LEAD THE WORLD

STANDING high above the Russian Pavilion at the pre-war Paris Exhibition there rose Madame Mukhina's fine sculpture of Soviet youth, forward looking, onward marching: triumphant young manhood and womanhood. Equal in size, purpose and intensity, a true picture of the change—possibly one of the greatest things that has happened in Soviet Russia—which lifts womanhood in a sixth of the world from the ranks of the unskilled, the illiterate, and the politically ignorant to a stature which in factory, in office, in laboratory and university places her on a parity everywhere with man.

And this miracle has been wrought with no sacrifice of woman's primary function as mother of children. Russia's womanhood demonstrates that women are in no sense naturally inferior to men. Women can hold their own both on the industrial productive front and on the Government front. Women can operate effectively in the wide affairs of nation and the world and yet prove perfect mothers to happy and contented children, consolidating a durable family fellowship. The choice is no longer marriage or career, but marriage and what career.

Women in pre-Soviet Russia stood low in the social scale, low in esteem of the State, low in esteem of husbands. In the old Russian Empire women possessed no rights. A wife could not even make her own will, nor receive a passport without her husband's permission. The attitude of working men to their wives occasioned one of Lenin's sharpest rebukes. Women had to toil harder than men in factory, home and field for less pay and with few if any aids in the provision of child care centres.

In one thing alone pre-Soviet womanhood equalled or surpassed manhood—her capacity for hard work. She has never lost it and when the doors to ampler life swung open she entered with a zest that swept her to victorious equality. The October Revolution accorded to women equal rights with men in all spheres of economic, cultural, social and political life. Article 122 of the Soviet Constitution ordains complete equality between men and women concerning the right to work, payment for work, rest and leisure, social insurance and education.

Women take an active part in Government administration. More than 1,700 women of different nationalities have been elected Deputies to the Supreme Soviet of the U.S.S.R. and to the Supreme Soviets of the Union and Autonomous Republics; 456,000 women are members of local Soviets. Thousands of women head factories, offices and scientific institutions. In 1940 150,000 women engineers and technicians practised in the U.S.S.R. and women accounted for half the students at universities and technical colleges, with at least ten millions more in industry. The process of women's emancipation took time. World war and civil war had left the Bolshevik leaders too weak and too poor to carry into effect the liberation they had designed from the first. Not until the Five-Year Plan had solved the problem of unemployment and created increasing demand for labour was it found wise or possible to persuade women to take their place beside men in productive industry.

Never save in the emergency of war, when Russian women like English women were mobilised for field and factory was a Russian woman compelled by law to leave her family and enter industrial life. Choice was always free. Persuasion, not force, was employed.

The urgent call for women to enter industry has its basis not only in the desire for greater production, but also in the belief that a wider life was beneficial to womanhood and to family integrity, as indeed it proves to be. Increased production due to women's labour has brought shorter working hours, greater amenities and greater leisure to both husband and wife. The wider activities of the mother have brought a more generous atmosphere into the home. The thirty million Soviet women who worked on farm or in factory prior to the war have found themselves enriched by new technical skill and by contact with the wider culture of the world. For a Russian factory or collective farm has its cultural side powerfully and deliberately developed. Leaving school does not mean leaving an educational environment. Factories provide free courses in cultural subjects, oftentimes with quiet reading-rooms and libraries added. By 1940 the Trade Unions possessed some 15,000 libraries; and factories possessed some 100,000 club-rooms.

As with factories so with farms. The woman drudge has given place to the woman worker receiving equal wages for equal work. A large percentage of women have become highly skilled workers. Out of 1,447 members of an important live-stock conference in 1936, 507 were women. Women engage in every kind of voluntary work. Immediately in front of *Voks'* headquarters and elsewhere in Moscow I saw voluntary women workers tidying up public gardens in squares, local housewives doing spontaneous social work on their own door-steps. There is no doubt whatever that one result of the war will be a great advance of women's activities in the U.S.S.R.

The war naturally augmented the tempo of women's work. Education and training before the war had prepared the ground. War gave the opportunity and provided the incentive. Women took a new plunge. The war thrust them into every conceivable kind of job, from civil defence to traffic-point duty, from radio operation to driving tractors on a farm. In Leningrad and Moscow they dug trenches, in the country they cooked meals for guerrilla units. Their main contribution, however, lay in the work of field and factory where they took the place of men and maintained a tale of production without which victory would never have been achieved. Very shortly women outnumbered men both in industry and agriculture.

As in England, women learned the new techniques of industry with surprising rapidity: 173,000 girls and women after intensive training were already equipped and at work on the railways in 1942. They even took on, with every precaution to health, the job of the miner. Many trades regarded as unsuited for women before the war can now be undertaken by women and girls owing to new techniques.

Women doctors already outnumbered men before the war. During war years women constituted 90 per cent of the entrants to the medical schools. Fifty per cent of women are assisting in one capacity or another in the laboratories of the Academy of Scientists, including junior women workers: 357 women in the Academy's research department hold the degree of Doctor of Science and Bachelor of Science. It was in war-time that Soviet womanhood finally found its feet.

4. CHILDHOOD IN SOVIET LAND

W A R M sunshine, blue skies, fleecy clouds and the soft air of spring caused us one day in May to visit Istra, a small town some forty-five miles west of Moscow.

A rough road, with tar-macadam centre, wrinkled and uneven, wound on through a typically Russian countryside of meadows, straggling wooden-housed villages, birch copses and pine woods to what before the war had been a lovely sylvan townlet built on rising ground in the curved arm of a small river and dominated by a superb church. The town lay in ruins, razed to the ground. The cathedral church, though horribly mutilated, still raised its dome in stately splendour from its green sward. Cloisters opening on to the church ran, not on the ground level, but on top of the huge Kremlin-like walls which completely encircled the sward and the outbuildings. Monks could walk or sit in sunshine all day long and gaze at the crowning dome of gold.

Istra had risen to fame through Archbishop Nikon, who built it in the seventeenth century and acquired a power almost equal to that of the Tsar, with whom at length he quarrelled and by whom was banished till permitted in old age to return to Istra to die. His tomb rests in the cathedral. The present building, erected after a fire in 1749, is a baroque structure of outstanding beauty. Entering by what had been the central door, we stood on huge piles of rubble beneath the dome, half of which was left and looked entrancingly beautiful, its cream coloured walls and golden illuminated frescoes bathed in sunshine and silhouetted against the azure sky. The other half was gone, wantonly destroyed at high expense and with devilish skill by mines sunk deep in masonry at the summit of supporting columns. Much of the ancient crypt with its warm barbaric splendour remains.

The peasant mayor, our driver and two peasant women joined us at lunch beneath the towering aspen trees whose spreading branches patterned themselves against the vivid sky. The mayor and most citizens had fled to the woods during the German occupation. Thence they carried on their Soviet functions as best they could and with no guidance from the centre. People still lived in holes and shacks amongst the ruins.

A sturdy, shy lad of sixteen, satchel on back, returning to school, passed us as we rested. I examined his books—physics and geography. He was continuing school till his seventeenth year, then plans to be a sailor. At my request we had sent the cars back to the cathedral and wandering thither on foot spoke to a little boy stumping school-wards on a wooden leg, his own lost through treading on a mine. Passing a large fine house recently patched up, almost the only one still standing, we stumbled across a bunch of children returning to school with spring flowers in their hands. One bonny child with fair hair and blue eyes set wide apart in a smiling face and aglow with health and youth ran up spontaneously and gave us primroses.

It was a moving picture; ruined church, ruined homes, withered old peasants sitting beneath the cloister walls in the spring sunshine, much impressed by my crucifix, a handful of adults sturdily and without complaint gathering up the threads of life. And there in the foreground, capturing the picture, these merry children, healthy, bonny and buoyant. Soviet Russia as it were in miniature. The child always in the centre. The first thought, as the Germans departed, had been of children and education, the first house made habitable, the house where children could assemble for school. Red Army men supplied the initiative and did the work.

It was the same wherever I went, north, south, east or west. In Moscow and Leningrad, in town and countryside: in Georgia, Armenia or Asia as well as in Belo-Russia and the Ukraine. Always the child first. Russia is the land of child and youth.

Soviet male babes, owing to love of children and an excessive birthrate which exceeds that of other civilised lands by 1.4 per cent, to-day approach numerical equality with all the male babes of England, her white dominions, Germany, France and the United States of America all put together.

The study of Soviet childhood and youth is of first-rate importance, and if the health of the Russian child had been my first quest, its nurture and education came next and I proceeded to examine from top to bottom the Soviet educational plan as it evolves to-day.

(A) *Soviet Education Breaks New Democratic Ground*

Two outstanding features characterise Soviet education: (1) its zest and (2) its wholly new democratic character.

1. No country in the world has taken education more seriously

than the Soviet Union, which in twenty-six years has transformed a sixth of the world, with a population approaching 200 million, from a land 80-90 per cent illiterate to a land 80-90 per cent literate. The increased school attendance from eight millions to thirty-six is reflected in every constituent part of the Union. Armenia's 34,000 schoolchildren of 1917, for example, becoming 320,000 in 1939.

Lenin from the first insisted: "We need a huge advancement of culture," and never once has Russia relinquished the goal of an educated proletariat.

Stalin's words in 1930, "The main thing now is to introduce compulsory education . . ." inaugurated a supreme drive for education, spreading from centre to remotest hamlet.

In four particulars Soviet education claims to have broken fresh democratic ground:

(1) As the first country in civilised history to remove all economic barriers to education. The first country to make education available to all from nursery school to university. "All citizens have the right to education," says Article 121 of the Constitution. And that is no pious aspiration. Education, even in its higher ranges, is available for all who can qualify to profit by it. State assistance, wherever needed, enables students to meet living expenses at low prices in hostels and dining-rooms. The following figures are eloquent.

In 1914-15 students in eight universities were classified thus: nobility and high officials 38.3; middle classes 24.4; tradesmen 11.4; rich citizens 14; clergy 7.4; manual workers—none.

In 1938 children of manual and office workers made up 97 per cent of students in all universities.

Four-fifths of Russian children lacked educational opportunity prior to 1917. No group of individuals in the Soviet Union to-day, willing to take advantage of a higher education and meeting the scholastic requirements, are debarred from doing so for economic reasons.

Capital has been made of certain small charges now attached to higher education. The principle of free education has not been fundamentally altered by the fact that certain educational classes have recently been scheduled for charge. A small charge is levied for education in the three highest classes of secondary schools, amounting to fifty roubles or 1.4 per cent of the average wage. And ample grants are given towards the 400 roubles fee imposed since the war for university education: with many fee exemptions, as for instance for the children of partisans or for orphans. It remains true that no child is deprived of the highest educational advantages by economic barriers.

(2) As abolishing any form of racial or colour discrimination. A Negro child suffers no handicap through the colour of his face, nor a Jewish child through the contour of his nose. All Soviet nationalities fare alike.

(3) As taking the lead in women's education. There is no kind of educational institution or field of learning from which women are barred. The proportion of trained women operating in various occupations and professions exceeds that of any country in the world. The 15 per cent of women students in Tsarist universities became, in 1938, 43 per cent.

(4) As establishing close relationship between school and institutions outside the school. These interlock. Hence there is a continuing demand for trained people turned out by the educational system. No fear of involuntary unemployment haunts Soviet youth. Young men and women are trained for higher positions in full assurance that appropriate jobs await them, with full security in exercising their trained powers. It would be highly dangerous for Russia to train these vast numbers of youth unless assuring their ultimate employment, and impossible to do so with the economic waste that unemployment implies. Soviet educational advantages do not operate in a vacuum. Soviet educational philosophy is part of Soviet general philosophy. Russia is a planned society and plans are made in the light of basic ideas.

Furthermore, to give equality of education to all races and colours in a society with racial segregation and colour bar is useless and dangerous. Russia is the first country in the world to make discrimination in the case either of race or sex a criminal offence.

(B)   *Structure of Soviet Education*

Soviet education, State financed and State controlled, is compulsory, universal, secular and free, save for the few charges already noted in the higher ranges.

In contrast to the illiteracy of the past and the barriers which prevented four-fifths of Russian children from receiving education at all the words "all citizens have the right to education" appeared of set purpose in the Soviet Constitution. As teachers and buildings become available education becomes compulsory. Thirty-six millions now attend school.

Education up to the eighth year of the secondary school is entirely free. From the eighth to the tenth year the annual fee of 200 roubles in Moscow, Leningrad and other republican capitals and of 150

(*Top*) In the Pioneers' House in Ivanovo, where young chess players
spend long hours at the game.
(*Lower*) Children in a holiday sanatorium, where they are always in
high spirits.

(*Top*) Pupils at a Moscow Girls' Secondary School.
(*Lower*) Uzbeck girls working on their diploma projects in the laboratory of the Samarkand State University.

roubles elsewhere is trivial. The fee for education in the universities and higher technical institutes of 400 roubles a year in Moscow, Leningrad and other Republican institutions, 300 elsewhere, can be earned by a youth in one month's work. All good students receive grants of 185 roubles a month for the first year up to 300 roubles a month for the last, with scholarships for brilliant work. School books are cheap: the price of four daily newspapers will buy a text book on arithmetic. Education is secular—the State remaining neutral in religious matters—and State controlled, its tasks determined by the State, its costs met from the State Treasury.

The core of the Soviet educational system is the general school with its three types: Primary, with classes 1–4; Middle, with classes 1–7; Secondary, with classes 1–10. Syllabus and text books are the same throughout, the child from the primary passing without change of books or teaching or special examination into the middle or to the secondary ten years' school. In 1938 the Soviet Union made the seven-year school universally compulsory in towns, with extension to eighteen years on local initiative.

Below seven years of age comes the kindergarten school for three to seven years, below that the crèche. These are not compulsory but their use extends as buildings are erected, equipped and staffed.

Beyond the secondary school comes the university and parallel with the secondary school, for adolescents whose tastes are practical rather than academic, are the vocational schools—trade schools, technical schools, teachers' training schools, etc. Boys and girls of sixteen and seventeen who have passed the seven-year school can enter technical schools of different specialities: teachers' schools, training primary or infant school teachers; or junior medical schools, training nurses or midwives. The course in these schools lasts three to four years. Co-education, still common in the majority of middle schools, especially in country places, tends to give place in large towns to separate schools for boys and girls. An order of 1943 aims at separate education for the sexes mainly on account of different rates of development. All subjects in the first four classes are taught by one teacher, thereafter by specialists. Marks are now given and annual examinations set and compulsory.

The subject matter of teaching—Russian language, mathematics, physics, chemistry, natural science, history, etc.—must be presented logically and methodically, with an eye to independent work with books, experiments and visual apparatus.

"Rules for pupils" regulate conduct outside school as well as inside. Children must not attend cinemas, or other places of entertainment, during school hours. Children are to be kind to old people

G

and smaller children and to offer seats in buses to elderly folk and generally to render assistance where need calls. Training of a "new man," or "character training," has its own importance. The late President Kalinin summed it up thus: "This new man must be infused with the best qualities of man . . . love for the people, honesty, courage, solidarity, and love of work."

Discipline demands observance of accepted rules. Persuasion is used, and rewards. Punishments also, where necessary, such as loss of marks, public reprimand by teacher, or by Teachers' Council, etc. Corporal punishment or detention which interferes with meals is strictly forbidden. Temporary expulsion must be authorised by the local educational authorities.

Clubs and circles for special pursuits, such as drama and botany, meet once a week outside school hours under supervision. Evening performances by the pupils take place monthly. The Pioneer and Komsomol (the Communist Union of Youth) Organisations aim at training for good citizenship. Pioneers, with special tie, banners and salute, are trained to study diligently in school and to help in house and school. Members of the Komsomol guide the Pioneers.

Special schools exist for the deaf and dumb, for mental defectives and other delicate children, special art schools also for the exceptionally gifted child.

Residential schools provide a general education up to fourteen years for orphans. A vocational or technical education with life in a hostel follows. Suverov military schools, with special drills, riding lessons, music and two foreign languages, with dancing lessons to encourage grace, deftness and carriage, in addition to the ordinary curriculum, are secondary residential schools for sons of officers or partisans killed in the war. The boys live a closely ordered day, with an hour's rest or games after dinner and story books before retiring to bed.

Higher education in universities, institutes and colleges admit men and women who have completed the secondary school course by examination or on attainment of full marks at the final school examination. Higher educational establishments, whose number has increased in twenty years from 91 to 788, train the personnel for key positions in economic life and culture. University study continues for four or five years and students who graduate are guaranteed jobs.

A special committee on higher education supervises the studies and equipment of all Soviet higher educational institutions. This centralised direction renders a planned training in accordance with every branch of the country's economic and cultural needs possible and practicable. Soviet enthusiasm for education never ceased even during the terrible years of war, though achievement was naturally less. Children were evacuated eastwards: kindergartens *in toto*, otherwise with parents or with school boarding establishments. One hundred thousand orphaned children were adopted by families, nerve-shattered children receiving special care.

Education struggled on despite all handicaps. Teachers diminished in numbers: in 1941, 1,222,205; in 1943-4, 774,795. Lessons were taken in shifts, class numbers rose from forty to forty-five. In Leningrad and elsewhere children attended unheated schools.

Rehabilitation followed hard on the steps of the retreating Germans. Peasants donated their houses for schools. Engineers and technicians erected new buildings. Large scale re-equipment began. In 1943 the schools of Stalingrad, Rostov, Kursk and Orel received 35,000 new desks. The Ministry of Education distributed 19,419,000 copy books, etc. Within four months Rostov had 524 schools with 50,000 children attending them. The total number of Soviet schools at its peak in 1941-2 was 193,025, falling as a result of German destruction to 116,548, but rising again in 1943-4 to 140,156. Teachers' remuneration was increased from a national total of 2,257,000,000 to 4,165,000,000 roubles. Nine Suverov schools were founded for orphans of soldiers or partisans. The budget for education in 1944 doubled that of 1943: 21,100 as against 12,700 roubles. In higher education reduced but intensified courses were introduced as an emergency measure. The syllabus remained the same as before. Certain alterations in fees took place to meet war-time difficulties.

(c) *Soviet Youth Feels Inter-Racial Unity*

One morning when wandering in the eastern area of Erivan in Armenia I came across a fine stadium. It was a hot morning with a fresh wind. The stadium was full of youth, young men and women of the sixteens and eighteens in the prime of vigour, half-stripped limbs tanned by the sun, hair tossed back, abounding in vitality heightened by enthusiasm. They were the sports teams preparing for a several days' journey to Moscow to join in the All-Republics parade on the Red Square, which takes place annually in July.

Several hundred youth will go from Armenia. Several hundreds more from Georgia and so on throughout the republics.

In Tbilisi, at the university, I came across more youth of these youth teams, preparing for Moscow. The Georgian team will be 500 or 600 strong.

From all republics youth will assemble in Moscow on a special day set apart for country-wide celebration of physical culture. Youth from Armenia and Georgia will meet youth from the Asian republics—Uzbekistan, Kazakistan and Kizistan; from Siberia and Karelia, from Kiev and Leningrad. In Moscow all meet—youth from remote corners of a sixth of the world, boys and girls of all tongues, of all shades of colour and from all environments. One and all they are members of the new Socialist order and proud of the fact. Youth becomes familiar with youth of other lands, learning the meaning of variety in unity.

As athletes they are members of a vast organisation of sport. Literally millions of young people are sports enthusiasts, eager among other things to win the C.T.O.—Ready for Labour and Defence Badge which seven million had won since 1934.

Never for a moment throughout the war has physical culture ceased. Though the Germans destroyed nearly half of the stadia sports grounds and club-rooms the sporting contests in the remaining areas actually increased the total number of entrants. Whereas in the cross-country races in 1942 five and a half million competed, in 1944 the number rose to eight million, in 1945 to nine million. The six million competitors in the ski races of 1944 rose to seven million in 1945.

The post-war enthusiasm has already begun the construction of seven gigantic stadia to seat 315,000 spectators.

Youth forms the bulk of the membership of a still greater organisation—the All-Union Society to Aid Defence, Aviation and Chemistry, an organisation numbering tens of millions of members in 230,000 initial organisations. In these clubs youth learns how to defend his country. Here Soviet flyers and parachutists took their early lessons in air mastery; here Russian snipers learned their skill and millions more learned how to defend themselves in air attack either by bombs, fire bombs or chemical gas bombs.

War is a supreme test of youth as well as of age. And the youth of Russia which met the youth of Germany in the Forces, though less well equipped mechanically at the outset, succeeded in wearing the other down.

How did they do it?

From childhood onwards German youth was trained in ideas of racial superiority; Russian youth in belief in the unique value of every national group. Hitler had said that the Germans must drive out and annihilate the Slavs. Rosenburg describes the English as degenerate and incapable of creative life, the French as not human beings and the Americans as a rotten race.

Hitler perfected the system of wholesale murder with his death technique at Maidenek, Auschwitz and Buchenwald. Soviet youth, however, was reared in another school and with another goal and with other methods. Initiative was linked with comradeship; love of one's own country with respect for other people's. Alien colour and alien language never infected youth who had marched with young men and young women of all colour and language on the Red Army Square. Instead of *Mein Kampf* and the burning of books Soviet youth had been fed on Shakespeare, Cervantes and Heine, on their own Pushkin, Gogol and Tolstoi and on all the great humanists of the race. Friendship of peoples replaced racial hatred. A spirit like that, other things being equal—and very often in spite of being unequal—was bound to wear the other spirit down.

And the same spirit which helped Soviet youth to win the war urges them on now to win the peace. Once again and with a zest never excelled before they set about the work of reconstruction. Back once more in the lands so long held in German hands, they neither sit and mourn nor stand and curse. They work.

5. SOVIET CULTURE

DRAMA

(A) *Moscow Art Theatre*

WHAT is your reaction to glamorous New York; its sumptuous shops, its air of plenty, its energy? I inquired of my neighbour, a young Russian trade delegate, at a New York banquet.

He replied after deliberation: "We Russians value physical amenities. In time we shall acquire them. Our real interest, however, lies in things of the spirit, in culture. Nor can we," he added, "enjoy physical amenities ourselves whilst others lack them."

Russia's cultural life, as one sees it in Moscow, or in the constituent republics, endorses every word he said. A rich cultural life still flourishes. As it had flourished through all the earlier days of economic stress and strain, so it flourishes to-day despite war losses. No post-war city provides richer fare than Moscow in theatre, opera or concert. On upwards of thirty nights I was enabled to study every kind of cultural entertainment. The contrast with London's provision of entertainment is gravely to our disadvantage. Russia's cultural life has always proceeded *pari passu* with her industrial life, never postponed till the day of industrial achievement, and, as far as drama was concerned, it has always found its focus in the Moscow Art Theatre, whence its influence has radiated far and wide.

The Moscow Art Theatre stands in a class by itself, not only as leader and pathfinder since the revolution, but as agent in provoking the revolution; exposing alongside of the inadequacy of the old dramatic set-up also the rottenness of contemporary Tsarist society.

Forty years ago Gorky wrote *The Lower Depths*, a deeply moving story of the underworld. The leaders of the Art Theatre determined to produce it and in preparation stepped down from their narrow theatrical circle, immersing themselves in the vagrant world, and sampling the grimness of the dosshouse at first hand and in their own persons.

A new movement which revolutionised the Russian Theatre had started. Stanislavsky as art-trainer and Nemirovich-Danchenko as producer—beginning their work in the nineties of the last century—were its creators and leaders.

Nemirovich-Danchenko describes the stage as he found it. In those days no preliminary talks introduced the actor into the soul of the selected play: the first rehearsal took place on the stage itself. Enlightened by no explanation of the artistic content of the play, work began with the vaguest notion of what it was all about, each actor being armed with a notebook containing his part and cue: "Stand by the table and say . . ." and nothing more.

The actor's culture at that time was on the ebb. His equipment inadequate. His standard of living low. His accommodation mean. A couple of box-office failures spelt disaster.

The Soviet Government gave every encouragement to change, spending money without stint. New settings and new costumes accompanied new plays. Adequate accommodation, adequate pay, adequate security became the actor's right: large public demands added the spur.

At their first memorable meeting Stanislavsky and Nemirovich-Danchenko envisaged the lines upon which Soviet theatres of to-day still operate. Both men had been steeped in drama from their youth. Stanislavsky learned the rudiments of dramatic production in his father's family mansion where he met and threshed out with Komissar-Zhevskayer, father of a famous contemporary actress, plans for a new type of theatre which should blend all the arts. These discussions led to the formation of a society of arts and literature, where Stanislavsky gained experience as actor and scope as producer.

Nemirovich-Danchenko also had loved the theatre since childhood. He acted. He wrote. And after a broad education received recognition as dramatic critic. His plays were accepted by the Maly Theatre, with himself as producer.

The two men had met at Nemirovich-Danchenko's invitation in 1897 in a Moscow restaurant: "A World Conference," wrote Stanislavsky long afterwards, "never considered important matters of State with such care and precision as we discussed the production of our future undertaking, problems of pure art, our future ideals, stage ethics and technique, organisational plans, draft of the future repertory and our mutual relations."

The talk continuing, after closing time, in Stanislavsky's country house lasted for seventeen hours and gave birth to the famous Moscow Art Theatre.

Stanislavsky and Nemirovich-Danchenko trod in those early years no primrose path. They sought to create a theatre which, emerging from old theatrical ruts, should serve the people, with charges not beyond the purse of the poorest intellectual. This demanded a subsidy. No public authority would give it. Nor did the rich help. A wealthy patroness to whom Nemirovich-Danchenko outlined his project dismissed him coldly. Nemirovich-Danchenko complains that "for the right to create a work of art out of Chekhov's play we had not only to perfect our talent as artists in years of hard work but also to humiliate ourselves in Varvaras Morosove's drawing-room. . . ."

In spite of all that they won through. After an uphill fight merit triumphed, the climax coming with a performance of Chekhov's play *The Seagull*. It was an outstanding triumph to turn what the critics had branded as an unstagelike and monotonous play into drama so thrilling that a noted critic, Gruzinsky, could write to Chekhov: "From the first act an out-of-the-ordinary and exalted mood gripped the audience. . . ." A seagull became the emblem of the Art Theatre; its white, wide-spreading wings which I saw so often upon its curtain still recall the evening of 17th December, 1898, when the Art Theatre was launched for its voyage across the stormy sea of Tsarist Russian life.

In tackling Gorky's play *The Lower Depths* the Art Theatre took its earliest steps in what Russia calls realistic art. For the play which dealt with vagrants needed more than photographic representation or vagrancy. Naturalistic art presents the surface of the scene; realistic art presents its soul. The actor must be able to say not "This is what it looks like from the outside," but "This is what it is in its inner reality; this is the thing as I experience it, as I live in it, as I know it for the fearsome thing it is." That was the secret of the psychological realism of the New Art Theatre and it carried immense conviction. It drove Gorky's message home. It harrowed the soil for the revolution. It taught that, though life may reduce man to the status of a beast, man still remains a man.

The Moscow Art Theatre, as a building, still retains the severe simplicity which characterises also the life of the Soviet artists. No glamorous bathroom, bedrooms, lounges in the Russian artists' homes. No sumptuous boxes in the Art Theatre.

The first play I saw in post-war years was Chekhov's *Three Sisters*. As the grey velvet seagull curtain parts we are in a sunny parlour whose flowered balcony overlooked a garden. A simple sturdy life flows before us. Irine, the youngest sister, seeking for love. Baron Tudenbach, a dreamy optimist, offering it.

Vershinin, a newly arrived artillery officer, speaks of Moscow. The three sisters, Olga the eldest, Irine and Marsha, who had been reading, awoke at the word Moscow. Moscow suggests escape from the rut of narrow provincial life. Vershinin tries to convince the others, and himself as well, that all are living for a happier future. The Baron speaks of a strong healthy storm creeping up, a storm which will scatter indolence, indifference and deadly boredom.

The reality which creeps up is, however, more than storm, it is tragedy. Dreams of joy yield to tragedy of unattainable happiness.

The very scenery of the second act forecasts the doom. The same, yet different; greyer, more dimly lit, and as the curtain parts, void of people. Natasha, the new wife of Andrei, the brother, enters with her husband. The petit bourgeois Natasha has lowered the whole tone of the household. Andrei has ceased his quest of a professorship. After a few strained minutes the couple leave the room.

Marsha and Vershinin enter. They are in love and you sense it.

Irine then enters, tired with work, dissatisfied with her job and ill at ease with life. "Work without poetry or meaning!" she exclaims. To which the Baron replies, in cold comfort, "Those who succeed us will be happier than we."

Each succeeding act, with subtle skill, increases the gloom. Natasha continues to ruin the home. Olga departs to a loveless life at a school. Irine, losing her youth, still dreams of Moscow but decides to marry the Baron. Marsha's love affair grows more hopeless as love increases. She comes out best. She at least knows how to rebel: "When you take your happiness in snatches, piece by piece, and then as I have done lose it, you gradually become hard and spiteful."

In the last scene the storm breaks. Autumn leaves flurry around. It is a day of parting, with awkward, aimless comings and goings.

The Baron is killed in a duel.

Vershinin's brigade leaves the town.

Marsha's bitter cry "An unlucky life!" rings out and the intolerable tension is only broken by Irine's last words: "We must work."

Thus ended Chekhov's vivid picture of the futility of Tsarist bourgeois life, only rendered tolerable as a play through its contrast with Soviet purposeful and hopeful work.

As I left the Art Theatre I knew the answer to the problem which a great English actress had set me before leaving home: "Find out if the Russian theatre has degenerated or not." My own emphatic answer formulated on that night and reinforced by all I subsequently saw was "not."

If it is true that only a healthy community enjoys the tragic plays which decadent society refuses, then Soviet Russia exhibits unusual signs of health, for tragic plays abound. And upon tragic plays the Art Theatre lavishes exceptional skill. I can never forget the production of Tolstoy's *Anna Karenina*, the woman whose unhappy end was predetermined by her social environment.

Nemirovich-Danchenko chose plays for their educational and social significance, seeking to wean the masses from the duty of slavish obeisance to the power of the propertied . . . to compel the masses to use their own heads . . . to develop a critical attitude towards all that had power over them.

Chekhov's and Tolstoy's plays suited his purpose admirably. They were written with passion, and Nemirovich-Danchenko reproduced them with passion. The rôle of the theatre in his eye, was not to amuse, but to educate for freedom, to revive man's faith in the future, in the ultimate triumph of good over evil.

Nemirovich-Danchenko knew that moral purpose must not be expressed in words but presented with subtle art. It must be overheard, not heard.

In the play *The Girl with the Dowry*, for instance, Nemirovich-Danchenko subtly depicts the life of a society woman, selfish and corrupt. The play itself awakes protest. Art which dispenses with moralising carries its own more massive moral appeal. And such high art dispenses with commonplace tricks, pathetic monologues, gags, formal entrances, exits and the like.

The Moscow Art Theatre stands still in a class by itself.

(B) *The Maly Theatre*

The Moscow State Troupe, founded in 1806, opened its season of 1824 in a small building in the centre of Moscow. Next year a huge Opera Theatre, the second largest in Europe, was built alongside it facing Theatre Square. The big and the little, in Russian the Bolshoi and the Maly.

The emblem of the Maly is an oval containing eight portraits: four famous dramatists, Griboyedov, Gogol, Shakespeare and Ostrovsky—who formed the theatre's basic repertory. The other four depict famous pre-revolution actors and actresses who helped to found the fortunes of the theatre:

(1) Pavel Mochalov, who sprang to fame at seventeen in *Œdipus of Athens*. "The play," says a contemporary, "was limping along in a stifling, overcrowded theatre when all of a sudden a young, vigorous voice was heard off-stage: 'Ah, where is she, lead me to her.' It was as though an electric current had run through the audience. The voice startled everyone . . . the applause was overwhelming and his triumph complete." Mochalov the tragedian died in 1846.

(2) Mikhail Sheherkin, who rose to fame as a serf, acted in Griboyedov's *Woe from Wit* the part of a typical Moscow aristocrat, arrogant and pompous. Sheherkin was forerunner of the subsequent realism: he had lived through the scenes he acted.

(3) Prov Sadovsky, who as a young actor at the Maly Theatre met Ostrovsky, then a city clerk, in a coffee house. The two are inseparably linked and, through Sadovsky, Ostrovsky's rich Russian speech caught the imagination of the Maly and created its fastidious care for the spoken word.

(4) Maria Vermolova, who as a child at the Maly Theatre School had neither the dancer's legs nor the dancer's smile. A serious-looking child, threatened with complete oblivion, her chance came through a happy accident which enabled her to take the part of the actress who was to play Emilia in Lessing's *Emilia Galotti*. The first sound of her voice established her career: "It was something utterly out of the ordinary and so unexpected coming from a frail young actress that the public involuntarily broke into applause before she had time to finish her first line," wrote a critic. "A debut like Vermolova's happens once in a hundred years and even rarer." Her passionate love of freedom revealed itself in Vega's drama *Fuente Ovejuna*, where seventy-two curtain calls broke the Maly record. The play was, however, banned by the Tsarist censor and remained unplayed for forty years.

Maria Vermolova lived on into Soviet days when in 1920, on completing her fiftieth year, she was greeted on the Maly stage by Lenin himself, who bestowed upon her, as its first recipient, the coveted title, "People's Artist."

The Maly, deteriorating in the early years of this century, rose with the revolution to the height of its founder's intention. It became a real people's theatre, creating, side by side with the reproduction of Russian and foreign classics, plays portraying Soviet people and Soviet energy and life.

The mechanism of the Maly organisation is briefly as follows: The work of the theatre, its creative development and the choice of plays, is controlled by the oldest actors sitting in council and presided over by the director. The staff is large—at present it numbers 163 actors and 1,000 personnel. The Maly School annually graduates twenty to twenty-five pupils. The budget in 1943 amounted to ten million roubles. It is self-supporting, though the Government has allotted five million roubles towards the complete remodelling of its buildings.

(c) *The Central Red Army Theatre*

New theatres spring up beside the old. In a spacious square, recently a labyrinth of squalid streets, now as noble as any square in Moscow, rises the huge Central Red Army Theatre, shaped like a five-pointed star. Every one of its 1,900 spectators has unhindered view of a stage equipped with every mechanical gadget, which is half as big again as the Bolshoi stage and can accommodate 1,000 people with room for an eight storied building or if need be for an armoured tank. The Red Army Theatre is appropriate for great spectacles. I personally miss the intimacy of the smaller buildings, though technical skill makes the huge stage shrink to accommodate small productions as well as great.

Plays revealing great military characters like Suvarov are popular here. The war has accelerated Russia's interest and pride in her past. In the present, too. In the Maly I saw *Ivan the Terrible*. Here I saw the siege of Stalingrad, which I confess was a great disappointment. Its emphasis upon intrigue, dishonesty and cowardice may be desirable as an education and a warning: they are less than credible in view of the result.

A happier performance was Shakespeare's *Taming of the Shrew*. English humour in general and Shakespeare's humour in particular find a ready home in Russia. The presentation, however, gave curious interpretations of the text. Not merely the wife, but the husband, and indeed everybody else, seemed in the sequel to be tamed.

The same tendency is seen in the novel and perhaps less credible though inspiring representation of Othello which depicts him not as a monster consumed with jealousy but as a believer in human nature who was pitifully disillusioned. Ostuzhev's acting contrives to insert in Othello's final cry of desperation, which makes the blood run cold, a recurrence of faith side by side with personal despair: Desdemona is innocent, faith in man survives.

In the Kamerny Theatre, which is smaller, I saw the *prèmière* of John Priestley's play *The Inspector Calls*, which had been translated in five days by Inna Koulakovskaya in collaboration with a friend. Mr. and Mrs. Maisky together with the British Ambassador and others were present. The play was well acted, especially the male parts, the reception enthusiastic. Details were often amusing and odd to English eyes—tail coats at a family dinner party, passionate exaggerated voices, port wine in corked undecanted bottles passing anyhow around and across the table, and drained glasses turned upside down to drip on to the carpet.

(D) *The Puppet Show*

I cannot leave the Theatre without a reference to Valentine Obraztsov and his puppet show. Obraztsov is a consummate artist. I attended his puppet theatre as often as I could, not only to watch the faces of his child audiences, but to see such plays as Kipling's *Mowgli* which could only be acted in a puppet theatre, where puppet wolves, tigers and serpents came really to life, leaping, climbing and crawling. No other medium could portray forest scenes so faithfully: the huge spotted cat-like tiger ready for the leap, the slow, lazy python for whom all made way, the graceful gazelles, the whimsical porcupine, the swinging, chattering monkeys and animals which moved stealthily and noiselessly, or with barks and growls, held adults as well as children spellbound.

(E) *The Cinema*

We spent a delightful evening with the cinema actress who plays Zoya in the patriotic drama modelled on a real eighteen-year-old partisan, a Moscow girl posthumously awarded the title "Hero of the Soviet Union": a play doubly interesting to me because I saw it on the evening of the day we had spent with an artisan family whose two young girls of eighteen and twenty had both, like Zoya, been decorated for heroism as partisans.

Zoya, written by Boris Chiskov, is a play of austere simplicity and vital realism. We see Zoya first as a new-born babe, weighed by the doctor. We see her at two, three . . . her years marked by doting parents in pencil on the door. Parallel with her growth and strength is depicted the growth and strength of Soviet society itself.

Born in 1924, her first impressions are of the huge Dnieper Dam. She sees the Soviet balloon fliers ascend to the stratosphere, continuing their scientific observations till they crashed. She welcomes the return of the heroic Arctic explorers and marches in the sports parade with her head held high.

Scenes, persons, ideas and aspirations which mould her character stand skilfully out: her mother, her schoolmates, and her diaries which provide authentic basis for the story. In an atmosphere of high morality, friendship, patriotism and a stern sense of duty she grows to womanhood. Her diaries record her love of Tolstoy, Shakespeare, Pushkin. "Everything about a person should be beautiful—face, apparel, soul and mind," she quotes from Chekhov.

A charming touch recalls an incident of Zoya in school as a child. A boy Boris refuses to let a "slip of a girl" sit at his desk.

"Move up," says Zoya in a quiet determined voice, a stubborn frown upon her brow.

Boris wriggles but snaps back a refusal.

"Go on, move up," Zoya repeats, more insistently.

Abashed, the boy drops his glance and moves. Zoya calmly sits down. They become friends. They become more and Zoya, raising her lips to his, receives her first and last kiss of love.

The torture scenes, never piling up the horrors, just portray them reflectively. Zoya's tortured brain reviews memorable episodes of her brief life: she hears her mother's voice ". . . even to die for other people's happiness. . . ." Cheered by her "voices," she refuses to betray her friends and dies.

In a clear voice she cries from the scaffold to the peasants who were forced to witness her death: "Why so downcast? Everything will turn out well at last. I'm not afraid to die."

As the hangman kicks away the box on which she stands she cries: "Comrades: be brave. Fight back. Resist the Germans. . . . We will win," and then: "Farewell, comrades. Stalin will come."

(F) *Russian Ballet*

The Russian ballet is, of course, superb, and has been so from the days when ballet was first created in Leningrad 150 years ago. Always first-class in Moscow, it is seen at its peak in Leningrad. It would be hard to say in which I enjoyed it the more, and I dare not trust myself to write of it at the length I should need were I to do it with any justice. Ulanova's dance in *Giselle* surpassed anything I ever saw as a spiritual expression of feeling through the motion of the dance.

Leningrad's famous ballerina Semyonova was older and physically
a trifle less supple; her technique was faultless.

I met both women and their husbands socially. Ulanova's husband
might at first glance easily have been mistaken for Sir John Simon.
He is a distinguished producer. Both women were entirely simple
and unselfconscious when off the stage. Semyonova was proud and
fond of her home and her several children.

6. LITERATURE

B E H I N D Russian drama lies Russian literature.

Books are the basis of Russia's cultural life. Books are creative.
Books pass thought from mind to mind and stimulate to action.
Russia therefore rightly lays stress on books of which she possesses a
rich heritage, especially books bred of passionate love of freedom and
equality.

In days of ferment, between 1855 and 1894, when Russia strove
for freedom from serfdom, poetry and literature illuminated the darkness of her social night. The rich thought and revolutionary spirit
of Pushkin, Lermontov, Gogol, Turgenev, Dostoyevsky, Chekhov,
Tolstoy and Gorky awakened the conscience of the people and prepared
the soil for Liberal and Socialist pioneers: for Chernyshevsky, Hertzen,
Bakunin, Plekhanov and Lenin.

Far back in the dark cruel days of Nicholas I Pushkin and Lermontov
the poets, together with Gogol, "Russia's Dickens," expressed their
faith in moral righteousness, their scorn at baseness and sensuality
and their abhorrence of autocratic administration. Stirring the Russian
soul to consciousness by consummate art, they set spark to tinder,
and Ivan Turgenev further fanned the flames, especially in the
"Nihilist" of his *Fathers and Sons*, where revolt against authority begins
to take absolute form.

Nekrasov, the poet, lashed out at Russian contemporary life, and
Dostoyevsky, who narrowly escaped death as a progressive in 1849,
interpreted the spirit of Russia in incomparable novels.

The literary critic Belinsky, the centre of a group which contained
Hertzen and Bakunin, together with Shevchenko, the Ukrainian
martyr-poet, seized the torch and handed it for the final round, before
the revolution, to Chekhov, Tolstoy and Gorky.

The political consciousness of the people now wide awake, Russia
was ripe for change. Liberal and Socialist pioneers plotted the course.
Prince Kropokin championed the peasant; Bakunin, the anarchist,

urged armed seizure by the people of the means of production. Hertzen
and Petrashevsky in the field of thought and Plekhanov in the field
of propaganda forced wider open the door which led to Russia's
Marxian Socialism. The period of revolt was not long as time goes.
An early photograph depicts as a group Tolstoy, Chekhov and Gorky
whose united life and work span the days from autocratic reaction to
Socialist triumph.

It is early yet perhaps for us in the West to attempt a just estimate
of Russian literature in the post-revolutionary period. We stand too
near to it, and the whole set-up of life in our respective worlds differ
too widely. But certain features and tendencies may be noted. First
there has been, and to some extent still is, a tendency in the Soviet
Union to confine the literary artist to too narrow a territory. To say
to him: "This or that you must do or must not do." To define his sphere
and his expression. In times of danger that is always so. Absolute
freedom of expression is of course impossible; it is even undesirable.
Certain short words, for instance, must never be shouted in public
or even appear in print in this most free country. Law disallows them.
And, still more important, popular opinion and feeling likewise
disallow them.

Do we feel thereby cramped? Certainly not. Extend this principle
slightly further. In times of war there is greater restriction on expression
both by authority and by popular ruling. So, too, in times of social stress
or upheaval. Anything that cuts across the main intention and purpose
of a people at any particular time is ruled out of order by authority
and banned as bad form by public opinion. And in the main the artist
acquiesces.

Such was probably the case with literary artists in the early days
of the revolution. Such to a certain extent may be the case to-day,
when the country suffers from terrible war scars and when a mass of
men are returning to their homes after long absence and after perhaps
having seen the beauty and comfort of German homes. Authority,
if not popular feeling, may impose restrictions and give forcible
expression to the imposition through authoritatively controlled organs.

With that caution in mind we may turn to modern Russian
literature and venture upon some broad generalisations. We may agree
with the present Russian analysis that true and complete artists have
a double aim. They depict. They also create. On the one hand they
depict reality as it spreads itself out before their eyes. On the other
hand in the light of the accumulated experience of what is valuable
and what is moral in the society in which they live, they aim at
changing the "what is" into the "what ought to be."

In capitalist society it is apparently hard to combine the two, and we get the phenomenon of literary artists tending to divide themselves into two groups: Those who depict things as they are, leaving the ought to be on one side. Or again, those who paint Utopian pictures of the ought to be with little or no link up with things that are.

Both call themselves realists. The first by expressing vivid experience; sticking to the facts as they are, but marshalling them according to their inner essence. The second by passing behind present imperfection to eternal and changeless realities.

One tends to mere portrayal of events seen tragically: that, and nothing more. Its effect is intolerable depression. The other tends to be merely romantic: its effect is a heady exhilaration. Both land us in futility. The one makes no efforts to create change. The other fails to do so because it lacks any connection with present reality.

In a society, however, where ideals are able to grow forthwith and proceed progressively into concrete realities, then the union of art which depicts and art which changes is consummated, with no violence to literary freedom. Present-day Soviet literary art, it is claimed in Russia, does precisely that. Soviet literary art is didactic, it aims at teaching, not merely at revealing. The Soviet literary artist claims to be a constructive engineer. Need that be bad? Need literature with a purpose be bad literature? Yes, if history itself lacks purpose. No, if history itself is purposeful.

And after all, what really great literature lacks purpose? Even if the artist endeavours merely to depict things as they are, he cannot escape the charge of being purposeful, though the purpose may be unconsciously felt and unconsciously expressed. For to provide no criticism of that which is seen and depicted is to express the passive purpose of acquiescence, tolerance, contentment with what is.

If indeed—to drive the Soviet contention still further home— art which inculcates a point of view instead of pure objective portrayal or subjective feeling is not real art, then many of the world's greatest writers from Plato onwards were not artists at all.

Good art is indeed always and powerfully purposeful, and more effectual by far for its purpose than cold straightforward prose, for it gets beneath the skin: "Truth embodied in a tale can enter in at humble doors." A child absorbs morality through stories like *Cinderella* and grown men through stories like *Othello*. It is the form which counts. Form is the artist's weapon for driving his message home.

Soviet literature has turned a new sod. Soviet literature differs from other literature in that it operates in a new environment, a Socialist environment; and in the new Socialist environment things are possible which never were possible before.

(*Top*) Students in the Library of the All Russia Art Academy in Leningrad.
(*Lower*) A volleyball game in the Central Park of Culture and Rest, Moscow.

(*Top*) A. Gauk conducting Rachmaninoff's First Symphony, at a
Festival in Moscow.

(*Lower*) The Vakhtangov Theatre marked its 21st anniversary with the
production of V. Solovyov's "Road to Victory."

In a society where ideals cease to be dreams in the air; where ideals find body and operate in concrete form; where we not only envisage a world where profit ceases to be the motive for toil and where man ceases to exploit the labour of brother man, but look out upon, and dwell within, a society in which that change has already occurred, then it is possible to write realistically about the world that is, whilst at the same time writing idealistically about the world as it ought to be.

In Soviet Russia society is actually and constantly changing. Socialist ideals are in process of realisation. Realistic and idealistic writing meet here and unite. The bleak realism from which we in the West are, it is to be hoped, at last emerging was content with portraying sordid reality untouched by faith or hope. Happier writing, we were told here, must be dismissed as wishful thinking. In reaction against these bleak realists were the head-in-the-air idealists who, despairing of the world as it is, spun beautiful stories of the world as it might be; sheer Utopias with no contact whatsoever with the world that is.

The great writers of the pre-Socialist age, men like Gogol and Chekhov, were realists, but their realism was not the realism of acquiescence. It was the realism of passionate revolt. "That," they said, as they drew lurid pictures of contemporary society, "is what the present is: revolt from it."

Socialist realism is a step beyond this. In the new Socialist order, where authority is on the side of ideals, where society itself condemns exploitation and fosters co-operation, artists can depict the life story of men and women who strive to make the new order a success. The things they depict have concrete reality around them already. They depict recognisable men and women.

But in addition to that they paint them, as it were, with art, with slightly exaggerated excellence; they paint them so that while contact with the present is obvious, so, too, the finger points on beyond.

Such writing is creative. It stirs men to live more noble, serviceable lives. It incites to action. Such writing not only depicts society, it changes society. That is why Stalin could speak of the artists as "creative engineers."

The new type of Socialist realism began even in the early days of the revolution: Gorky himself started it with his novel *Mother*, where his hero's spiritual growth develops through the early stages of the proletarian struggle.

Gorky was able to give this struggle concrete form because there were men around him actually living the thing out; men devoted to building up the new Socialist order. He could also give his writing effective form. It was intentionally purposeful, and actually achieved

H

its purpose in its readers. It set men and women working, as the characters in Samuel Smiles' books worked, but with a nobler goal.

In Ostrovsky's *How the Steel was Forged*, for instance, the passion for work and invention was no less keen than the passion which drove Stephenson to harness steam for transport; but the goal—the integration of man with man—was nobler and greater. Ostrovsky sees the ideal and aids it by his art.

Russian authors write for no coterie who crave cleverness and subtlety. They write for the common people. They write in the vernacular, with the vocabulary of everyday speech. Their heroes are men and women of the people and not lonely intellectuals of the upper class struggling against the whole stream of life for a new order. Their heroes are in the stream and directing its flow. Naturally their story is often a transcript of their own lives told artistically: Soviet writers are themselves in the stream and understand it.

Therein perhaps lies one of the biggest differences from our own between-the-war writers, and poets particularly. Much modern poetry and some modern pictorial art tend to move farther and farther away from the people, almost deliberately so, using modes and words incomprehensible to the masses and deliberately designed for obscurity but regarded by the critics as clever and profound.

Great art never did that. When a man burns with a message, a truth, a new understanding, something within him seeks to share it broadcast with brother-man. That hot message and that urge to express it creates, as Bernard Shaw once pointed out in the case of Isaiah, great art.

Too many modern Western poets, striving after an originality they do not possess, fall short of great art. Probably that is why their very names are unknown to the wide public—so different from the days when the names of great Victorians, whether novelists like Dickens or poets like Browning and Tennyson, were household words. They spoke and strove to speak in the vernacular.

Such is undoubtedly the aim of the Soviet writers. To fall short of that, to run away from the common people, despising their language and their emotions, awakens the rebuke of Soviet critics: and an increasingly cultivated proletariat is itself the critic.

The measure of this cultivation is the clamant demand for literature in the Soviet Union and the vast output of books to meet it.

For many months and even years now a vigorous discussion which throws much light on what has been said and on present trends and dangers has raged in the Soviet Union on literature and drama, a discussion in which many creative writers, the critics, the public and the authorities take part. In the main it is writers, readers and critics overhauling their work, disclosing its weakness, planning its improvement and clarifying its theory. The Central Committee of the Communist Party initiated the discussion. They did not, as Hitler would have done, decide the question and execute the judgment apart from popular opinion and discussion. They did not apply a censorship. They did not intimidate. Books, plays, operas and films have been permitted to appear freely, and as freely are criticised. Publicity precedes discussion and criticism. It is no question of the rigid control of a totalitarian regime. That, from our point of view, is the supreme factor.

Zoshchenko's works, a case in point and one mainly commented on in England, have not been banned: they have been widely and severely criticised. A frank, sincere, fearless discussion proceeds, conducted by the writers themselves, who also themselves seek a new movement in the literary world. A review of Zoshchenko's *Before Sunrise* appearing in January, 1944, describes his work as utterly alien to the feelings of the people. He is preoccupied with himself and forgets that he lives in Society. He finds solace in recalling past emotional thrills. He relates sixty-two indecent escapades. He describes the lechery of an old and dying man. He gives examples of unmentionable vulgarity.

The reviewer wonders how a Leningrad writer could walk our streets and find, in face of the struggle of the people and nameless sacrifices in defence of their city, nothing better to write about than that which needs no recalling and had better be forgotten. When Zoshchenko first wrote in this strain it was thought that he wrote to illustrate the triviality, foulness and futility of the old dying world, his heroes being shady adventurers awaiting better times. Then it became apparent that Zoshchenko was writing for people of kindred nature—apathetic, melancholic, self-indulgent, contemptuous towards the people and holding womanhood in poor esteem.

What angered the people and critics still more, Zoshchenko wrote these unworthy tales in remote and beflowered Alma-Ata, where guns never roared or shells whined. The people of Leningrad felt shame for such a writer who formerly worked as one of themselves.

The war had played havoc with normal life in the Soviet Union. Authors had scattered. Some had been using their pens in the front line in aid of their land and cause; others had been evacuated to safer areas; others yet remained and endured nameless hardships. Leningrad, Soviet Russia's chief cultural area, had suffered to a peculiar degree in a long and devastating siege; members of the Writers' Union, along with the rest, had been concerned with elemental physical needs. Ordinary standards had lapsed. Literary anarchism had reigned. And then dilettantism.

Soviet writers themselves call for a halt and a redirection. Soviet writers seek once again writings worthy of their country's quality, writings which will spur men on to post-war tasks. Zoshchenko, it is claimed, has forfeited his right to membership of the Writers' Union by his open contempt of the Soviet way of life. He is not exiled or sent to a concentration camp. The worst that happens is that he cannot get published the writings that offend, not the authorities merely, but the people and the writers themselves. Indignant protest arises not against Zoshchenko the writer of sparkling humour as once he was, but against Zoshchenko who now outpours sordid and cynical trivialities.

To understand and appreciate the situation as the Soviet people themselves see it, we must remember that much which we call liberty Russia would call licence, and that Russia in general accepts the communist creed in precisely the same way as we accept modern science. The public no more questions the communist creed than we question anti-septic surgery. The Communist Party feel they have as much right to recall artists to their faith as to recall a doctor who disregarded anti-sepsis in his surgery. They protest by criticism and persuasion, not by sending the artist to Siberia. Nor do Soviet literary men themselves resent the criticism. What in reality we see is the whole literary world putting its house in order. The people as a whole also resented the easy-going attitude of literary men who uttered no protest against what they knew was evil writing.

The agitation came to a head when the Central Committee of the Communist Party of the Soviet Union passed a resolution on 14th August, 1946, expressing its grave concern that the chief literary journals of Leningrad, the hero city, famous for its advanced culture, had so seriously lost touch with the life of the Soviet people and forgotten the educational rôle of literature in the Soviet State. The resolution re-emphasised the fact that the task of Soviet literature was to aid in the education of the people, especially the youth, and to answer their questions. Its chief function was to inspire people with courage and faith in their cause and to arm their determination to overcome all obstacles in reconstruction. The executive of the Union of Soviet Writers was blamed for failure in their responsibility for maintaining the highest level in their journals.

The Leningrad writers answered to the spur and themselves sincerely sought for high purpose in literary work. They declared war on so-called "pure" art, calling for criticism based on principle and for the re-forging of the links between writers and the broad strata of the working people.

A general clean-up followed: a resolution of the "Præsidium of the Board of the Union of Soviet Writers" passed a resolution which included in its censorship several journals, the Sovietsky Pisatel publishing house, a number of authors for "writing empty pot-boilers," the scenario writer Nelin and certain other dramatists for plays which show "Political neutrality and a superficial and flat treatment of great vital themes."

The Soviet Union of Writers itself suffered stern rebuke for forgetting that literature is a mighty weapon in the task of educating Soviet people; for passing slipshod work without rebuke, and for permitting unquestioned the wide circulation of poems such as Pasternaks', which are devoid of significant content.

Among the main tasks laid down by the Præsidium are these: to recall writers to themes of the present day; to themes of heroic labour in restoration; to conduct among writers systematic propaganda of the Party's policy in basic problems of internal and international life; to encourage the fighting spirit of active, militant ideology of Communism; to castigate works which reflect the influence of decadent Western European tendencies and to reject careless work.

All this will naturally be judged by our own literary standards and by our own conception of the function and responsibilities of literary artists. Are artists, such as poster designers, who do work directly serviceable to the public and to industry to be despised as on a lower category than those who follow their own more subjective fancy? Is the artist to be regarded as a responsible member of society or as a law to himself? Is art to function in complete independence of politics? Are modern artists never to be prophets of revolutionary change as undoubtedly were Plato, Dante, Shakespeare, Milton, Cervantes, Swift, Defoe, or Tolstoi, or even most conspicuously of all, the writers in the Bible itself?

In Russia the people are so closely knit and welded together into a unity unknown here that the whole outlook on the freedom of art, as on economic freedom, differs radically from ours. The freedom claimed here by the rich to do precisely as they like would be called licence in Russia: similarly in Russia the freedom to write precisely as one likes is called licence and as strongly discouraged.

In an old-fashioned white-columned building in Moscow is the All-Union Book Chamber whence comes every book and pamphlet published in the U.S.S.R. Some 386,000 books and pamphlets in editions totalling 10,339,000,000 copies have been published between 1917 and 1946. Pushkin's works in 76 languages totalled 32,749,000 copies; Maxim Gorki in 66 languages, 43,000,000 copies, and Leo Tolstoi in 60 languages 25 million copies. Shakespeare in 20 languages 1,615,000 copies. Editions in 1946 were 57.8 per cent more than in 1945.

7. INSTITUTIONAL RELIGION IN THE SOVIET UNION

R E A L I S I N G the paramount importance of close and careful study of the problem of institutional religion in the U.S.S.R. I sought out in turn the heads of the several religious communities, naturally approaching, as head of the Russian Orthodox Church—by far the largest religious community in the Soviet Union—Alexei, Patriarch of Moscow and all Russia.

We met, as I have already stated, on Victory Day, and, by his own invitation, in the Patriarchal House. I also met on Victory Day, and on other occasions, Mr. George Karpov, the Chairman of the Council of the Affairs of the Orthodox Church.

From what I learned from these and others there emerges a clear-cut picture of the Russian Church in post-revolutionary days. To understand which in true perspective one needs further knowledge of the history of the Russian Church.

In its earliest days the Orthodox Church was, in intention at least, an independent institution with a purely religious function, existing within the State: its secular head was the Prince and later the Tsar. The Church with its Patriarch stood over against the Government with its Tsar in a healthy tension. Peter the Great broke up this symphonic relationship, abolishing the independent Patriarchite and putting in its place a Holy Synod whose members were appointed and could be dismissed by the Crown. The Church was secularised, its business handled by a State Department of Religious Affairs, the chief Proculatorship of the Church held by a man with the rank of a Cabinet Minister, its bishops and high clergy paid by the Government. The Orthodox Church became in reality a department of the Civil Service. The Church was absorbed by the State. And when the Tsar's Government collapsed the Church collapsed with it.

This position has now been reversed. The Church has moved back to its earlier and happier position of independence within the State. From the first, State and Church in the Soviet Union have been separated. But the earlier relations were not happy. Archbishop Sergius was doubtless right in his main contention that "from the moment when Soviet power was established in 1917 the Soviet Order and its constitution guaranteed freedom of conscience to all its citizens, a law universally observed." But tension and excesses existed. In my discussion with him on religion in Russia, Stalin said: "At first the Church anathematised the State, forbidding payment of taxes. The State was bound to act.

"There may," he added, "have been excesses on both sides. It is, however, different now. Church has seen patriotism in the State. State has seen patriotism in the Church. Former tensions have disappeared."

The excesses were indeed real, but have been much exaggerated by enemies of the Soviet Union. Archbishop Sergius, in his too little publicised book, published just before his recent death, said these words: "The enemies of the Russian Orthodox Church have falsely affirmed that the Bolsheviks seized and shot Bishop Andrei Ukhtomsky whilst travelling. The bishop survived this so-called execution, as did Archbishop Simon of Ostag, said to have been tortured."

In 1943, Stalin invited a Committee of three Orthodox Bishops to the Kremlin to discuss with him and Molotov the relations between the Orthodox Church and the Government. The conference, conducted in a friendly spirit, led to official approval to the Orthodox Church to hold a congress of bishops for the establishment of a Holy Synod, which would be empowered to elect a Patriarch, and the Church accepted and welcomed the further ruling of the conference that a State Bureau on Church Affairs should be created. Permission was received to open theological institutions and pastors' schools and to publish a monthly magazine, the *Journal of the Moscow Patriarcate.*

The Congress of Bishops was summoned and the Metropolitan Alexei of Leningrad was unanimously elected Patriarch of Moscow and all Russia, and enthroned in the Cathedral of the Resurrection on 4th February. Born in Moscow in 1877, Alexei had graduated in the Moscow University Department of Law and in the Ecclesiastical Academy. In 1926 he became Archbishop of Novgorod. He was appointed Metropolitan of Leningrad in 1933 and stayed in that city through the 900 days of enemy siege. He organised the assistance of the clergy and believers at the front and for this has been awarded the Defence of Leningrad Medal. In the autumn of 1946 he was decorated with the high Order of the Banner of Labour, for his patriotic services during the war.

Before his enthronement, Mr. Karpov in his speech of welcome to the bishops made this important and clear declaration: "The Council of Affairs of the Russian Orthodox Church under the Council of People's Commissars of the U.S.S.R., formed by decision of the Government, maintains contact between the Government and the

Patriarch of Moscow and all Russia on questions requiring Government decision.

"Not interfering in any way with the inner affairs of the Church, the Council makes for the further normalisation of relations between the Church and the State, supervising its correct and timely execution of the laws and the decisions of the Government in respect to the Russian Orthodox Church."

The appointment of a Council of Church Affairs needs careful understanding. It is liable to give rise to serious misconceptions. The Council is in no sense regulative of the internal affairs of the Church. It never meddles with doctrinal questions or matters which strictly belong to the clergy. The Russian Church has not become an Erastian Church. The existence of the Council is due solely to the exigencies of a socialist economy, where all capital investments, buildings and lands are owned by the State or the collective in trust for the people. Neither individuals nor institutions can live on income from endowments in the Soviet Union. The Church owns no property in its own name: its clergy must live off current offerings or fees for services and the like. Buildings are leased to the Church, free from tax, but subject to maintenance in good condition.

Inasmuch also since in a socialist country all production and distribution are under the control of the State and must fit into the general plan, therefore all material used for fabrics, vestments, ornaments, all paper for printing, all electricity for light, heat or power, must find their place in the State budget or they cannot be procured. Apart from some joint arrangement confusion was bound to arise and it was precisely to avoid this confusion and to regularise the provision of the Church's material needs, and in no sense to interfere with the Church's spiritual and internal affairs, still less to dominate Church teaching and doctrine, that the Council of Affairs of the Orthodox Church was established under the headship of Mr. George Karpov with branches far and wide.

The Church, for instance, sought seminaries in Moscow and Saratov. The Council considered the needs and passed on the recommendation. The Government ordered the local representative to prepare the needed accommodation.

Training centres are desired and are granted in big towns from Leningrad to Odessa. Four hundred priests will shortly be in training and four hundred new churches were opened in 1945. Eighty-nine monasteries now function. Pastoral schools are providing a simple training for the rank and file of the clergy. Whatever may have been the restriction in earlier days upon the teaching of religion to children other than by parents or in small numbers by a priest, such restrictions have now ceased. Mr. Karpov, categorically speaking, said children of any number of parents may gather and be gathered for religious instruction. Whatever ban existed against the printing and distribution of Bibles, service books and religious literature in general, has now been raised and the Church has received explicit permission to order any quantity of testaments, prayer books and liturgical service books which it may require and make representation for the needed quantity to the proper rationing authorities. No restrictions prevent the circulation of religious literature.

When visiting the aged Archbishop Gregory of Leningrad in his small room high up in the south-west wall of Leningrad Cathedral, I asked bluntly whether it was really true that the Church could print Bibles if it so desired; he reached down a New Testament and pointed to the date and place of issue, Leningrad 1922. At that date at least the freedom existed. It exists again. Lastly, whatever ban existed on preaching and propaganda has now been removed. Again, in this case as in the case of the children's instruction, Karpov states that "priests may engage in proselytising work without any restrictions except those placed upon every orderly citizen in the U.S.S.R."

The production of a film illustrating every phase of the election and enthronement of the new Patriarch advertises the deliberate intention of the Government to express its friendly attitude towards the Church.

$$*   *   *   *   *$$

It has, however, been no one-way track that brings Church and State together in sympathetic accord in Soviet Russia. The Church moves sympathetically towards the State as the State moves sympathetically towards the Church.

When Sergius was asked "Have any changes occurred within the Church?" he replied: "Naturally. The members of the Orthodox Church are by no means inclined to view the Soviet changes in the light of 'persecution,' but in the light rather of a return to the times of the apostles."

Alexei strikes the same note.

"Communism," he says, "aside from its materialistic and atheistic theories, is quite acceptable to the orthodox. Monasteries are based on Communist foundations."

The Russian Orthodox Church is by a very long way the largest single Church in the Soviet Union. But other communities exist, Baptists and Evangelical Christians—now said to number three millions—Jews, Episcopal Churches in Armenia and Georgia, and Moslems in Asia. I visited all. I made contacts with the heads of each.

The Baptists and other sectaries suffered more than the Orthodox.

The Baptist Movement, beginning early in the second half of last century, reached considerable proportions despite the Tsarist persecutions. It exists in two groups, differing only in name and origin and now united under the title of Union of Baptists and Evangelical Christians.

Never tied closely to the old order, and not disposed, like the Orthodox Church, to defend it, the Baptists received considerate treatment from the State in the early days, when divide and rule was policy in high quarters. The Baptists, for their part, welcomed the separation of Church and State and enjoyed the new freedom not only of worship but of religious propaganda and association. Bibles could be printed. The Bible in the Baptist Church in Moscow bears the imprint "Leningrad 1926"; the concordance imprint 1928. And if the separation of school from State forbade the carrying on of any classes for instruction below the age of eighteen, yet children's services, apart from school or class register, were permitted and bridged the gap.

The outbreak of pacifism as a result of war-weariness complicated the position at a time when the Red Army of National Defence was being organised. It savoured of tacit obstruction at a dangerous moment and many young Baptists were shot. Then came relief: both groups repudiated pacifism; whilst the State on its side made conscientious objection permissible.

Fresh trouble arose, when in the winter of 1928–29 the collective farms were in process of formation. The natural desire of Baptists to form collectives out of their own members led to misunderstanding and produced the repressive enactment of 1929 which regards religious bodies as existing for one sole purpose: the performance of rites. Cultural and economic activities were forbidden together with services for children and meetings for Bible study. The printing of Bibles ceased.

Naturally, when we remember that Baptists in common with much Western reformed Christianity lay primary emphasis on teaching, doctrine, thought and not as the Orthodox Church does primarily on ceremonial and acts of ritual—visually, Orthodox Churches exhibit altar and no pulpit and extremist Protestant Churches pulpit and no altar—the Baptists were the chief sufferers. These restrictions happily progressively disappear. Classes for religious instruction are permitted now where desired.

I visited the Baptists in their chief place of worship in Moscow, sharing with them a two-hours' service one Sunday morning in a 300-year-old church, in Mali Busorsky Street, rebuilt in 1700 for the German Reformed Church and handed over by the Soviets to the Baptists in 1923. In this simple, dignified church, I listened to, and afterwards met, Jacob Zhidkov, Chairman of the All Union Council of Baptists and Evangelical Christians.

The crowd at the service was dense and devout: the occasion the monthly collection for war orphans. The preaching was simple, earnest, moving. Emotional hymns were sung, set to familiar English and American evangelistic tunes.

Zhidkov, a tall sparsely built man, rugged and worn, his sincere face crowned with thinning sandy hair, wore a black alpaca jacket with lay collar and tie. Born of the lower middle class at Stalingrad, then known as Tsaritsin, he had served, in Tsarist days, as agent for the British and Foreign Bible Society. Of his five children he had lost three in the war: all had served the war effort in one capacity or another. His wife had taught in the schools. His daughter had worked in the Stalin plant. One son placed the Red Flag on the Berlin Reichstag, another had descended as a paratrooper in Hungary. A third son winning recently a distinction and a medal, had been elected a member of the local Communist Party. His father was proud of it.

Baptists and Evangelical Christians—Zhidkov maintains—enjoy under the Soviet Regime privileges of religious equality which they never enjoyed before the Revolution. Baptists, and indeed the smallest religious communities, now receive precisely the same consideration as the vastly greater Russian Orthodox Church, a thing never known previously.

Asked later by one of my friends who likewise attended the morning service in the same Baptist chapel: "Since when have you been free to preach as I have seen here to-day?" Mr. Zhidkov answered: "I was baptised in 1903, and commenced to preach five years later, since when I have always been free to preach." My friend found it difficult to believe his ears. "Were you free to preach through the Revolution and immediately after?" he asked. It was Zhidkov's turn to look perplexed, and then he laughed, and said: "Of course."

As to Sunday schools there had been none, said Mr. Zhidkov, before the Revolution: every mother is accustomed to give religious instruction to her children, and every mother does so. "Your Sunday schools," said Mr. Zhidkov, "are a purely English and American institution."

Mr. Ivan Vassilievich Polyanski, acting through the Council for

Affairs of the Religious Cults, aids the sectaries precisely as Mr. Karpov aids the large Orthodox Church. His Bureau handles the affairs of the Armenian Church, the Gregorian Church, the old Belian Roman Catholics, the Greek Catholics, Lutherans, Jews, Moslems, and Buddhists, as well as the Baptists.

"Not only," says Zhidkov "do we find no barriers to our work, we receive aid in procuring churches practically free of charge: to heat them and keep them in repair being our sole responsibility. Even in the hardest days of war our Moscow Baptist Church never lacked fuel. Our meetings are free to all. We have the right to proselytise. We can print new books. We can initiate training courses for our clergy. Where one such course and one alone was allowed in Tsarist days we had in the Soviet regime two for 300 students in Leningrad in 1924 and one in Moscow.

"During 1926 and 1928 indeed we had suffered persecution and had sent a protest to the world Baptists. That day has gone. We now work happily with the Soviet authorities and tackle with them the tasks of reconstruction and peace."

This Union of Baptists and Evangelical Christians is exceedingly active. One permanent delegate sits at Kiev, and with the title of Elder Presbyter he presides over fourteen elders at Kharkov, Poltava, Odessa and other widespread towns, organising congregations as citizens return and securing churches for their worship. Another elder presbyter directs activities in Byelorussia from Nminsky, others in the North Caucasus, and at Tashkent and Alma Ata in Asia.

Jews form no inconsiderable number in Russian life and I visited the chief Rabbi of the Soviet Jewish Community. He showed me his synagogue, housing now an ancient Jewish library. He outlined the material aid the Soviet authorities gave to religious Jews, new library accommodation for their books; new bathing rooms for ceremonial ablutions.

Anti-Semitism is a thing of the past in the land where pogroms began. Stories of recrudescence of anti-semitism are false; demonstrably false, when related to the Ukraine, where Germans killed the entire Jewish population. Cruelly false, when related to Government action in Odessa, where, knowing the treatment of Jews at the hands of Germans, the Soviet Government itself removed the Jewish population as a priority act eastwards from Odessa and other threatened towns.

Investigation of the religious situation, and other studies, took me far beyond the Russia proper and far beyond the orbit of the Russian Orthodox Church. I visited Armenia, Georgia and Asia.

Learning whilst in Moscow that delegates from fifteen countries—

whither Turkish persecution had driven large elements of the Armenian population—were to assemble in mid-June at Etchmiadzin, Armenia's ecclesiastical centre, to elect a new Catholicos, I sought to visit Armenia. Moscow sent me by plane, and I spent two weeks in closest touch with Armenian people and Armenian Church.

Nowhere perhaps does Soviet Order shine more happily and splendidly than amongst formerly backward people. Poverty-stricken Armenia has stepped with one stride into new life, prosperous, cultured and proudly national. Of that visit and election I shall write more fully on a later page. Here I would only add that the seventy-six-year-old newly elected Catholicos, proudly wearing his "Defence-of-the-Caucasus" medal, had quite recently spent two hours with Generalissimo Stalin threshing out details of a new Church Charter, Stalin adding notes in Aramaic in his own handwriting.

By that charter the Catholicos regains his former residence, and the Church many of its former buildings. Some new ones, too, and a seminary for forty priests, together with library and a printing press.

At Tbilisi in Georgia, meeting a group of Academicians, I had opportunity to speak with Professor Cornelius Cecelidze, who gave me his 1,000 page volume on the history of the Georgian Church and Georgian literature.

"Something other than history," a young graduate told me, "comes through the Professor's lectures and it excites students to visit the Cathedral." There they listen attentively to the old Catholicos Patriarch and to a young priest who, short-haired, clean shaven, and dressed as a layman in white duck clothes preaches with eloquence and persuasiveness.

We visited the Catholicos Patriarch in his small verandaed home beside the cathedral and high above the silent swiftly flowing river. A short but dignified old man, with long, silvery hair and beard, and kindly smile: he welcomed cordially our Anglican desire for an œcumenical council on which his Church would be represented with other churches throughout Europe. Toasts were drunk to our Anglican Church, to international unity, to the young guests, to the young priest.

"It is homely, healthy village wine," said the Patriarch when I spoke of "doctor's orders" forbidding further toasts, and he added "one more we must have. We always conclude with a toast to our Lady" and we emptied our glasses.

Church and State move smoothly together in Georgia and I learned with interest that it is now contemplated to found at the Tbilisi University a chair of Church history. There remained the

Moslems and the Roman Catholics. Moslems I visited both in Moscow and in Asia, spending a whole day in Tashkent with the aged Imam, the Head of all Asian Moslems. With him I walked through the clean still streets of mediæval Tashkent to worship at a Mosque much too small for the worshippers who had gathered and spread their prayer mats in neat rows in the open air. But of that service, that feast and that friendship I shall also write in its appropriate setting. The essential fact to mention here is the feeling of gratitude expressed by the Eastern Moslem world. Formerly lacking both civil and religious liberty; they now possess both.

The Roman Catholic Church is mainly centred in the Baltic Republic of Lithuania.

The following statement was made to a Tass correspondent by the Catholic Archbishop of Vilnius, Mgr. Reinis:—

"The Catholic Church enjoys perfect freedom in Soviet Lithuania. The local authorities are assisting us in restoring and repairing churches destroyed by the German invaders, and supplying building materials. Our clergy are provided with all necessities.

"There are at present two archbishoprics in Lithuania—those of Vilnius and Kaunas. The Catholic Church organisation has remained unchanged. All 711 churches are functioning with their staff of 1,332 clergy. The Kaunas Ecclesiastical Seminary, headed by the prominent theologian Ventskus, is graduating scores of young Catholic priests annually."

BOOK VI

SOVIET PLANNING

1. PLANNED INDUSTRY

A L L the foregoing benefits: benefits of health, home, education and culture are made possible because Russia now possesses a planned, socially and scientifically controlled, implemented and conducted industry.

The dominant word in Russia is PLAN. The Russian world is a planned world. A Moscow babe enters a planned world at birth. Planned for nourishment, shelter and education. Plan secures a child's birthright of human milk in infancy and subsequent appropriate nourishment as years proceed. Plan supplements his mother's care by accumulated traditional nursing and educational skill in crèche, kindergarten, school and in all ranges of higher education. Plan orders his work in adult life. Plan integrates one man's activity with that of others, assuring him of useful work, free from fear of unemployment. The Plan is the most original Soviet contribution to civilised living.

Households need their plan. Households without a plan are muddled households. The dominant class in England knew it to perfection. The pride of the English country magnate lies in the ordered rhythm of his mansion; where kitchen ministers to dining-hall, home farm to kitchen; where nurse and governess in appropriate quarters supplement maternal care and where library, music room, and ballroom serve a many-sided cultural and social life. Plan need never cramp: plan liberates.

Countries need plans no less than households, and Russia provides a plan which stands well the test of time. Russia's whole economy is run to ordered plan. A sixth of the world is a planned sixth. Jolts and jars naturally occur as in the best ordered household, or the best ordered factory. Worth-while order is never built up easily and over-night. Difficulties arise and must be overcome, dangers avoided, adjustments made. It is no more easy to integrate a country than to integrate an orchestra. Much more difficult in fact. And Russia has constantly tripped. Nor has war helped the integration. But Russia, keeping her eye on main essentials, has pioneered and still pioneers towards a fully planned economy, as lovely in its own way as the economy of a country house, and not limited to any one small class.

Since Russia's planned economy and planned industry was only possible on condition that the mass of the country's productive machinery and the land was socially owned, Russia at the outset secured the social ownership either by State or by co-operative organisations of 98 per cent of all Russia's productive apparatus.

The Soviet people sought for and are achieving a society free from want and exploitation, a society where each is at liberty to work according to his ability and receive goods according to his need; a society of wealth, culture and fellowship where human personality can grow and operate. The eighteenth and nineteenth centuries gave cultured life to a few and based it upon exploitation of the many. Russia is in process of giving cultured life to all and bases it on power-driven machines. The Soviet people, in short, seek by a State plan to secure and increase public wealth, to better the conditions of all who work, to raise the cultural level of the whole and strengthen resistance to hostile attack.

The formulation of Russia's plan began in the Council of People's Commissars in October 1917, the task passing to the Supreme Council of National Economy in December of that year.

In 1921, at Lenin's invitation, the State Planning Commission—known for short as GOSPLAN—was set up and still operates as a permanent commission of the Council of People's Commissars of the U.S.S.R.—Russia's equivalent of our Cabinet. It consists of eleven outstanding planning officials and scientists; a body charged with preparing the national economic plans, advising the Government on similar plans prepared by the separate republics, and supervising the fulfilment of the plans after their adoption.

The study of the plan, however, to which this chapter is devoted must not stop with the study of the authoritative formulation of Gosplan from above, though it must begin there. It must consider, as an intrinsic part of the plan, the share of the mass of the people in its formulation and execution. It must not look merely at the wide range of the scheme for a well-thought-out domestic or family economy which regulates and plans for the well-being of a sixth of the world. It must pay regard also to the share which millions of workers and common people have, not only in executing the plan but also in its formulation. It is just that fundamental feeling that the plan is their plan, that they have had a share in its formulation and are therefore directly responsible for its execution, which makes the plan workable.

I have therefore reserved a separate section to make clear this important point, which has also a direct bearing on Soviet conceptions of democracy. It is mentioned here merely as a matter to be borne in mind when considering Russian Planned Economy lest it should be regarded as totalitarian direction solely from above.

Now turn to the principles which regulate the formulation of the Soviet Five-Year Plans.

The fundamental task of economic planning is to determine: (1) what must be produced and in what priority; (2) how production shall best be distributed to serve the country's need. How best to mobilise raw materials. How best to secure that regional distribution of enterprises which avoids superfluous transport.

More concretely the plan must determine:

How much coal, oil and iron-ore must be extracted.

What crops must be grown and in what quantities.

How much metal, machinery and finished products of several kinds—bread, boots, houses—must be manufactured.

What proportion of human labour shall be directed to capital development and what proportion to producing consumer's goods.

Where to build factories for most economical use of raw materials.

How to transport commodities.

To meet these tasks Gosplan has long-term and short-term objectives each with its own plan for fulfilment.

Power as Lenin saw, was a first priority. How to convert Russia's water power into electrical energy demanded in 1920 a formidable long-term plan called Goelro, covering the next ten or fifteen years.

Of the possibility of executing this plan H. G. Wells was sceptical. When he visited Moscow in 1920 he wrote in his diary that Lenin had succumbed to the Utopia of the Electricians. "I cannot see anything of the sort happening in this dark crystal of Russia, but this little man at the Kremlin can." Lenin was right. The war was the final test. Without Goelro the Russia of 1942 would have lacked machines. Without machines Russia would have lacked guns. Without guns Stalingrad would have fallen, with Russia at Hitler's feet and Britain on the brink of annihilation.

Vast events depended on Russia's early plan and it stood the test.

Russia accused of undue haste, knew the world better than her critics. She hurried and arrived in time.

The year 1928 saw the first comprehensive, all embracing Five-Year Plan, supplemented by annual and quarterly plans, with scope for the readjustment by political developments east or west, or to meet scientific changes supplanting some processes and accelerating others.

Gosplan determines the quantity of production required for each branch of industry and sets the targets; Regional planning aims at a rational and all-sided development of resources. The first, Gosplan, which is called "Branch planning" estimates, for example, the quantity of boots needed; the quantity of appropriate machinery to make

I

them; and, working backwards, the quantity of metal to be mined and power provided for these purposes.

"Regional Plans" are complementary to "Branch Plans" and have an eye to the needs both of the region in question and of the Soviet Union, as a whole. For example, arctic areas need green foodstuffs: transport of cabbage from farms a thousand miles southwards increases costs and monopolises rail waggons needed elsewhere. Hence the successful experiment of arctic hothouses for arctic needs. Consequential plans for local supplies of necessary glass, fuel and chemical manures for arctic hothouses followed as matter of course.

Yet again, Asia is Russia's prime source of cotton. Formerly cotton crops as a whole travelled northwards to the Moscow and Gorki cotton mills. Part of the finished cotton goods to meet Uzbek, Tadjik or Kazak needs, travelled back again to Asia with heavy drains on transport facilities. Thousands of truck miles were saved when Regional Planning built cotton mills in Tashkent to meet Asiatic needs for finished cotton goods.

Three priorities—the metal industry, the power industry, and the transport industry—overshadow all other elements of the plan.

The humblest cabbage patch demands a steel spade. Broad wheat lands demand complicated steel combine harvesters. Production of spade and combine harvesters demand metals. Metals demand fuels for smelting. All call for haulage by road or rail. Metal, fuel, power and transport are therefore from any point of view primary.

These simple illustrations, spades calling for steel; steel calling for mines, iron and coal; each calling for railroads and motorways, combine to form a delicate network of activity, they reveal the need for balance in industry. Balance is a primary word in Soviet planning.

Two important elements of planning proceed *pari passu* with the fundamental needs of production; elements frequently overlooked elsewhere but never overlooked in the Soviet Union—cultural needs and scientific needs.

Lenin ranked education with electricity and mechanism as a priority. An educated proletariat is an all-important element in the Socialist State. Educational needs therefore based upon analysis of the growth of population are carefully planned. Science again, like education, was a priority from the first. In 1920 Lenin enlisted the services of 200 scientific specialists. Many of these doubted the wisdom of the new Soviet economy; some doubted it to the end, though many more changed sides as time went on. One and all, however, were, in general, encouraged and implemented in their scientific tasks.

In preparation for the Second Five-Year Plan, Gosplan convened in the years 1932 and 1933 no fewer than twenty-four national scientific conferences. Intensive scientific development took place year by year up to the time of Hitler's attack. At the outbreak of war the tempo quickened. Among other scientific activities an intensive study of the Urals and Western Siberia and Kazakstan was conducted by the Academy of Science. A group of prevalent misconceptions as to the meaning and working of Soviet planned economy need dispelling. Soviet planning does not for example apportion a fixed amount of consumable goods to each individual. Neither, at any rate before the war, did Soviet planning dictate what task each individual should perform. Only in war emergency was labour directed in the Soviet Union, as with us, to appropriate tasks. Neither does Soviet planning deliver out an equal quantity of goods to each individual. Least of all has the Soviet Union effected any fundamental change, any fundamental movement—as is frequently alleged—in a capitalist direction as a result of the war.

Soviet planning, to revert to the misconception that a fixed amount of consumable goods is allotted to each individual, merely determines that so much of consumable goods of various kinds shall be produced and allotted for general use in a given period. Each individual has access to his or her own share of these goods as and when they desire them on the basis of the cash they earn through the quantity and quality of the work they themselves perform. This merely carries into practice the basic principle of Socialist economy, "From each according to his ability: to each according to *his work*." The goods a man receives, or the cash to purchase them is the reward, or pay, for the work he performs; the total income received by the workers through wages being planned and distributed in quantities sufficient to purchase the total amount of consumable goods produced, with adequate margins to provide workable elasticity.

Money, in a word, is only created against goods produced and acts, as in strictness it should act, as mobile tickets or tokens for the easy and appropriate movement of commodities. Money is never a commodity and where prices are fixed inflation is avoided.

Money, however, serves an additional purpose. The accountancy of money supplies the needed check on inefficiency. As each enterprise must cover its cost of production and accumulate its resources through the sale of its products, strict economy on expenditure is essential. Accurate financial accountancy applied to all operations serves as a wholesome check.

The problem of incentives is supremely important, and the plan provides for it. Over fulfilment of plan in factory or enterprise brings additional reward. Factory workers strive to hit or over hit their target. Workers encourage one another in effort. It is not a case of my success *or* yours in a factory. It is my success *and* yours. If you succeed in increasing output, I gain. If I succeed, you gain. If I succeed, I earn increased personal pay. I also share in the collective increase and the collective reward. My egoistic instinct is satisfied. My altruistic instinct also, for I know that my increase of production increases total production, in which my neighbour shares as well as I. Both I and my neighbour are thereby incited to discover quicker modes of production and cheaper processes, reducing still further cost in terms of energy expended. For, after all, at the heart of the drive for increased production lies the fact that the workers in the Soviet Union are the owners of the industry and know it. The factory is ultimately the workers' factory. The collective farm is the workers' farm. Workers as owners of industry know that as production grows their share in the increase grows. The worker knows that the increased standard of life which he seeks is intimately and directly bound up with production in his factory and other factories. Hence his desire to increase production not only in his own factory but in neighbouring factories as well. Mutuality of interest becomes apparent and appreciated. A cotton collective in Uzbekistan knows that textile mills in Moscow depend on efforts in Tashkent; whilst they in turn depend upon Moscow factories for the textiles they wear. The process comes nearer home when textile mills are built, to spin and weave in Tashkent the raw cotton the farmer himself supplies into finished fabrics which the farmer himself needs. Coloured cotton which eliminates the process of dyeing altogether, brings immediate benefit still nearer to farmer and textile worker alike: that knowledge adds zest to work and invention and to belief in and encouragement of the science which produced the miracle. To these material incentives for increased production we might add many other motives, such as pride in craftsmanship, love of country, and sense of duty, higher motives which gain impetus with time.

The Five-Year Plans have long since passed the experimental stage. Approving themselves in days of peace, with equal success they have approved themselves in the supreme test of war. Progressive in character, they started when Goelro, launched in 1920, aimed at doubling electrical output by 1935. Goelro actually achieved a sixfold increase. That led on to the Five-Year Plan whose course has been roughly as follows:

1. The First Five-Year Plan in 1928 transformed the Soviet Union from an agricultural to an industrial land, lifting it from the mediæval to the modern technical level. Nation-wide socialism was the goal.

The results passed all expectation. Industry was shifted eastward, lessening the dangerous concentration of 90 per cent of mining in the Donbas and 60 per cent and over of manufacture in the central area. Industry, located nearer to raw materials on which it operated, rapidly modernised the backward areas. Production targets were overshot. Industrial production doubled the 1928 level. Industrial output, as against agricultural output, rose from 48 per cent to the total of 70 per cent. After five years the Soviet Union had become an industrial country with a socialised agriculture. Agriculture itself likewise by no means lagged behind. Russia now possesses the largest-scale agriculture in the world.

Wages rose 67 per cent. Unemployment and extreme poverty were conquered. Further planning was eagerly welcomed.

2. The task of the Second Five-Year Plan which aimed at completing the technical reconstruction of the national economy, speedily hit the target. Soviet industry had grown eightfold since 1913 and 80 per cent of all production came from newly created enterprises. Goelro's task was completed. Industry was electrified and fittingly redistributed. The coal output of Siberia, Kazakstan and the Urals exceeded that of the Donbas in Tsarist days. Giant industrial units arose in the east; the Magnito-gorsk and Kuznetsk iron and steel combines, the Gorki motor works, the Chelyabinsk tractor works and others. Eastern oil was tapped. Asian-grown cotton was woven in Asian weaving sheds. Great farms on the Volga, in the Urals, in Siberia and in the central Asian areas were mechanised and virgin soil brought under the plough. By 1938 Russian agriculture was already operating 483,000 tractors and 130,000 complex threshing machines.

New populations arose in the East and new radial rail lines served them. The production target for grain and cotton was overshot. The Soviet Union grew technically and economically independent. Real wages increased 101 per cent. Illiteracy departed. Forty million children and others received schooling in 1938. Scientific institutes grew: the Georgian Academy of Science was founded in 1941; that of Armenia in 1944. Scientific research establishments numbered 2,265.

3. The Third Five-Year Plan for 1938-42 aimed at overtaking and surpassing the most highly developed western countries in the production, per head of the population, of pig-iron, steel, fuel and electric power. National production was to be raised by 50 to 100 per cent with corresponding increase in wages and retail trade. The cultural level of the masses was to reach the standard of technicians and qualified engineers.

4. Finally, the general plan for fifteen years from 1940 was to "overtake and surpass the most highly developed countries in production per head of the population of all principal goods."

The era so eagerly longed for, so persistently worked for and so patiently suffered for was about to dawn. Russia at last would confront a sceptical world with an accomplished fact. The justification of Russia's system would be plain to all. Russia would step proudly out beside the foremost peoples of the world. Russia would *lead* the world, not by force of arms, but by force of her successful experiment in a planned life and a socialist economy.

Then came the war and all the bright hopes were dashed to the ground. German armies surged across the frontiers. For 800 miles Russia retreated, yielding yard by yard only after fierce battles. A third of Soviet territory and that the best third passed into German hands robbing the Soviet people of a third of her former food supplies, and more than a third of her coal, iron and steel. Russia fought on, and did so precisely because of the vast achievement of her First Five-Year Plan. Russia's planned economy had been utilised up to the limit of her power.

Russia's plan had provided heavy war industries with adequate equipment, had built up powerful metallurgical and fuel bases in the East, had united the many small agricultural holdings into larger units, had mechanised the land, multiplying harvest yields to the point where soldiers could still be fed despite the loss of the Ukraine and the Caucasus, had redistributed industry, bringing millions of virgin acres under the plough, had trained specialists and workers on a mass and hitherto unwonted scale, had redistributed resources of every kind, giving first priority to the front, had enabled speedy evacuation of machinery from the Ukraine to the Urals there to continue undisturbed the production of goods. And when victory came Russia's planned economy switched over without a jolt from war to peace production. No strikes. No unemployment. Russia's planned economy is mobile in war and mobile in peace. Mobile in war. The loss of the Donbas had demanded a speedy change in Ural metal manufacture. It was made. The Kuznetsk iron and steel combines were changed overnight and rolled out armour plating. Scientific research providing Kuznetz in the meantime with local iron-ore and manganese. Mobile in peace. The swing back to the Donbas sent farmers, miners and factory workers surging along in the wake of the victorious Red Army with the same remarkable spontaneity.

Miners did not wait till pithead shafts were built, they learned the art of building pithead shafts themselves. Machine hands became masons and, quickly mastering a new craft, built their own shops and factories. Women laid bricks, plastered walls, cooked meals, tended children. Russia's planned economy is amazingly adaptable and amazingly mobile: certainly it enlists to the full the enthusiastic support of the workers, who know now what they are working for and for whom they work.

Reconstruction is the keynote of the Fourth Five-Year Plan. Industry had moved eastwards during the war, accelerating a pre-war eastward drive. It still moves eastwards to the Urals, to Siberia and to the Far East. But this by no means implies that the Western areas will be superseded as powerful centres of industry. They are and will remain essential to the Soviet economy and therefore must be restored. Hence the key word of the new plan is not construction but reconstruction, especially in heavy industries and rail communications. Development will, of course, proceed at the same time: reconstruction will take precedence. So with consumer goods. Expansion is to take place, but only after recovery has taken prior place. Production of an abundance of goods of primary necessity to the consumer is to be priority production.

Careful analysis of the plan from a social and political point of view reveals three important principles at work:

1. A deliberate effort at decentralisation with a view to intensive development of the republics and the greater economic wealth of the Soviet Union as a whole. Industry in Moscow for instance is to be pruned, that in new districts with resources in raw materials and power to expand. Lithuania's total production, for example, is to increase 3.9 times—far in excess of Moscow's: greater local economic autonomy is to accompany this expansion.

2. As most of the damage was done in the vulnerable western areas, from the Ukraine to the Baltic States, rebuilding on the vast scale planned—the Ukraine alone is to absorb 20 per cent total capital expenditure under the plan—would not take place if military considerations alone ruled, or if Russia anticipated that war with the West was imminent or even probable.

3. Output of goods in bulk is evidently a determining factor, with a view to the transition from socialism to communism with its goal "to each according to need" which postulates a wealthy community. Hence economic and social considerations tilt the balance against military considerations in the western areas.

The losses during the war have been immense. The Soviet Union must, as it were, start again, as it started after the Revolution. But with a difference. Then it had to build on the ruins of a capitalist economy. Now it builds on the foundations of a socialist economy which still stands despite the war and its losses. The speed of recovery will therefore bear no comparison with the speed of the earlier work. Trained personnel, in large numbers despite the losses, still remain, with trained technique and knowledge gained by experience. No groping now.

The new plan carries on the former tradition with regard to the republics, aiming at the full development of their reconstruction and the re-establishment of their productive capacity to secure a manifold development of the several economies within the economic system of the whole Union.

The heavy metallurgical industry in remoter districts, in the Urals, Siberia and the Far East is to increase still further, with a metallurgical plant in Georgia and a pipe-rolling mill in Azerbaijan, as parts of the self-contained bases of iron mines in the Far East, Siberia and the Caucasus. More is also contemplated, for geological research is bidden to seek fresh reserves of iron-ore and metallurgical raw materials. Electrical energy is to be increased 70 per cent above pre-war output. Light industry is to be increased, with a consequential increase in foodstuffs and articles of common consumption. Grain crops are to be increased to 107 per cent in comparison with 1940; sugar beet to 122 per cent; cotton to 125 per cent; flax to 139 per cent. Horses at the end of the Five-Year Plan will have increased by 46 per cent; cattle by 39 per cent; sheep and goats by 75 per cent; pigs by 200 per cent. A large increase of tractors, agricultural machinery and chemical fertilisers is to facilitate the increase. Heavy industry, light industry and agriculture all depend on transport. The density of Soviet communication is to be increased: a total freightage by rail, road or water of 657,000 million ton kilometers is envisaged in 1950 as compared with 483,000 million ton kilometers in 1940.

The plan calls for an increase in the real national income of 38 per cent above the pre-war figure, made possible by a rise in the total producing capacity of the Soviet Union, a higher trade turnover, an increase in expenditure on housing and social service as well as in the Accumulation Fund—the money spent on capital development—and the Consumption Fund.

As usual Russia thinks ahead in matters of skilled personnel, in the training of skilled workers. The plan provides for 7,700,000 new skilled workers by the end of the Fourth Five-Year Plan with an advance in the technical standard of the 13,900,000 workers already engaged in production.

Special arrangements are made and inducements planned to encourage the transfer of labour power from agriculture, which has become prosperous and popular, to the various branches of industry. Expenditure on cultural services is to be increased, together with expenditure on social services for workers and clerical employees—260 per cent for the whole above the 1940 expenditure.

An increase in the number of students in general—the plan enters students at universities, high schools and technical colleges—is to advance to 1,954,000. Cinemas are to reach 46,700; clubs and libraries 284,900, hospital beds 985,000; and places in sanatoria and recreational centres 450,000.

The figures for the second quarter of the State plan for 1947 are highly significant and perhaps, as the *Times'* newspaper suggests, partially account for Russia's self-sufficiency in recovery. The overall plan was fulfilled 103 per cent for gross production of the entire industry of the U.S.S.R. Many industries reached high percentages; chemical industry 115 per cent, electrical equipment 113 per cent, rubber industry 114 per cent and so on.

2. PLANNED AGRICULTURE

(A) *The Scientific Soviet Farmer*

HITLER promised and sought disaster to Russian farming and starvation to the Russian Army. He failed. Despite incredible destruction Russian production in general, as we have noted, and Russian agriculture in particular struggled on. By reaching Stalingrad Germany had robbed Russia of 600,000 square miles of best agricultural land, two-fifths of her grain supplies, half her potatoes, 85 per cent of her sugar beet and 60 per cent of her sunflower seed.

Nevertheless hunger, which had destroyed the Tsarist, failed to destroy the Soviet Armies. Backed by Soviet factories and Soviet farms the Red Army had turned the tables and Hitler was destroyed. Collective farms had outworked and outwitted him. "Plant new acres; increase fertility" had been the slogans. Work and science—women's work, children's work and work of the old—had saved Russia.

Soviet wives and daughters are strong and intelligent: 10,000,000 women have qualified as specialists in agricultural work. Acreage and output increased even throughout the war. A Ural family of four made more "work days" after the father's departure than before. The 4,000,000 acres increase of 1941 became 6,500,000 in 1942 and 16,000,000 in 1943.

Scientific farmers replace ignorant peasants. All share the work and all share the prosperity.

Mr. Tsitsin, Russia's leading agronomist, told me the story of his own contributions to output, his latest achievement being perennial rye. With the American Professor Hanson, I handled experimental specimens in 1937. Planted in the autumn of 1939 Tsitsin produced four crops in two years with a total of eighty-three bushels per acre.

Perennial rye now reaches the industrial stage: thousands of acres were under cultivation by 1945.

Interesting work at the Michurin Central Genetic Laboratory in 1946 included the crossing of apples and pears with hawthorn. The vitamin content of the fruit thus obtained considerably exceeds that of lemons.

Professor Dunin's graft planting of potatoes had saved thirty-six million pounds of seed. Children, taught by Lysenko, planted potato eyes and saved another 150,000 tons.

The Central Asian Republic had planted 2,000,000 tons of grain with no diminution of cotton crop.

Sixty-five thousand farmers at Fergana had built a thirty-five-mile irrigation canal bringing 90,000 acres of rich land under cultivation.

No branch indeed of Soviet activity had shown or shows better results than the collective farm. The wooden plough stick has gone. The sickle, too, and the bullock-drawn stone roller for threshing. Strip culture also, where a peasant, even where rich enough to own fifteen acres, might find his property divided into a dozen or more parcels of land a mile away from his own home and from one another.

Kolkhoz or collective farms replace peasant holdings. Not indeed without a struggle did they win against the richer peasant, who burned tractors and fired collective farm barns, harried Soviet organisers and enlisted religion against a farm calendar based, not on Saints Days, but on scientific study of the seasons.

Kulak sabotage and the drought of 1932 brought on a crisis. The Government forcibly seized the foodstuffs contracted for and stopping sabotage saved the country. Serious hardship was experienced. Rumour abroad said that one million died. A gross exaggeration, disproved by cold statistics, which record no decline in population in 1930-34 when mass collectivisation took place.

The strict censorship—in which Eugene Lyons concurred—during the most critical years was due not to Soviet secrecy over brutal methods but to fear lest Japan might stage an attack based on Russia's food shortage and internal difficulties. Good harvests in 1933 marked the change and the triumph. Collectivisation had been harder to achieve with agriculture than with industry and demands close study. Here is an outline of its structure.

Farm units consist of a group of families banded on a voluntary basis, receiving land appropriate to their numbers and held *in perpetuo*.

No purchase price and no rent is demanded. A tax on the produce being the farmer's contribution to the national revenue.

Machine and tractor stations, serving the needs of many local farms lessens cost of power, conserves machinery and frees capital for fresh livestock, orchards, vineyards or industrial crops.

No marketing anxiety or fluctuating prices harass collective farmers. They sell to an ever available market at a known price. A fixed minimum quota at a fixed price to the Government is obligatory: surplus beyond the quota may be sold to factories or municipalities or private consumers at the price it will fetch, with the Government always ready to purchase it at a fixed minimum price. Hazard goes.

Price, and plan readjustment, protect the Government—which needs the food for the Red Army and other such purposes—from over-abundance of any one commodity. Obligatory insurance of 1 per cent protects the farmer against unforeseeable disaster. He may increase it at will and gains greater benefits.

Ample incentive exists. Each worker of sixteen years and upwards has equal share in electing the management and making basic decisions. Each worker can specialise according to taste and aptitude.

Jobs are evaluated according to difficulty, experience and skill demanded; the datum being the average piece-work of a semi-skilled worker. This "work day" is paid, not in money but in harvest shares, with advance payment for current needs whilst awaiting harvest time and subsequent settlement.

Before profit distribution, reductions are made for taxes, machine-rentals, seeds, fodder reserves, capital expenditure, insurance and cultural needs. The remainder being divided, according to "work days," among the members, with consequent incentive to all to increase both the number of "work days" and the prosperity of the farm. One man's success means another man's benefit on a Soviet collective farm.

Machines in the Soviet Union, accompanied by no fear of unemployment through displacement of human labour, are welcomed. New tasks await released labour. Industrial crops, chicken runs, grapes, orchards, or fresh modes of rearing fish or breeding cattle constantly call for fresh workers.

The more progressive collectives run local power plants, local laboratories or the like. They may even possess an airfield or a modern housing estate. Each family owns its private garden for vegetables, chickens, a cow or for growing the more precious kinds of industrial crops. Farms tend to specialise, to compete, and to break records; record breakers often winning high preferment in the State. Two hundred and sixty-one such competitors met to pool their experiences at the Constitutional Congress of 1936.

Since increased efficiency yields increased harvests for less manpower with higher earnings and dividends, farm earnings advanced from 4.568 million roubles in 1932 to 18,798 millions in 1938, with consequent advancing standards of living—radios, bicycles, clothes, books or musical instruments. Ampler houses were built; longer holidays enjoyed. Farm workers developed a culture previously wholly unknown.

So popular indeed has become the collective farm that special attractions are needed now to lure adequate manpower to the towns.

Behind the vast network of collective farms, each with its local plan, lies a master State plan, which regulates the total bulk of any commodity grown.

The local plan makes an inventory of all inhabitants, with age and capacity; of livestock with expectation of increase; of area to be sown for home consumption, etc. The sowing of the remainder is based on the needs of the particular area and the needs of the national plan.

Machine and tractor stations also serve other purposes besides preserving valuable machinery and utilising it up to the hilt with consequent lowering of overhead charges. Self-supporting, but making no profits, tractor stations serve as collecting stations for grain for Government use, each farm rendering payment in grain not cash. Middlemen depart.

Tractor stations, yet again, become agricultural headquarters where experts meet, where lectures are given, where seeds are bought or new livestock exhibited and explained. The late President Kalinin was right in his statement that in industrial production Russia copied the best models in other lands. He was also right when he said that "in farming we are leaders on a new road." Scientific farming, as Prof. Levy urges in *The Times*, reaches its peak in the U.S.S.R. Vernalised seed avoids autumnal sowing. Early grain is scattered by plane in dry areas upon the melting snow. By plane also, pests are fought, day-old chicks transported a thousand miles, seedlings flown from the Black Sea to Leningrad and Moscow. Soviet agriculture fights and conquers deserts and dust bowls with hard subsoil plants, with tree belts hundreds of miles in length, with trench planting, cool by day and warm by night. Snow is captured and retained in dry places by snow fences and snow mounds ploughed at right-angles to prevailing winds.

Agriculture pushes east and north. Stump-pullers clear the ground, weather charts guide the pioneers who carry with them pest-proof potatoes and specially produced nothern plants, new varieties of flax, hemp or sugar-beet. Wheat, rice and cotton move north to solve the transport problem: potatoes move south. Rubber, so essential in modern life, is produced from native sources; Kok-sagyz yields its harvest after one year's growth with still richer harvests in the second year. Sugar-beet produces excellent rubber, the 30 lbs per acre in 1941 is now 150 lbs. One million acres of sugar-beet for rubber was the plan for 1942.

The Ukraine, terribly desolated—Russia never dwelt upon her losses, perhaps fearing to rouse suspicions of dangerous weakness—makes vigorous strides at rehabilitation. In less than half a year after liberation in 1943 the Ukraine numbered 1,723,000 head of cattle, with 800,000 calves added by the Government from the central east. To meet the urgent needs for skilled workers three million farmers took intensive courses in 1943 and 1944. New and higher standards are the aim all round. Soviet agriculture is a high spot indeed of Soviet life.

(B) *Forced Landing*

"They only show you what they want you to see," is a frequent charge by the critic.

Of course they do. We do the same. But it by no means follows, as is so often implied, that what you see is a sham, a dressed piece. And I had innumerable chances to check up what I was shown by what I was not shown. Let this narrative from my diary suffice.

I write in a Russian meadow. It is 5 a.m. The grass is heavy with dew. The lark sings. I am where I could wish to be. In the heart of the Russian countryside; 350 miles from Moscow, 6 miles from the nearest town. An unexpected visitor, dropped unannounced from the skies.

Our plane made a forced landing last night. We were bound from Tbilisi to Moscow. A rough journey; over Caucasian mountains and across the Black Sea. We were only two hours from home. Many had been sick. I observed and called attention to a trickle of oil from the propeller case. Then a spurt, which grew in volume. Engineers and pilots acted instantly. We swung round, seeking level ground. Not a soul was alarmed. We made a perfect landing on a flower-bespangled, breezy isolated meadow.

Within a few minutes children surrounded us as if they had sprung from the ground. Peasant children. Bonny children. Boys and girls, friendly and smiling. Boisterous too when the propeller revolved to make wireless connection with Moscow and sent a rush of air which laid the meadow grass flat. Children struggled with the wind-

stream as men struggle against blizzards, and then, yielding, were
hurled back like chaff, screaming with delight.

Girls desisted first and gathered round us, eager to ask and answer
questions.

"Were the Germans here?" we asked a pretty child of Ukrainian
parentage, who looked fourteen but was only twelve.

"They were," she said.

"And did you go away?"

"No, we stayed. The Germans took our houses and we lived in
holes."

"Did the Germans kill any people in your village?"

"They killed my uncle. He was head man. They cut off his hands
and feet and then shot him," she said with childish directness.

An old man came hobbling up. No other adult arrived and we
asked the child: "Where is your father?"

"At the front."

"Are many fathers at the front?"

"Yes."

Looking around the eager faces I said: "Put up your hands if your
father is away."

Every hand, with scarcely an exception, went up.

Village and collective farm here is run by women and children
with a few old men.

To escape the roar of the engine we wandered to a group of distant cottages. The village lay out of sight beyond. Some cottages
were wrecked, a few were intact. They were old and simple but full of
charm, white-washed and thatched with rushes. Three small windows
on each side of the four-square house, cased in unpainted, weather-
bleached wooden frames with well-moulded decoration.

The garden was large with sturdy potato and marrow plants.
White chickens pecked around. A calf awaited its mother.

We asked a pleasant-faced woman in the garden if she had milk.

"Not till the cows come home," she said.

"Who tends all this garden"—it was large—"and who tends the
great collective farm?"

"We women do it," she replied. "Each woman is responsible
for five acres of the common farm besides her own private garden,
and her own farmyard."

The woman was forty-five. A widow for fourteen years. She had
a boy of fourteen and a girl of sixteen.

"Were the Germans here long?"

"Five months. Foot and mouth disease drove them away. They
put a cordon round the village."

Just then a child came up with a cracked jug full of milk and the woman invited us to eat our sandwiches in her cottage. We gladly entered.

A pleasant cottage, reminiscent of Wales. A four-roomed house. Sitting-room, bedroom, brick-floored kitchen and an entrance porch used by chickens and humans alike.

We sat on a broad couch in the sitting-room, big enough for a bed and covered with a rough rug beautifully woven in check pattern with dark rich colours of home-dyed hemp.

A white-hempen cloth charmingly embroidered covered the table. "My own work," the woman said with pride.

Two plain rugs covered the spotless deal floor.

We asked the woman to share our sandwiches of white bread taking care to give her the only meat sandwich left.

She ate it, remarking that she had never seen white bread like that in her Kolkhos. Thinking of breakfast, we asked if she had any eggs. Yes, she said, and potatoes and sour cabbage. She bade us take breakfast with her. Two other things struck me. A large chest, waist high, stood against the opposite wall. As we talked a fine girl of sixteen came in and selecting from the chest a coat of modern cut and donning it and with a red scarf round her throat, she led the pilots to the village. "At what does your daughter work?" I asked. "She does not work, she is still at school," the mother replied. Sixteen and still at school!

In a corner behind some tall india-rubber plants, hung around with dainty muslin curtains, was an ikon, a picture of Christ.

Learning that I was a minister of religion—my dress was "lay" on account of the hot journey—the woman left the house and eagerly returned with a bowl of newly dug potatoes, lit a fire, fed it with straw and stiff reeds, and heeding no remonstrance cooked a dishful there and then.

Three bowls, three spoons, three forks were placed on the table—potatoes in one bowl, sour cabbage in another, sour milk in a third, and then a jug of warm milk straight from the cow. "Kolkhos fare," the woman said with a smile.

We helped ourselves straight from the dish with our own spoons: crockery is scarce after the German invasion.

A healthy meal. And that fare with eggs from the fowls, bacon from the pigs, and the coarse bread, accounts doubtless for the bonny sturdiness of our hostess who stood before us with crimson apron, green belt and white blouse: a comely woman with plaits of flaxen hair coiled up, Russian style, on either side of her head and peeping out from the white kerchief which the peasant women always wear.

She had been beautiful when young. Her portrait with a chain of small pearls hanging round her neck, taken on her marriage day seventeen years ago, hung on the wall.

Had no war come it would have been a richer home: the bedstead witnessed to that.

But the essentials of a home were there. Security of livelihood. Ample private farm and garden. Her wage for work and her share in the proceeds of the collective farm. Her children's future also secured; each being educated to a high standard. A boy of fourteen and a girl of sixteen still at school. Music and culture in the home: the boy had his balalaika and the girl her pretty frock. No doctor's fees. Medical attention free. Full security for mother and children in sickness or old age.

The Germans gone, there was a carefree, happy look on the smiling face of our hostess. There may be richer homes in the so-called millionaire Kolkhoses, and there maybe and alas there are many far more miserable as the inevitable result of German barbarity, but here was something broadly typical in this simple peasant home, graced with its peasant artistry, happy in its security, in its honest but not hopeless toil, with its well-fed, well-educated children, whose virile future is assured. This is the fundamental wealth to retain which Russian soldiers fought so valiantly in the peoples' war.

I was sad when a great plane roared overhead at 7 a.m. and alighted gently beside our crippled craft; sad to leave the breakfast that awaited us in the cottage, and to miss the smile which our charming hostess would assume for her unexpected guests.

It would take a good deal to persuade me that a forced landing occasioned by my own observations had been arranged to "show me what they wanted me to see," especially as it happened to be the second surprise visit to a Kolkhos within a fortnight; the other in Armenia, where we ate our meal with wine, bread and fruits of the sunny south on lovely eastern carpets spread beneath the cherry trees.

3. PLANNED SCIENCE

SCIENCE dominates Soviet thought. Science is regarded, and has from the first been regarded, by the Soviet authorities as a necessary part of the social organisation, demanding of Soviet rulers and administrators, a certain scientific training and much scientific understanding.

Not so in the Western countries. Not so in England. The majority of English students—as Mr. J. G. Crowther, the Cambridge scientist, pertinently points out—training at Oxford to be politicians or administrators, study ancient and modern history and literature, with economics now added, but largely to the exclusion of science and technology. In Oxford ambitious students aiming at political careers learn how to hold their own in influential circles by speech and manner; how to master the technique of public speaking and the art of public debate.

This "verbal method of education" had its virtues in the past, and was most effectual when the art of managing people was the chief part of politics. It is an idea of government, however, which to-day persists in spite of that vast extension and influence of science and technology, which is the leading characteristic of modern civilisation and calls for radical change in governmental or administrative outlook.

The governors of Western Europe do not, in their theory of government, consider technology and science as an essential part of the social organism. Science and technology are just two more factors for the administrator's manipulation.

That attitude was out-moded from the first by Soviet Russia's rulers and administrators, who regard science and technology as sources of power which transform the very nature of political problems and who enthrone planning rather than verbal argument as the prime requisite in the art of government. The modes of thought which produced modern science and technology have dominated Soviet administrative thinking in a way not yet recognised as necessary here, despite all efforts of the late Mr. H. G. Wells.

The permeation of modern science and technology into Soviet political and administrative thought is reflected alike in the wide range of Soviet scientific work and in the organisation of science existent in the Soviet Union to-day.

The range is most impressive.

In 1915 Tsarist Russia contained altogether 120-150 scientific research centres, the majority being departments of ten universities with a sprinkling of higher technical schools and academic museums. The Soviet Union possesses 2,256 independent scientific institutes. Within twenty-five years the Academy of Sciences alone has raised the number of its scientific workers from 95 to 4,000 in 152 scientific institutes, organising in addition ten affiliated bodies in different places, including twenty-two institutes, 139 scientific laboratories, five national parks, seven observatories with, in 1940, 3,000 workers and 300 post-graduates. Nor is this extension of science confined to the old centres: it has spread to hundreds of towns throughout the Soviet Union.

The organisation of science is no less significant. Science is socially

K

organised. And it is precisely here, in the matter of social organisation, in the relation of science to social life, that science in Soviet Russia differs most widely from science in England or America. It differs not at all in tools and laboratory practice. Research in the Soviet Union is conducted as here with the same instruments, the same chemical reagents and in general with the same well-tried tools. It is, however, related to the whole social life in a way unknown as yet amongst us. and thereby occupies a position of greatly increased importance, receiving from the State ample material and economic assistance.

Pre-revolutionary science in Russia was as chaotic as pre-revolutionary production, and from the same cause and with the same effect.

Galileo had led the scientific world of his day in introducing isolated experiments for investigating phenomena. Unlike the mediaeval philosophers, who desired only a comprehensive account of phenomena, Galileo decided to isolate simple phenomena and obtain accurate knowledge concerning them, leaving on one side the relation of this or that particular phenomenon to the phenomena of the universe. That meant subdivision of labour in the scientific world precisely parallel to the subdivision of labour in the industrial productive world, with results similar in each case. Vast accumulation of goods in the one case, and vast accumulation of knowledge of facts in the other. Lacking synthesis, these unco-ordinated facts led to intellectual chaos in the scientific world parallel to the chaos of unordered production and unordered distribution in the industrial world.

Solving the unco-ordinated and ruinous struggle in the social life, the Soviets claim also that they have solved the inefficient and wasteful unrelatedness of study and exploration in the scientific world.

And that brings us back again to the social organisation of science, the second significant feature of Soviet scientific activity. Soviet science is socially related. That is fundamental. Soviet science is closely tied up with the practical affairs of life, with industry, agriculture and medicine. Soviet science deals with practical problems, pioneering with new industrial, agricultural and medical conceptions and possibilities; striving however no less than the isolated pioneer to penetrate to ultimate problems whose solution will again react beyond all imagination on the various activities of human life, as for instance in the knowledge and control and beneficent application of atomic energy.

Working thus in close alliance with the main activities of Soviet life, and financed to an extent which rouses envy in scientists elsewhere, the Academy of Sciences, the most influential scientific body in

Russia, has expanded its operations out of all knowledge: twenty-five years ago it had fifty-two investigators working on physics and mathematics, now there are 217; where two formerly worked on chemistry, 367 now work; where eleven on geology, now 302; where twenty-nine in biology, now 639, an increase ranging from four to 180 times. Higher educational institutions, which are centres for the development of scientific knowledge rose from ninety in 1915 to 750 to-day, with a total of 600,000 students undergoing higher education as compared with a former 100,000.

The production of books prior to the present war was about 40,000 titles a year; half of this output dealt with technology, agriculture, natural science and mathematics. The Academy of Sciences alone produced the largest group publication of scientific literature in the world.

Furthermore, all this scientific activity penetrates to the remotest parts of the Union. I was enabled to study it in Georgia, Armenia and Asia as well as in Moscow and Leningrad.

The close tie-up between science and the activities of daily life in the Soviet Union and throughout the Soviet Union may be illustrated concretely by examination of the principles regulating the need for, and the size of, scientific institutes.

The Soviet planners both of institutes and industries start from a calculation of the needs of a population which may be expected to grow during the next forty years to 300 million people. How much food, housing and clothing will they need? How much bread, milk, boots, suits, bathrooms, motorcars and dwelling space. . . .? The figures are immense and in vastly greater proportion than the present population receives, for a great increase in the standard of living is planned for.

The wide scope of the State Planning Commission, which tackles the colossal problem of production makes much the same claim, with promise of the same prestige, on ambitious Soviet youth that political position makes upon ambitious youth at Oxford. Positions on the State Planning Commission are coveted.

This State plan, which is indeed the most original product of the Bolshevik Revolution, is closely tied up with development of scientific institutes in the following way. When the quantity of consumable goods has been calculated, an estimate is made of the scale of agriculture and industry needed for their production: so many factories, so many machines, so much metal; so much transport; so many farms, so much cattle, so much seed, so much power.

The Metal Industry must expand to meet the demand. The power units must also expand. Likewise the output of electrical machinery.

The related demand for agricultural products will also be reckoned together with improvements in plants and animals. Soviet resources of men and materials consequently need careful scrutiny for their full economic utilisation. Hydro-electric stations must be planted where power is available; mines and metal works located where minerals exist. Tens of thousands of workers must be trained and fitted for the gigantic operations contemplated. Research is needed everywhere. The aid of science in every activity is eagerly looked for.

Men with genius or talent for research are singled out and cherished as sedulously by rulers, administrators and those who fashion the plan, as are new sources of chemical materials or new metal deposits. The chemist of genius is as much a national resource as the deposit which he discovers or exploits. All this then explains the growth and disposition of scientific institutes and aids us to understand many interesting and valuable characteristics of Soviet scientific activities.

Research stations and institutes we should notice, on the one hand, are not placed arbitrarily here and there but are definitely planted where practical needs call for scientific help. The individual, on the other hand, finds his niche, and wide scope for initiative, not only in an ordered whole but in the precise spot where his initiative is most needed. Research knowledge is mobilised at the point where need dictates.

Heavy metal industries for instance are faced with daily problems, whose very nature invites research into the properties of metals, and into the ultimate nature of matter. So we find powerfully and ably directed Research Institutes growing up side by side with the great metal plants and in close connection with particular industrial concerns.

Many of the best physical research institutes are attached to the Commissariat of Heavy Industries, the research laboratories maintained by this Department being organised in a division named the Scientific Research Sector of the People's Commissariat of Heavy Industry. This organisation finances many of the best-known laboratories in the U.S.S.R., such as the Physico-Technical Institute of Leningrad directed by Prof. Joffe or the Physico-Technical Institute of Kharkov.

The duty of these particular institutes is to conduct research into those fundamental principles of the physical sciences which underlie the technique of industrial processes, these being under direct control of the industries with which they are connected.

Three-quarters of first-class research in the Soviet Union consequently is at present located in Moscow, Leningrad and Kharkov where industry is also in the main located. Large new institutes, however, now arise in places where new industry develops, at Dniepropetrovsk for instance or in Tashkent. This process of decentralisation rapidly proceeds.

The great central institutes still, however, in the main tackle the more fundamental problems such as the constitution of matter itself.

This procedure, this development of scientific institutes cheek by jowl with factory and farm wrought a slow but profound change in Soviet science. Whereas previously science had been divorced from practical tasks and scientists too often distracted by mere abstract questions, scientific theory became organically bound up with requirements of technique and practice. Science and scientists became accessible. Science and the knowledge of it was more widely spread in its scope and contacts by being applied so closely to the needs of life.

Also though the individual scientist was given wide scope for initiative and more assistance than in other lands in the line of his gifts and studies, he had his place in the whole range of science, and kept to it. He was less inclined to dogmatise about matters outside his sphere. And from the public point of view, though the special individual's name was well known, it became customary to speak of the school rather than the man: the school of Pavlov, the school of Kurnakov. The collective nature of Soviet science was thus instinctively revealed and emphasised. Though valued more highly even than formerly the individual of genius stood no longer as a solitary figure, like the great Lomonosov in earlier days, but as a guide and teacher of a scientific school.

This collective work became and becomes increasingly necessary owing to the complexity of scientific knowledge, with a literature, running as it does into tens of thousands of articles a year, a complete grasp even of individual tendencies lies beyond the powers of any single individual worker and necessitates the organisation of collective work.

And there is more to it even than that. The benefit of a school of science clustering around a man of marked talent is twofold, stimulating the young whilst keeping young the old. The product is a healthy mingling of tradition and adventure. The knowledgeable older man inspires respect for the tradition of science; youth supplies the courage and will break away from the past, when necessary, with revolutionary boldness.

This adventurous, explorative spirit, which is fostered in Soviet laboratories, wins daily triumphs. A simple illustration is seen in the reversal of the attitude of the older generation of geologists as to possible mineral wealth in the Caucasus. Too young in geological time were these mountains, the older men theoretically urged, for accumulation of valuable mineral deposits. The younger geologists challenged this verdict, and exploring the high mountains found not only lead, zinc, copper and arsenic; but the more rare and much besought minerals molybdenum and wolfram. A like audacity has conquered the supposedly bleak and useless arctic north.

A direct and intentional product of the juxtaposition of science and industry, lies in the principle that true science can no longer be content with description and contemplation. It must be up and doing as well as down and thinking. Assistance in up-building the national economy has replaced "Science for its own sake" as the prime motive, though resolute pursuit of this end brings Soviet science daily, and more than ever before, up against ultimate problems.

That the world is knowable and logical, that all natural phenomena are related and inter-related, that there is a cause for all processes of nature, are rooted beliefs of Soviet science. These beliefs yield useful results, at times dramatic results. The discovery of the largest potassium deposits in the world in the Western Urals, affords an admirable illustration.

Under the old science a vast number of individual and isolated discoveries were made. Minerals were found, described, and plotted on the geological map. The findings were random and gave the impression of an orderless collection.

Soviet science probes deeper to-day. What is the significance of those points on the geological map, is the miner's practical question when he seeks new mines and wishes to know where to find them. Soviet science has now revealed that these scattered minerals are due to no mere accident of past geological forces, they occur in a pattern; they bear logical relation to one another and to their context; their occurrence is associated with the laws of distribution of atoms in the world. The discovery of those complicated laws is fruit of the work of Geochemistry, a new science arising where two sciences coalesce. By the laws of probability—mathematics being drawn in—it has been found possible to predict, and thus to guide the miner's pick and shovel.

Theoretical progress founded on the probability of discovering potash deposits in the peculiar conditions of the Western Urals led to the establishment of the world's largest potassium industry.

It did that for the Soviet Union. It did more for the scientist: it supplied him with fresh data in solving the complex problems of mathematical chemistry. Practice furthers theory and theory aids practice when wedded in the new Soviet science.

Unco-ordinated detailed scientific investigation was made the rule of the past. Detailed investigations are the rule to-day, but they are co-ordinated, and lead to the profounder approach to the essential nature of individual phenomena. Facts are collected as vigorously as formerly, but always with a view to the formulation of new theoretical generalisations. These theories are of course submitted to rigid proof.

That is so, naturally, with scientists everywhere; theory and practical proof are inseparable from modern science. But in the Soviet Union the association between theory and practice is closer and more unbreakable: it lessens the gap—so disastrous elsewhere—between discovery and application. Private interest of individuals which in the Western world not infrequently hinders immediate applications of new theories and discoveries—even if deliberate sabotage is not practiced—is never sufficient to hinder advance or benefit application in a land where the interests of the country as a whole is alone at stake.

This gives immediate and practical direction to scientific work and scientific discovery. It also increases popular knowledge of and interest in scientific achievement. The most abstract theories assume a new complexion when seen in relation to beneficent application. Contemporary physics in its attempts to understand the earth and its surface formulates profound theories which at once assume significance and awaken interest when applied for instance to procure fresh sources of crude oil and minerals. The discovery of oil in the Urals, like the discovery of potassium, is the direct result of fundamental theoretical conceptions and mathematical methods of modern geophysics and geochemistry and no time need be lost in coming to terms with private interests before work commenced.

This chapter has been devoted so far to organisation rather than to the achievements of Soviet science and rightly so. The foundations of a nation's science are always more important than its immediate achievements. With foundations well and truly laid to-day the peaks may be sought to-morrow. And it is just that extensive and intensive thought for foundations which, in the Soviet Union, is building up a whole people, led by their legislators and administrators, into the scientific attitude of mind which is the significant thing about Soviet science.

In the extension of higher education, in the range of new scientific institutes and activities, in the training and increase of scientific workers, in the lavish outlay of money and in the promotion of popular interest in science stimulated day by day with stories of scientific achievement—therein lies the hope for the future.

Not that present achievement is wanting. Fresh discoveries occur daily, not only theoretical triumphs, but these advances in productive power which find immediate employment in industry and immediate publicity in the Press. The discovery of potassium salts and oil in the Urals are not isolated triumphs. Other lines of progress which can be readily appreciated by average laymen constantly open up.

In the realm of physics, for instance, Professor Joffe's recent work promises provision of materials for buildings and machinery indefinitely lighter and stronger than those in present use. Seeking the cause of low mechanical strength of materials which should, theoretically be immeasurably stronger than they are, he finds it in microscopic surface faults and cracks. Solid bodies in reality consist of closely packed collections of atoms. Shown by X-ray analysis to be crystalline their strength can be calculated. They should be several times stronger than they are and Soviet scientists are hot on the scent of the weakness. The cause discovered and removed, architects and engineers would be supplied with revolutionary materials; structures would grow cheaper, lighter, stronger and might become indefinitely more graceful and elegant.

The weakness has already been traced to surface fracture. Hot water, for instance, affecting the surface of rock salt on immersion, increases its strength twenty-fold. Glass with suitable surface treatment likewise increases tenfold in strength.

Another achievement of Joffe and his school arises from his investigations of the electrical properties of different substances.

An enormous amount of solar energy reaches the earth. Plants absorb only 1 per cent of it. They are inefficient as means to harness energy. "Every square metre," says Joffe "of surface of the earth placed perpendicular to the sun's rays receives about one kilowatt of energy." How shall we harness it?

If we are nearer the answer to-day it is largely through Joffe's work. An experiment at the end of last century showed that light shining on a zinc plate produced an electric current in a nearby wire net. Einstein, by means of the photo-cell, enabled light to be turned into electric current. Very feeble as a power unit, it serves excellently as an "eye," guiding ships in fogs and aeroplanes to their targets. But why not power? Why a loss of power so great that Joffe likens it to "pouring water into a sieve; only a few drops remain"?

Joffe still pioneers here. Led by theoretical reasoning he has been able to select new materials better fitted than others to change light energy into electrical energy. Better solid photo-cells are the result. Used in "talkie" cinemas they give greater clarity of sound. Used in mines they give instantaneous warnings of the presence of dangerous gases: the sensitive photo-cell detecting the minute rise in temperature of a heated platinum wire when the smallest fragments of combustible matter impinge upon it.

A further interesting application is the sensitive needle-shaped photo-cell to test the difference of temperature between a plant and its surrounding atmosphere and ring an alarm when the danger point is reached.

Of Kapitza's probing work into the nature of matter through extremely low temperatures with their slowing down of motion of the electrons, I have already written on page 55. It will be seen that he and Joffe and other physicists are constantly concerned with long range work, work which shows no immediate utilitarian results. They continued this work even throughout the war, and received government encouragement and aid in doing so.

The marked encouragement again shown by the Soviet authorities for pure mathematics and astronomy, especially of those branches which promise no obvious application, point in the same direction. Fundamental research receives as much support as applied science. The famous observatories at Pulkovo near Leningrad and in the Crimea are to be rebuilt without delay.

Similarly Russia probes deep into the earth and soars high into the air. Professor Krayov makes borings twenty miles deep and now deeper still to investigate the earth's compositions; other scientists, with delicate electrical technique, peer into the sky far beyond the eight miles reached by super-searchlights.

S. I. Vavilov, President of the Academy of Sciences, when in July 1946 he outlined the present Five-Year Plan, said, "In 1946, the age of atomic energy, radar, rocket propulsion and tele-mechanics, it is hardly necessary to explain the emphasis laid on physics in our five-year programme. Soviet scientists will continue their investigations into the structure of matter, the problem of elementary particles, the structure of atomic nucleus, crystals and fluids. Special attention would be paid to atomic energy and cosmic rays."

He also spoke of attention to be concentrated on the outstanding present-day problems of the stability of motion and the theory of oscillation.

Of immediate practical importance is the work on soil structure with a view to change and regulation.

Appropriate physical treatment for example can turn sand into soil, or an admixture of a gum, prepared from the turf and the waste products of paper and artificial silk, can make soil out of clay.

Colours, it is found, have a marked effect on heat radiation of soil, white material reducing heat absorption and moisture evaporation in hot Central Asia, and soil blackened with an emulsion of bitumen adding 11 per cent to the yield of the cold soil of Leningrad through eliminating heat absorption. Russia pioneers in soil science. Other countries copy her methods and her nomenclature. Russian engineers also experiment on high-pressure boilers. Two Loeffler boilers providing super-heated steam at a temperature of 500 degrees—not much below red heat—and at a pressure of three-quarters of a ton per square inch, give 60,000 kilowatts of power to a neighbouring turbine, which, several feet in length, is only two feet in diameter looking ludicrously small for so great a power output.

Russian geologists and engineers spurred on by wartime shortage of fuel, saved the war industry of Saratov on the Volga, when its coal supplies ceased through German bombing, by tapping subterranean gases at the village of Yelshanka. They brought the gas through a quickly improvised pipe line ten miles to Saratov. To-day an abundant flow of gas from the same almost unlimited source traverses ninety rivers and numerous lakes in large diameter pipes to light and heat Moscow. Other lines are planned to supply Stalingrad from the same source.

Chemistry and biology also have marked achievements to show.

Talmud, the chemist, makes interesting experiments on the hardening effects of layers of absorbed substances on sand. He foresees important applications of this process for the strengthening of materials for house-building and for foundations of roads by modifying the properties of soil. He anticipates the preparation of liquids, which when sprayed will harden earth, a matter of vital importance to Russia where lack of road-building materials constitutes a grave problem.

Professor Vavilov, President of the Lenin Academy of Agricultural Science has directive control of a staff of 18,000 research workers, seeking to examine, modify and extend the plant resources of the Soviet Union, and of the world as they get access to plant materials for experimentation.

All plants of the world are to be examined. Three hundred traveling botanists will have, in ten years' time, made a collection of 300,000 plants, including thirty species of wild potatoes from South America. Soviet scientists note that of the 700-800 plants of industrial importance, 150 occur in China, other countries contributing various and lesser quantities. Persia, for instance, though small contributes eighty varieties, and is wonderfully rich in wild species akin to domesticated trees suggesting the physical backgrounds of the story of the Garden of Eden.

By reasonable deduction the origin of any particular species is indicated by the number of varieties growing in the neighbourhood. If this is true, then soft wheat, rice, broad beans, and apricots come from South-West Asia; oats, barley, soya from South-East Asia. Onions, peach, olive and figs come from the Mediterranean area. Hard wheat from Abyssinia, and the sunflower from South America and Mexico.

Wheats vary in their properties. Wheat from 3,000 feet up in the Transcaucasus is highly resistant to rust and mildew. Wheat from Abyssinia is early in ripening. Resistant wheats also occur in Syria and Palestine. Dutch and Scandinavian wheats are high yielding, with large grain, good storks, but late in ripening and of poor quality. Scientists seek to produce new types by selection and cross-breeding, trying to combine the early maturing together with the high yield and the rust resisting properties of the various wheats.

Let this selection from a large number of published statements of British scientists visiting post-war Russia conclude this chapter. Professor E. D. Adrian of Cambridge says: "In years to come the U.S.S.R. with its large number of trained physiologists will have an output of research exceeding anything in Europe." Dr. Julian Huxley says: "The U.S.S.R. is taking its place as one of the foremost countries in biological research." He anticipates that it will soon be leading the world in some fields. Professor C. N. Hinshelwood of Oxford says: "Perhaps the strongest (impression) is that of a numerous and enthusiastic community of scientific workers, led by the most eminent scholars of the country, housed in excellent buildings, well equipped with all the facilities necessary for their work, and enjoying a nation-wide prestige which must be almost unprecedented in the history of learning."

4. LABOUR IN PLANNED COMMUNITY

T H E organisation of Soviet labour is the task of the Soviet Trade Unions with their enormous aggregate membership.

Until late in 1946, the Chairman of the Central Trade Union Council was Nicolai Schvernik, short, thickset, with firm, determined but not unkindly face, whom I met personally in Russia. I had met him before, in London first, when he had accompanied the Russian trade union delegates on their visit to meet English trade unionists. I had met him again at receptions in Moscow. He received me on a special visit at the Kremlin.

Like Stalin, Schvernik, at that time President of the trade unions, now President of the U.S.S.R. greets his guests with cordial simplicity, neither effusive nor offhand. There is nothing either overbearing or self-conscious in his manner, and he gave his guest no hint that as Number One Secretary of the All-Union Central Council of Trade Unions, whose membership on the eve of war was twenty-five and a half million workers belonging to 191 unions, he was the administrative head of one of the world's greatest corporations.

A trade union movement of such vast proportions, organised on an industrial and not a craft basis could be a powerful weapon in fighting; a strike called out by such a union would paralyse the whole of industry.

Yet, there are no strikes.

Why?

Are strikes illegal? In peace-time certainly not. No anti-strike law stands on the Statute Book. Why then no veiled or open warfare as in other lands? Precisely because there is no combatant to fight and no point in striking. Differences and hot tussles there may be to settle this point or that of administration or organisation, but fundamental warfare is absent because there is no enemy to fight.

In capitalist industry elements of clash are always present because two divergent interests are always present. In capitalist industry labour is a cost, a charge on industry. And since the price of a commodity depends on cost of production, costs must be kept low to yield competitive prices. Hence the perpetual incentive to keep wages low.

But the worker desires a rising standard of living, which means a rise in the cost of labour. Hence strife. New processes cheapen production, the owner desires the benefit in profits; the worker in higher wages. They fight. When tension reaches breaking point we get the strike or the lock-out.

In the Soviet Union it is radically different. There is no owner seeking profit over against worker drawing wages and seeking higher living standards. The men who draw the wages are the part owners. You do not fight against yourself; you do not strike against yourself. You fight against administrative inefficiency or bureaucratic tendency or personal difficulty. There is no fundamental clash of interest.

It might otherwise be asked why there is a trade union at all. The answer is simple. Because even when industry is owned by the people there are questions of organisation to be solved and adaptations to be made and the workers have an interest in the body which makes them. Wage rates need settling, skill must be classified and wage rates determined. Houses, conditions, health, and safety need protecting if the workers are to be maintained at high efficiency. Social insurance and sick benefits need fixing and administering.

Zest needs cultivating in work and cultural development outside of work. For all these things the trade union exists. And the State not only recognises the right of the trade union to engage in these types of activity, but gives positive encouragement in their fulfilment: Article 126 reads:

"In conformity with the interests of the working people, and in order to develop the organisational initiative and political activity of the masses of the people, citizens of the U.S.S.R. are ensured the right to unite in public organisations—trade unions, co-operative associations, youth organisations, sport and defence organisations, cultural, technical and scientific societies."

That is a real charter of democracy and the trade union gives it substantial embodiment. The vast membership of the trade union is more than any mere book membership. Members attend meetings and share in elections: even amidst the rigours of war 78 per cent of all union members voted at local elections of officers. And more than five million union members—one in five—serve in one capacity or another on a wide variety of Committees.

The organisation of the Soviet Trade Unions is extremely simple in theory. As producers each man or woman of any nationality can become a member of a trade union, which embraces, not his craft, say as bricklayer or plumber, but the whole industrial unit in which he works either as bricklayer, plumber, clerk, carpenter or office cleaner.

In the Soviet Union every reasonably sized State farm or factory is a small, central settlement with its own schools, nurseries, public kitchens, hospitals, clubs, and even theatres—planned, built, staffed and administered by the workers themselves in their capacity as trade union members.

The vast majority of workers—twenty-six million—are enrolled in 164 Soviet Trade Unions; any worker save those who have authority to engage or dismiss members are eligible. Each union is as wide as the Soviet Union itself. No local union exists, only local branches. Regional divisions exist in some of the largest industries such as coal mining or steel on account of the vast extent of territory: three steel unions for instance organise the steel workers in the south, eastern and western areas respectively.

In every establishment all groups on a common job organise themselves in brigades. They meet periodically for discussion of trade union matters and elect officers and delegates to the factory committees twice yearly. Every two years elections are held for the all-Union Congress of each trade union. This Congress, meeting in Moscow, decides general policy and elects a standing committee for everyday administration.

In the All-Union Congress of *all* unions, which meets bi-annually, each union is represented according to size, in 1937 one to every 15,000. Composed of 2,000 delegates, the All-Union Congress of all unions is the supreme assembly of all trade unions. It appoints its own executive committee and determines the broad lines of trade union policy and advance.

The delegates carry information and recommendations on the upward stream to the All-Union Congress and through it to the All-Union Congress of all unions. This All-Union Congress, through its All-Union Central Council of Trade Unions, originates the downward stream of regulations and suggestions to the central committee of each union and through them finally to the factory or office committees. It concerns itself with directions as to hygiene in workshops, with cultural activities and insurance, but primarily with collective agreements.

5 . PLANNED DISTRIBUTION

WHEN the people own land, minerals, water, timber, means of production and means of transport, two major problems still confront them.

First the problem of production. What to make: in what order, in what proportion, in what bulk and where best sited to avoid costly transport. Secondly the problem of distribution, of trading the things made. The one is the problem of field and factory: the problem of supplanting a profit-making industry. The other, the problem of the shop, of supplanting a profit-making trading. The latter proved to be the harder task.

*   *   *   *   *

In early days the problem was solved by excessive and inelastic centralisation. It was a makeshift method and unsuited to normal times, though essential in the early emergencies when need for food was urgent and primary. At the outset the State seized all food and delivered it for distribution, mainly through the co-operative stores, many of which were already in existence, having originated when, in order to avoid excessive traders' profits, individuals had locally banded themselves together to buy goods in bulk and deliver them at cost price to each member. Though essential at first this State centralisation was cumbersome and rigid and beyond the immediate, need for food, inefficient.

A safe, flexible, efficient mode of collective trading was sought, and, whilst being elaborated, new rein was given temporarily to the private trader who entered the field with alacrity and captured 93 per cent of the retail trade in towns and 80 per cent in the country. The co-operatives sold cheaper; their organisation, however, was inadequate. The co-operatives failed to meet the need of the market. Trade is an art and must be learned.

     *   *   *   *   *

The engineers of the new Socialism understood, however, that trading was crucial, stating in momentous words that "never has the co-operative movement had such vast and decisive importance as under the present conditions and particularly in a country like ours, with an enormous number of petty peasant farms which can be led to Socialism in no other way than through collective forms of organisation, i.e., through consumer and produce co-operative." The Government therefore threw its whole weight behind the co-operatives. Socialism itself was at stake.

Happily, co-operative stores were no new thing in Russia. As far back in 1864, only twenty years after the Rochdale pioneers, a group of miners at Kynovsky in the Urals had joined together to buy and distribute amongst themselves good tea at reasonable prices in Moscow. The movement spread. It received impetus after the Revolution of 1905-6, when the people of the countryside awoke and thence onwards constituted the bulk of the membership of the new Co-operative Societies. Membership, on the conclusion of World War I, had sprung from one and a half millions to five millions, growing by January 1918 to nine millions.

Two specialised forms of co-operatives, agricultural and producer, had hitherto grown up side by side. In agricultural co-operatives peasants who grew flax, potatoes and such like and who needed seeds and implements formed themselves into associations to market their produce and purchase their farming requirements.

In producer co-operatives workers of special handicrafts joined for collective marketing of their products. In 1924 the State began to make deliberate efforts to strengthen consumer co-operatives by price reduction, tax reliefs and improved services. By 1929 large-scale industry had become a substantial force. A determined effort was made to balance it by collective and co-operative agriculture, first in marketing their produce. Success was achieved in both spheres, and two years later private trade ceased. The State and the co-operatives held the field between them.

Wages in the meantime had risen, and with their rise came the demand for more foodstuffs and more manufactured goods. The State trading enterprises and the co-operatives adapted themselves to supply the demand. At first, and especially in urban areas, the State trading establishment outstripped the consumer co-operative in growth and extent. From 1930 to 1935 State stores and kiosks increased from 23,600 to 108,900; the consumers' co-operatives from 119,300 to 158,100 units.

The State gradually became, and now remains, the predominant trader in the towns. By 1937 it handled 95 per cent of retail trade with 27.9 per cent in the country, where consumer co-operatives predominated with 71.3 per cent. On 9th November, 1946, the Council of Ministers of the U.S.S.R. restored co-operative trading in the towns, and extended it to the countryside. Centrosoyus is empowered to purchase village surplus products with a view to selling them in the towns at State-fixed prices, with additional facilities enabling the co-operatives to extend their own manufacturing processes to supply both town and country with an increased range of consumer's goods. Supplied with raw material and relieved from certain taxes the target aimed at was 2,500 new producers co-operatives in 1947, producing this year, among other things, 500,000 beds, 4,000 tons of crockery, five million pairs of felt boots, twenty-three million pairs of socks and stockings and fifteen million pairs of leather footwear.

The first big job of the consumers' co-operatives was to improve rural trading facilities, and in 1936 it was given the countryside to look after and relieved of responsibility in the towns. By 1946, however, its responsibilities were again enlarged, as outlined above. The consumer co-operatives of the Soviet Union are to-day, with a membership of seventy-six million, the largest co-operative movement of the world, with a carefully co-ordinated structure rising up from the broad basis of *selpo*, as the village co-operatives are called, to the co-ordination of these in district consumer co-operative unions, and thence to the regional or territorial union, all of which are in turn united in one central body called Centrosoyus, the Central Union of Consumer Co-operative Societies of the U.S.S.R. and the R.S.F.S.R. Regional and territorial unions of the Russian Federation are directly represented in Centrosoyus, those of the Republics through representatives of the Republican Consumers Co-operative Movement. Selpo, the local rural consumer society, is controlled by the General Membership meeting, assembled not less than once in three months. If it includes a group of scattered villages it is controlled by delegates elected for one year.

This General Membership Meeting, which has for its Executive

Committee a Board of Management of five to seven members, endorses by-laws, elects boards and auditing committee, admits members, adopts business plans, distributes profits, etc. The meetings, which cannot legally be held without the attendance of 66 per cent of the members, are lively and well attended: 87.7 per cent of all members attended the 18,695 rural consumers' societies in 1944. Membership is open to both sexes and all ages from sixteen years upwards, with an entrance fee of three roubles and a share-holding of not less than fifty roubles. With Selpo and its town equivalent, as the basis of the pyramid, Centrosoyus at the apex leads and plans for the entire system of consumer co-operatives, purchasing agricultural produce, organising production of consumer goods, bread baking, and public catering, distribution of capital investments, placing of orders, or planning for distribution of credit.

The shops of the village co-operatives bristle with goods—bread, meat, fish, game, fats, eggs, tea, coffee, wine, beer, tinned goods, woollen goods, boots and clothes, stationery and window glass, iron-mongery—with a range and variety of commodities which increases year by year and are received in bulk from the district co-operative unions, which buy them from the regional and Republican unions.

The consumer co-operatives purchase and sell to their members town-made goods. They also purchase agricultural produce for the peasants and for the towns, thus forming links between country and town. They process and preserve foods. They dry and salt vegetables and fruits. They undertake baking and bread-making and free the housewife for productive tasks and social activities.

Profits at the year's end are divided and distributed by decision of the General Membership Meeting, between payment of dividends, provision of club room, playgrounds, training of personnel and financing the bakehouse and other occupations. The balance, which must exceed 50 per cent, is added to basic capital. The cultural and educational side of consumer co-operative activities is large and increasing.

As may readily be supposed, the efficient control of so vast, so rapidly growing and so varied an organisation demands highly skilled personnel. This need is recognised, and provided for, as chief among the many educational activities of the consumer co-operatives.

1. Institutes are run by the co-operatives where the high personnel are trained. These offer a four-year course in either (a) economics and accountancy; (b) economics and trade, including planning and (c) department of trade with specialist training in agricultural and manufactured commodities. All departments offer general courses in political economy, higher mathematics, statistics,

L

history, book-keeping and Soviet trade organisation. Each department teaches the specialities of its own departmental knowledge. Candidates must have graduated with the full secondary school course of education up to seventeen years of age.

2. Less advanced courses, for pupils of fourteen to fifteen years, are the vocational high schools, forty-four in number, with a total membership of 9,700 and with a three years' course. These train book-keepers, commodity experts, etc.

3. Finally the seventy-one co-operative business schools, with a student body of 5,090 members, open to students of thirteen and fourteen with a six-year education behind them. In addition there are correspondence courses.

This work of educational activity is administered from Centresoyus and financed by a fund built up from village and district contributions after retaining at least 20 per cent for its own district educational activities.

These latter general cultural activities though the co-operatives share in them are, however, first and foremost the responsibility of the trade unions.

6. PROGRESSIVE DEMOCRATISATION AND THE PLAN: ELECTIONS

THE Soviet plan is not only the authorities' plan. It is the people's plan. The plan indeed is useless without its firm basis of popular support. And that support exists. The plan depends on its cellular strength, that is on the existence of an immense number of local centres of thought and activity which feel they have a direct share in the formulation and execution of the plan.

Russia's cellular organisation stood the ultimate test of war. War indeed revealed the popular or cellular support of the plan. War produced the partisan, underlining the fact that the whole economic set-up lived on the goodwill of the people, and could work on if only a few cells were left. And the moment the war ceased the fuller organisation returned, through the determination and knowledge of the people themselves, not waiting for direction from above. This cellular strength, this people's support of the plan, this popular drive in its execution demands and deserves the closest study. For with it is bound up Russia's conception of democracy.

Soviet authorities refer to the process of planning as the progressive democratisation of their society. It is this consciousness of participation in the plan and its execution which makes the rank and file feel as they never felt before, that they possess actual power to mould their own future. Popular flow of power upwards which is revealed in the people's share in making the plan, is one of the most characteristic features of Soviet life, registering the radical difference between Communism and Fascism, where authority is only exercised downwards.

The widening freedom of the people is seen in the extension of power to local elected authorities, to trade unions in the factories, to collective farm committees in country districts.

The elected local authority always answerable to the rank and file, forms the real source of Soviet power in peace and in war. This is the cell. In war it maintained the organisation, even when by invasion the locality was severed from the centre; in returning days of peace it renews its relation to the centre, which comes increasingly under its influence. The cells inject ever recurrent life into the formulation and operation of the plan. The tens of thousands of small committees, or local councils, enjoying wide powers over their own affairs are also the local executive body busy to-day rebuilding villages and roads, re-equipping workshops, factories, schools or churches. The central organisation attends to the rehabilitation of capital machinery.

The elected representatives of the people in Russia in this way exercise a control over the administrative heads entirely unknown here. They exercise it in the workshops and the field; in the administration of local affairs, and increasingly in the administration of regional and central affairs. If it has far yet to go, it is well on the road. Already close observers on the spot point out that in March of 1946 the Supreme Soviet itself was characterised by an altogether franker and more audacious atmosphere.

This process is precisely what Lenin projected when he willed that every cook in the land should know how to govern the land. To encourage people in the exercise of their local power and local responsibility has been a ruling objective of Soviet authority from the first.

The primary problem indeed which Lenin and the builders of the new Soviet order had set for solution had been precisely this: How were the common man and the common woman, all men and all women, to be drawn into the daily task of government as citizens, as producers and as consumers? That task was tackled as follows: Citizens, of either sex, over the age of eighteen were empowered to elect members of the Village Council, or Soviet as the Russians call it. Every village had its own elected Council, one member for each hundred inhabitants. This is the primary organ for government, empowered on the one hand, to carry out governmental instructions from above, even to the setting up of its own courts for local administration and justice.

The Village Council keeps an eye on the efficient working of collective farms, industrial enterprises, and consumers co-operatives. It inspects and audits the accounts of local concerns, instituting where necessary fines and penalties for non-observance of law or plan. In its area it is omnicompetent. Beyond its area it is urged to understand and gear itself to the larger affairs of district, province, republic, and finally to the Soviet Union as a whole and the international world beyond it.

On the other hand it is also empowered and encouraged to send forward recommendations on any matters which concerns it to the higher authorities. This is a principle of supreme importance. For the existence and power of this local council, coupled with the fact that every citizen in town or country has a voice in the direct election of representatives to the district parliament and also to the parliament of nations, provides the foundation of really democratic forms of government. A flow of power upwards accompanies the flow of authority downwards. The elected body at the top, which is not only kept informed of the wishes of the majority at the bottom, but can be withdrawn if it fails to execute those wishes, is thus enabled to make rules and recommendations which are sent down again through each elected body to the village Soviet itself. The various stages of this hierarchy of legislative and administrative bodies, the village or the town Soviets, the districts, the provinces, are all elected directly by the people themselves.

The same principle operates alike in the matter of the plan, which is discussed from top to bottom, and from bottom to top. A provisional plan and the place occupied in it by each industry, village or individual, and based on information already in hand, is circulated for discussion and observation. These observations pass on their upward course and in turn generate power from below; power showing itself in the upward movement of knowledge of local circumstances and needs, and power generated in the general understanding of and interest in the finally formulated and authorised plan. Each individual in the community feels that he is assisting in making the plan and is therefore vitally concerned with its proper execution.

Precisely, the same principle, more or less fully developed and operative, is at work in the trade union, in the collective farm, in the co-operatives and in the Communist Party. A surge of vitality from below, free expression of opinion, formulation of desire; expression of will. Furthermore, and this point will be developed in its appropriate place, the same principle is at work throughout the whole union and among the more than 150 nations or groups throughout the Soviet territory. An Uzbek, for instance, working in a cotton mill in Tashkent, receives careful explanation of the overall plan and of his industry's part in it. He develops a sense of association in nation-wide constructive endeavour.

It is upon this principle of the power of each member of the committee to share in the control of his destiny, together with the complete equality in the U.S.S.R. among minorities and between the sexes; on the absence of any kind of discrimination; on the economic and social rights and opportunities guaranteed to all Soviet citizens and on the absence of powerful monopolies of press, radio and movies, that the Soviet Government bases its claim to democracy.

The wide differences in the Russian electoral system from our own demand close scrutiny. Theirs is a one-party system, ours a system of two parties or three. It is easy on first glance to assume suppression, to assume that freedom of expression is absent, and that the unanimity of a vote where nearly all go to the poll and where majorities run to upwards of 99 per cent are a fake.

It would be difficult, on the other hand, to suppose that this universal interest in the elections is a sham, that this mass attendance at the polls following weeks of mass meetings and vigorous discussions is all engineered from above and built on a mass-terrorism and dragooning. Talk to any intelligent Russian and you will soon discover an unshaken belief that the vote counts and that the possession of the vote represents real power to the voter. The thing needs examining closely and let us start with an examination of procedure. Candidates are nominated, not by parties but by organisations, of which a wide range exists. The Communist Party and the young Communists; any branch of any trade union; any sports or cultural society; any staff of a theatre or the union of writers; or by a specially convened statutory mass meeting of any large plant or factory or farm. Discussion takes place weeks before nomination day, and at various centres of activity, to ascertain which candidate could best serve the neighbourhood. A selection conference is then held of delegates from every possible nominating body in the division. Discussion ranges around the decisions as to which candidate would be the most acceptable to the greatest number of organisations. The candidate thus selected by show of hands becomes the candidate of the bloc composed of party and non-party and receives forthwith the support of all organisations.

Candidates come from every walk of life and their merits are freely discussed with full biographical details by the newspapers weeks before the election day. The Communist Party naturally possesses the greatest pull, though not infrequently important local bodies can and, for sufficient reasons, do reject the Party nominee. And it must be recollected that the Communist Party itself consists of the central core of all the organisations, voicing their special require-ments and commending them to the rest of the country.

One consideration of great importance must never be forgotten. It takes us straight to the heart of the whole problem of our differences in electoral method. The absence in the Soviet Union of groups of people with competing interests in any economic or social sense is something unknown to us here and difficult to appreciate. There are no rival classes in the Soviet Union. There is no demand therefore for political groups to represent major interests as here. Hence there is no quest for rival parties. That by no means rules out discussion, however, which is vigorous and often heated, but turns upon such questions as the best way to stimulate production and the best leader to augment it. The fundamentals of socialism are universally accepted as axiomatic, as little questioned as anti-septic surgery is questioned by doctors in England to-day. The interest aroused by discussion is the best proof of the democratic basis of Soviet rule. Sixty million copies of the draft Constitution of 1936 were asked for and provided in all the principal languages of the Union and suggested amendments amounted to 130,000—a plebiscite without parallel. A people which uses its opportunities of debate so thoroughly has the prime requisite for a working democracy. In this discussion of what should be done in the best interests of farm or factory ordinary men and women become in the fullest sense citizens.

The extent and depth of this interest is shown in the huge percen-tage of citizens who go to the poll on Victory day. As I said earlier, when so large a percentage attend the poll—it was 99.7 per cent on 10th February 1946—and when 99.18 per cent of those who went voted for the candidates selected, there must be some living reality behind an election where voting power is equal, where the ballot is secret and where election is direct.

The fact that occasionally more than 100 per cent of votes is recorded, is not as is sometimes suggested proof of a fake election; it is due to the fact that a visitor to that constituency on election day can carry his vote with him and in industrial areas an influx of workers frequently takes place.

Government of the people, for the people and *by the people* is the basis of the Soviet conception of democracy and undoubtedly the Soviet people believe that they possess a vital say in government and act on their belief.

For the election of the Soviet of the Union there are approximately equal constituencies of 300,000 inhabitants, covering the whole territory. Thus every 300,000 inhabitants of Moscow, and every 300,000 inhabitants of Uzbekistan, each have one Deputy in the Soviet of the Union. Three hundred thousand inhabitants means approximately 200,000 adult electors.

The Soviet of Nationalities, which ensures adequate representation of the smaller nationalities is elected on the basis of one Deputy from each Union Republic, of which there are sixteen; eleven Deputies from each autonomous Republic, autonomous Republic being a substantial grouping of national population entirely surrounded by Soviet territories and without a common frontier with non-Soviet States; five Deputies from each autonomous province, and one Deputy from each national region.

The Union Republics are:

> The Russian Soviet Federative Socialist Republic.
> The Ukrainian Soviet Socialist Republic.
> The Byelorussian Soviet Socialist Republic.
> The Azerbaijan Soviet Socialist Republic.
> The Georgian Soviet Socialist Republic.
> The Armenian Soviet Socialist Republic.
> The Turkmen Soviet Socialist Republic.
> The Uzbek Soviet Socialist Republic.
> The Tajik Soviet Socialist Republic.
> The Kazakh Soviet Socialist Republic.
> The Kirghiz Soviet Socialist Republic.
> The Karelo-Finnish Soviet Socialist Republic.
> The Moldavian Soviet Socialist Republic.
> The Lithuanian Soviet Socialist Republic.
> The Latvian Soviet Socialist Republic.
> The Estonian Soviet Socialist Republic.

Whereas on the basis of population the Russian Republic holds approximately half the seats in the Soviet of the Union, it only has the same representation as Armenia—which has only one-seventy-fifth of her population—in the Soviet of Nationalities.

7. TAXES, WAGES, SALARIES, INCOMES AND PRICES

WHENCE does Russia procure money to finance free education, free medical service and all the other free amenities which continually expand and constitute the progressive realisation of Communism: "to each according to his need?"

No question is more frequent than that in face of Russia's social achievements. Whence does Russia get the money? Education free. How is this paid for? Medical aid free with no contribution. How is this paid for? Theatre, opera and ballet available at prices no box office receipts can justify. Who makes up the difference? An army which smashes the German war machine. Whence came the money to equip and maintain it? Whence comes Russia's money for Russia's activities is a question of many ramifications. It demands an answer, and the answer is illuminating. The money does not come from personal income tax. Emphatically not, and that we can see at a glance when personal income tax figures are examined. In general, personal incomes are taxed but lightly. Limited income tax levied in certain particular cases for important social reasons which I shall make clear later, touches a comparatively small number and yields no more than 5.7 per cent of the total Soviet revenue. An income tax producing 5 or 6 per cent towards the Budget would be small help to England. It would be small help to Russia also.

The bulk of the revenue required to maintain defence, education, medical service and social amenities comes not from income tax but from the profits of industry collectively owned. Technically these profits are called "accumulation" in Russia. "Accumulation" means the difference between production costs and marketing price. We call it simply profit. This accumulation or these profits account for 91.9 per cent of the State Budget. Taxes and levies account for only 8.1 per cent.

The supreme problem of the Soviet financial system was how to fashion a reliable instrument for mobilising the accumulation or the profits of industry, and at the same time increase industrial and agricultural activity.

A word first on the past, and its history. Soviet Russia had inherited a bad and inefficient taxation system. Tsarist taxation was at fault socially: it was ineffective nationally. Socially bad because it laid the whole stress on indirect taxation—taxation on the essentials of life, mainly on food and drink. Indirect taxation placed the heaviest burden on peasant and industrial worker, men least able to bear it. Indirect taxation, together with customs levies, accounted for 87 per cent of Tsarist tax revenue in 1913: 59 per cent of this came from taxes on alcoholic drinks alone.

Nationally indirect taxation is bad because it is inflexible in operation. And while indirect taxes had practically reached their limit before World War I and could not be further expanded, direct taxation had been and remained so framed that the possessing classes, those most capable of paying, had escaped, and continued to escape, if not scot free, at least without serious inroads on their resources, leaving no appreciable margin to make up for the decreased revenue from the failing yield of direct taxation, let alone increasing the total sum available for war exigencies.

The fall in receipts from the decrease in consumption of alcoholic drinks alone was a disastrous blow at Tsarist Russia's financial stability; Tsarist Russia's war-time taxation failed to add a single rouble to Russia's coffers. Her only resource was to issue paper money, with consequent inflation, and rise in prices. The real estate of the land-lord remained intact, whilst the real income—that is, the purchasing power of income—of the working and professional classes fell disastrously. Production decreased, paper money increased. Fewer goods on the market demanded more money to claim them, prices rose.

Barter took the place of money. Money having ceased to represent anything real, people left money aside and began to exchange one real thing for another—eggs for knives, corn for soap. A sound and trusted currency was and is a prime essential for a civilised community. Money was reinstated by 1924, one of the means for its reinstatement being the compulsion upon the peasant to pay at any rate a part of his tax in money as well as in kind. A quest for money ensued, money had a new value. In this situation, a situation aggravated by civil war, the new Soviet Government began to lay the foundations of new modes of taxation, modes at once economically efficient and socially beneficial. One of these new modes, indeed, and the earliest to be applied, was of merely temporary significance. It had, however, an important political bearing. This new mode was income tax, tax on the personal revenue of the rich, who had hitherto escaped almost entirely from taxation—their claim upon essentials, like food, being a negligible proportion of their total income.

This extraordinary income tax, as it was called, was deliberately aimed against those who were accumulating large sums of money. It was essentially a war-time measure. It was a political tax deliberately aimed, not merely at producing a source of new revenue, but at crippling the power of the major opponent of the Soviet Society.

Outwardly there did not appear to be much change in taxation under the new Regime, direct taxes and indirect taxes remained. In reality, however, the change was radical. The centre of gravity was shifted, and shifted to the direct tax. The direct tax, always negligible in Tsarist days, when the holders of wealth escaped, became the most important item in the new Soviet Budget. It became the major source of all the money needed and spent in the Soviet Regime.

The wealth in Tsarist Russia was owned by private persons, and so was the wealth-producing machinery and land. In Soviet Russia the wealth-producing machinery and land is owned by the State and by the groups of workers in their collectives. For Soviet industry was of two orders. Some State owned, some owned by co-operatives, that is by groups of workers owning and working co-operatively. Thus the direct tax from which all these former owners of wealth escaped was now levied on Socialist industry, which did not and had no desire to escape. The direct tax took the form of a tax on all goods sold after the last stage of their production: goods sold over the counter as it were—an automobile in an automobile factory, shoes in shoe factories. This direct tax on finished products levied at the moment of sale, and known as the Turn-over Tax, is the most important of all Soviet taxes, and yields the bulk of all revenue.

Turn now to income and wages. And let me say at the outset that wages differ in amount in the Soviet Union. Inequalities exist. They are intentional. Wage inequality acts as incentive.

Nor is this any new thing. Sixteen years ago, as far back as 1931, Stalin pointed out that wage equalisation removes the prospect of advancement, the unskilled worker lacks incentive to acquire skill, where wages to skilled and unskilled workers are equalised. Wage inequalities, however, are based on a carefully thought-out plan and if in certain rare cases certain individuals can earn very high money in comparison with others they do so according to plan and not through accident or favour.

Neither does wage differentiation lead to class differentiation. Mr. Edward Crankshaw, with the Military Mission in the U.S.S.R. during the war years and writing on "Privilege in Russia" in the *New Statesman* in May 1946, rightly says: "There is no discernible crystallisation of new classes around these different income levels. There are inevitably broad classes, corresponding with the different types of labour—white collar labour, agricultural labour, artisan labour, unskilled labour, intellectual labour and revolutionary labour—as I suppose one might call professional communism. But these classes are not differentiated by the sharp income discrepancies which generally occur within them so that a Stakanovite foreman, an individual, may earn more than the manager of his factory."

Wage variation rewards workers whose productivity exceeds the average. They vary from industry to industry, from category to category and from place to place. In the linen textile industry for instance—one of the lowest rated of all—wages are scaled considerably below those in the heavy metal or oil extraction industries. If the index figure of the average earnings in the textile linen of 1938 is 100, that of heavy industry would be 161.

Wages again vary according to category. If 100 is the index for average earnings of artisans in the engineering industry, then a draughtsman's salary might be upwards of 350, a senior engineer upwards of 600, a director of big enterprise upwards of 2,000.

It is, however, very important to notice that money wages do not constitute the whole of a man's salary or income. The whole, that is, of his ability to win for himself and his family the power to command goods and services. Besides his basic monetary wage—most carefully fixed for each industry after prolonged and thorough discussion, in which he has his share—there is also his piecework earnings, or bonuses and his share in the distribution of profits. Few are content or need be content with the average day wage.

Yet again there is his share in what is called socialised income. His share, that is, in the things he receives without money payments. That fringe of commodities and services coming under the heading of "to each according to his need" which are already distributed free. It is a varied fringe of benefits, and an expanding fringe. Its expansion, depending on the worker's efforts, constitutes a further incentive to work and skill in every category. The greater the productivity of labour the more extensive becomes the social benefits a man receives as well as the higher wages which industry can afford to give him.

It is not possible here to give a complete catalogue of social income, but the chiefest amongst these items are sick benefit, old age pensions, medical service, maternity service, family allowances, education, also crèches and kindergartens, holiday camps for children and meals at canteens, all provided at lower than cost price. Rent also, which normally includes central heating, water and radio and is based upon income, not upon competitive price, and which never exceeds 10 per cent of the monetary value of his income.

A man's total income, to put it another way, as I pointed out in the previous chapter, consists of two parts, one of which—his wages—is at his own disposal, he can spend it as, where and when he chooses. The other part he cannot spend as he likes but it is spent for him as he ought to like, spent in providing for himself and his family the things all really need—defence from enemies, a share in all that doctor and hospital, school and college can give, together with pension and sick benefit.

The reward of a man's productivity comes to him thus in two parts, personal wages and social amenity. The growth of both, in which the individual has direct and immediate interest, increases as the productivity of industry expands. The desire for expansion in both forms of income, the wages which he receives according to the quantity and quality of his work and the social amenities which he shares

equally with others, acts as a powerful and ever-present spur to the
Soviet worker as he grows in knowledge and intelligence.

The inequality of wage payment is based upon the principle of
payment by results. Piecework is the mechanism by which it operates.

Piece-work in England has a bad record but is now accepted by
many of the trade unions and even demanded. Piece-work rates which
formerly were fixed by inciting the most skilled artisan to work
intensively for a short period, thus erecting a standard which overdrove
or undercut the less skilled and less strong and were consequently
hated as unsocial, are now fixed after collective agreement and welcomed. Whilst overdriving none, they provide an indispensable
incentive to increased production.

The fixing of the piece rates is a highly technical task and based
on many considerations. There is the skill of the workmen. Workers
are divided into eight classes. There are the conditions of work, some
shops are pleasant and of equable temperature, others by the nature
of their operation, as in cotton weaving, are hot and less pleasant.
All these and many more matters must be and are carefully weighed
before the rates are fixed.

In the fixing of wage rates the workers have a vital interest and an
operative share through their trade union. Changes in rates must be
approved by the trade unions before they are applied, and in each
shop a wages committee scrutinises carefully the way in which the administration applies the agreed scale.

Bonus of some kind is given to all workers, clerical and
administrative as well as machine operatives and craftsmen. In a
retail shop the bonus of those behind the counter will depend on skill
of goods display, on freedom from customers' complaints and the like;
others who work outside the shop on turn-over. On the railway there
is also an ingenious system whereby the great bulk of the workers
enjoy bonus or piece-work rewards in addition to the basic wage.

A curious but reasonable feature in Soviet piece-work is that excess
of output over the minimum required is rewarded progressively.
When the rate is exceeded by 10 per cent the worker receives double the
basic rate. If he exceeds it still further he gets treble the basic rate.
This is stimulating to the worker and reasonable because, "overheads"
remaining the same, more reward can be afforded. Reward on the
collective farm has already been described in the chapter on farming.

One root factor is fundamental. Every worker in the Soviet Union
is a shareholder and he knows it. He has a share in the profit and a
share in the management. In the management through his trade
union delegate. In the profit, either, as already explained, directly
in wage or indirectly in social service. Some of this social service

comes from the State, some from the enterprise. Two per cent of the estimated profit—for a profit is budgeted for—goes into what is called the Director's Fund. Fifty per cent of any surplus profit over and above the budgeted figure goes also into the Director's Fund, the remaining 50 per cent being used by the ministry for capital machinery and reduction of prices. The Director's Fund is spent for the worker in various forms of social amenity—crèches, libraries, canteens, etc.

Certain principles rule the present situation in late 1946. The desire for increased production is paramount. The need for acquisition of more ability as a means to increased production is akin to it. And so is the provision of incentive to earn more and learn more. War-time tax has gone. That helps. No special taxation saps desire to earn more as here. But while price for rationed and necessary goods is exceptionally low, varied items of diet are scarce and costly. And so are ordinary goods which make for amenity of life, gramophones, for instance, or radio sets.

These things provide the spur. The Government sells at high prices all suchlike consumable goods as remain after priority needs have been met. The difference between low wage and high wage may only mean the difference between a radio set or none. It may only mean the ability to enjoy one night a month at a costly café or none. And men are willing to work hard for these small luxuries, and no one begrudges them the reward. No one saves. No one needs to save.

Of course, the Government's ultimate aim is to provide all desirable goods at a uniform and low price and thus give incentive to production and raise the standard of life for all. It paves the way for the future and kills exorbitant prices—peasants will charge highly for food grown on their own allotments and sold on the open market—by itself entering into competition in the open or "commercial" shops where unrationed goods are sold. The drop in prices in the "commercial" shops is often phenomenal as goods become available. Clothing was reduced 40 per cent in one day. It is anticipated that by the end of 1947 rationing can safely cease.

8. PROPERTY AND OWNERSHIP

PROPERTY in England and in the Soviet Union and in any other civilised country is of two kinds, carefully distinguished in the U.S.S.R. and subject there to different laws. Less carefully distinguished here in popular imagination and in legal enactment.

I possess an Austin motorcar. It is my property. Its possession is assured by law. It is possible for me also to possess a share certificate in the company which makes Austin motorcars. My possession of that share would in England be permitted and assured by law. Car and share are both property. We do not disentangle them or set them under different legal categories. We are permitted equally to hold either or both.

And there we differ from the Soviet Union, which does distinguish them and sets them under different categories. The Soviet Union recognises the first right, but not the second. The Soviet Union recognises the right of all to own cars. It aims indeed at bringing cars, or anything else of personal use, within the range of all Soviet citizens. The possession of a share in a motor-producing company however, is impossible in the Soviet Union because such a share represents ownership of a major means of production and that is illegal.

The Soviet constitution divides all property into two major groups, means of production and means of consumption. The means of production are land and all that is beneath it, every natural deposit, mines, oil, subterranean gas, also waters and forests, factories and machinery, means of transport by rail, water or air, post, telegraph, telephones, shops and trading, banks and insurance institutions.

Personal property on the other hand, that is articles for personal use or personal consumption, are the things we need for subsistence and for ample living, houses to live in, food to eat, clothes to wear, furniture and cooking utensils for convenience, books and pictures, pianos, radio sets, bicycles, motorcars and suchlike things for the enlargement and enrichment of life.

All the major means of production in Russia are socialist or public property. They belong, together with their revenues, to the State, or to a co-operative enterprise or to a public organisation.

I say major, because it is possible for a peasant to own and use in perpetuity a small strip of land for productive purposes, or for a tinker to own his own workshop where he makes, mends or sells kettles: but neither the one nor the other may employ hired labour to help them. Such ownership therefore is negligible, it cannot in any significant way influence the economic life of the country as a whole. All other means of production and their revenue and products are public property. They are worked, not for the selfish benefit of any individual but for the public at large. This Socialist ownership is the foundation upon which the whole economic life of the Soviet society rests. It is this which facilitates and makes possible the planned economy. which is the outstanding contribution of Soviet Russia to the economic history of the world. For as each socialist enterprise is run for the benefit of society as a whole and as the plan is made for the same purpose, their joint aims coincide, they receive from one another mutual support. The management of each industrial and agricultural unit knows that they have an interest in the plan. They also feel that they have a share in making the plan, for their observations and advice are sought when the draft plan reaches them. They give support to a plan, therefore, which is framed in their interests and fits their own small unit into the working of the mighty whole, leaving nothing to chance or accident, ruling out speculation or hazard, ruling out also boom and slump whilst giving perpetual incentive to the workers.

In precisely the same way the workers in each unit know that the plan is made in their own interest, and that its smooth and progressive working assures for them an increase of wage, and a cheapening of consumable goods: that increased production per man employed gives greater facilities to all with no fear of unemployment to any.

Though the Soviet citizen does not own for his exclusive personal use or administrative right the individual share in the motorcar-producing works, he does share as a member of the Soviet community in the collective benefit which accrues through that or any other factory, a benefit which comes to him in a variety of ways, through public amenities in which all share. For the collective revenue provides an army to protect him, free medical attention for himself and his family, and free education for his children and many more facilities. Though he does not own this property directly in any exclusive way he owns it very substantially in an indirect but highly beneficial way. And he is well aware of the fact. For that reason he puts up with hardship when he is told to tighten his belt in order that much revenue must be reinvested in more capital machinery, in order that at a future time more consumable goods at a cheaper price may come to him and his children. He knows that the collective capital in which he shares is growing. Each citizen progressively understands—he is taught to understand—that though he has no outright ownership of any part of the productive machine he has an intimate share in its product itself. And he knows that when the collective machinery grows and its output grows, his share in the collective ownership grows. That gives the common worker incentive to work and secures his aid for the plan.

To put it in another way. Wealth comes to the Soviet citizen in two parts. The one part comes in his wage, which he can spend on the things or in the ways that he likes. The other part is spent for him on the things or services that he ought to like. His wage is at his sole disposal. His share in the collective revenue comes in defence from external enemies, in free medical attention and education, in sick pay and old age insurance and a hundred other things which are essential to him and spent for him as a parent spends wisely for a child. A proportion of this second part again is reinvested in fresh capital machinery for future enrichment.

Just as the head of a private factory in England, building up a new concern, stints himself and his family to augment his capital with promise of subsequent enlarged benefits in which all will share wins family agreement in the present duress, so the Soviet super-parent wins agreement of the Soviet citizens in their present duress in the interests of future abundance. For to him the Soviet State, the co-operative enterprise or collective farm is really an enlarged family concern.

The revenue from the revenue-producing property which the State owns is so ample that the Soviet society sets aside annually large sums to increase the productive capital of the country. The money thus allocated in the years between 1933 and 1937 doubled the capacity of industry, multiplied the aggregate number of tractors employed in agriculture nearly three times, and increased the carrying capacity of the railways two and a quarter times. This wise and far-sighted development of their capital resources has enabled the Soviet Union in a very short space of time to build up a first-class industry and a highly mechanised agriculture. It enabled the Soviet Union to out-produce and to smash the Hitler machine.

Of course, increase in revenue-producing capital means still further increase in national income and that again means an increase in the national standard of living. In 1913 the national income was 21,000 million roubles; in 1933 it was 48,500 million; in 1937, 105,000 million roubles. In 1950 it is to be 205,000 million roubles.

Wages rose during the same period. At the beginning of the First Five-Year Plan the average wage of an industrial worker was about 800 roubles per annum. By 1933 it rose to 1,513, by 1938 to 3,477. Amenities increased. In the period between 1933-37 the State built 20,500 more schools. The budget appropriation for health services rose during the same period from 900,000,000 roubles in 1933 to 6,927,000,000 roubles in 1937. Shopping expenditure of the citizen again grew in the same period from 61,300 million roubles in 1933 to 162,900 million in 1937. The Soviet citizen, in short, as part-owner of collective property finds himself possessor of a rapidly growing and prosperous concern which provides him, in return for increasingly effective work, with rising wages, falling prices and an augmentation of personal property over which he has absolute control.

Property of both kinds, socialist and personal, is jealously guarded by law. Article 131 of the Constitution reads: "It is the duty of every citizen of the Soviet Union to safeguard and strengthen public socialist property as the sacred and inviolable foundation of the Soviet system, as the source of the wealth and might of the country, as the source of the prosperous and cultured life of all the working people. . . ."

It is a mistake, it is well to note in passing, to think that all public property belongs to the State. It does not. Some belongs to co-operative organisations—collective farms, producer and consumer societies, trade unions or youth organisations. It is a kindred mistake to suppose that these organisations are able to do precisely as they choose: their activities are regulated, in accordance with the plan, for the benefit of the whole community, as well as for the benefit of their collective owners.

A collective farm is held in perpetual tenure and the law sets no limits to the amount of property a collective, either farm or co-operative, may accumulate. In 1938 the average income of such property was 70,000 roubles. In 8,623 cases the collective farm income ranged from 250,000 to 500,000 roubles: in 769 cases it exceeded one million roubles and the number of millionaire farms was rapidly rising in the period 1939-41.

Turning to personal property and its legal aspects we note that the rights of property are carefully safeguarded by law: "the owner has the right, within the limits established by law, of possessing, using and disposing of his property." He may sell, exchange or give away his property. He may use his property as he likes providing that use does not transgress law; for example, he may not use it for speculative purposes or derive unearned income from it. Certain obligations are attached to ownership: the owner of a house must keep it in repair, the owner of cattle must cover their insurance. In war or national emergency, the government may requisition personal property, with proper compensation. The same government right applies to distraint for debt or non-payment of taxes. Though even here restraint may not touch a definite minimum of household goods or a definite percentage of wages.

It might seem that the laws relating to personal property, whose outline is thus briefly stated, would be short and simple. They are not. There must be and is much needed definition and enactment for specific cases. Personal property may not be used, as we have already noted, for exploitation of others. Precious metals may only be sold to a State bank. Objects of art may not be destroyed or sold abroad. Owners of pedigree cattle may not slaughter them without permission from the veterinary authorities. Houses must be kept in repair. Personal property of any amount and description may be left to heirs, or as legacies. Inheritance tax is no longer levied, having been

M

abolished since 1942. Membership of a co-operative does not pass to heirs, only the refund of the share contribution.

Property may be bequeathed to persons of choice, save that it must not be willed away from legal heirs—and these cover a wide range, wife or husband, children, grandchildren, great grandchildren, parents, dependants, brothers or sisters—though within limits it may be distributed amongst them according to choice, with, however, no injury to the interests of minors. Bank deposits may be willed at pleasure and the same applies to all property if legal heirs are absent.

The law of inheritance provides in the first degree for the partner in marriage, the children, parents (if unable to earn their living) as well as maintenance for other dependants of a year or more standing. If no partner or child or dependant survives, the parents inherit. If none others of prior claim survive the estate passes to brothers or sisters. If no heirs survive and no will is made all property passes to the State.

BOOK VII

SOVIET FAMILY OF NATIONS

1. FROM COLONIES TO NATIONS

M Y final quest concerned the Soviet Nationalities and most of my time was spent in the Caucasus and Asia. The Soviet State had inherited a Colonial Empire of vast extent and dominated by principles embodied in the phrase "One Tsar, one religion, one language." An area of 8,700,000 square miles, embracing 177 distinct races or nationalities or tribes, speaking 125 different languages and professing forty different types of religion, had been forced by an iron autocracy into a single mould, which had thwarted industrial development and ironed out the cultural languages of all non-Russian people. How fared the nationalities under Soviet rule?

Lenin and his companions accepted the situation they had inherited and with great courage faced the task of reshaping the Russian Empire on lines never attempted before. On 15th November, 1917, the Soviet Government, immediately upon coming into power, issued over the signatures of Lenin as Premier and Stalin as Commissar of Nationalities "The Declaration of the Rights of the Peoples of Russia," which projected the equality and sovereignty of the nationalities, the right of separation, the abolition of religious privileges or restrictions and the free development of all national minorities. Moslem people, for example, were assured that their belief and customs and cultural institutions were inviolable and would be protected by the Soviets of the workers, soldiers and peasants' Deputies.

It was a politic move. The new Soviet Union needed manpower and material resources and the colonies provided both—Asian cotton, Ukrainian coal, Siberian timber. It also needed the aid of the nationalities in the task of smashing Tsarist autocracy.

That it was also a policy based on principle, however, is seen by the persistence of the same policy long after the Tsarist power was broken, and by its developed fruition to-day. "The crux of the national problem," said Stalin in 1921, "lies in the obligation to put an end to that backwardness (economical, political and cultural) of the nationalities which we have inherited from the past and to afford the backward peoples the opportunity of catching up with central P ussia politically, culturally and economically."

If the nationalities were backward it was because they never had the opportunity to be forward. The effort to give them that opportunity began forthwith and it took tangible concrete economic form. From the outset the plan provided that each national division should have products peculiar to their own climate and resources, it was also encouraged to develop an all-round economy with a balanced industry and agriculture.

Article 123 of the 1936 Constitution reads as follows: "Equality of rights of citizens of the U.S.S.R., irrespective of their nationality or race, in all spheres of economics, state, cultural, social and political life, is an indefeasible law. Any direct or indirect restrictions of the rights of, or conversely, any establishment of direct or indirect privileges for, citizens on account of their race or nationality, as well as any advocacy of racial or national exclusiveness or hatred and contempt is punishable by law."

By carefully elaborated machinery that policy has been persistently pursued, supplying the Soviet Union not only with vast material resources but also with that unity and solidarity which, upsetting all the calculations of Hitler, helped to secure his defeat. The peoples of the Soviet Union fought for victory as one whole. The Soviet colonial policy had in fact produced a family of nations.

Soviet principles of minority development ran on all fours with Soviet principles for the development of the Russian majority, subject in both cases to the overriding principle that all must be carried on according to socialist pattern—the pattern which meant public ownership and administration of material resources and industrial productive machinery, which abolished class distinction and forbade exploitation of labour for personal profit.

That was the Socialist content and it was invariable. The forms it took within those limitations, varied with national tastes, traditions, and cultures. It was multiform. "Socialist in content, nation in form" was the slogan, and granted its Socialist content, Lenin's principles for democratic administration in the nationalities were as follows:

(1) Political activity was to be secured for all. Not just the exercise of the vote every few years, but a direct share in day to day administrative business, drawing all, in their respective capacity as producers, consumers or citizens, into the daily task of governing.

(2) Cultural autonomy was the second principle of decolonisation, and this implied the use of the vernacular as the official language, preference for natives as teachers in schools and administrators in the government machine, in every grade of industrial production and management 50 per cent of the personnel must be natives. Negatively there must be no interference with religious services and rites. Positively natives were encouraged to publish newspapers and books in their

own language, to set up their own theatres and create a native mind familiar with modern knowledge and attitudes.

(3) Working-class supremacy was to be secured by means of socialised economy. Universal industrialism under the dominance of collectivism had a levelling effect; power was no longer concentrated in the hands of the few.

(4) The principle of national self-determination was also enunciated. Nations are sovereign and all nations are equal said Stalin: Nations have the right to federate or secede, provided they possess a common frontier with a non-Soviet State.

The same problem confronted the nationalities as had confronted Russia proper: "How was the common man to be drawn into the daily task of governing, as citizens, as producers and consumers." It was tackled in precisely the same way.

All citizens, over eighteen, as in Russia proper, have power to elect members of the village council, the primary organ of government, keeping an eye on the efficient working of collective farms, industrial enterprises and consumer's co-operatives, omnicompetent within its own area and encouraged to gear itself successively with district, province, republic and finally with the Soviet Union as a whole.

Each citizen, as in Russia, has a direct voice in electing representatives to the District Parliament and to the Parliament of Nations. There is also in each republic the same upward flow of power and downward flow of authority, keeping the elected body at the top well informed of the wishes of the majority at the bottom.

Each individual also is taken into consideration concerning his share in the plan. Plans of the several Republics are formulated in the manner already described in the chapter on Planning. The plan for the Republic interlocks with the greater plan for the Soviet Union as a whole, which takes full account of the potentialities and needs of the several Republican areas side by side with the needs of the whole.

Trade unions are constituted and operate precisely as in Russia. All workers on a common job, organised in brigades, meet for discussion and election of officers twice yearly, election for the All-Union Congress of each trade union taking place every two years. The All-Union Congress of each trade union meets in Moscow, as does the All-Union Congress of *all* unions. Politically, economically and culturally each constituent Republic is treated precisely as Russia proper is treated. Colonial dominance has given place to a true and vigorous form of national life, wedded likewise to a true and vigorous internationalism.

2 . A R M E N I A

(A) *Antiquities*

I T was cold and dull when we left Moscow on the long flight to
Stalingrad—our first refuelling stop; sunny and hot when we landed
at Rostov, and hotter still at Krasnodar where rising ground and hills
were first encountered. Sharp rocks and thickly-clad wooded hills
soon brought us to the Black Sea Riviera and we coasted past Sochi,
Gagri, and other watering-places to the eastern shores where the
plane rose steeply to cross the lofty Caucasian ranges.

By 2 o'clock we had crossed the Georgian border and the steep
seriations and wooded crags of the Caucasus gave place to widely
spaced and richly fertile valleys rolling smoothly up on either side to
steep crags and ridges. In one of these the pilot pointed down to a
village dominated by a castle perched high on a rock at the confluence
of valleys: "Stalin's home," he said. Ten minutes later we descended
to refuel at Tbilisi, the capital of Georgia.

We left Tbilisi at 4.15 p.m.

Forty minutes of green valleys, wooded hills and high mountains
brought us to a vast expanse of water ranging from deep blue towards
its centre to fascinating shades of green, when, clear as crystal, the
waters approached the shore. A curious white streak just about
the water-line ringed the lake as far as the eye could see.

It was Sevan, the highest large lake in the world, bigger than all
the Swiss lakes put together, the white streak of the strand being the
chalk deposit left by its receding waters, as the lake's level subsides,
the calculated result of Armenia's hydro-electric schemes.

Twelve minutes' further flight and Yerevan appears below, a
large town regularly built around a semicircle created by a basin in
the hills on the northern side and sloping away on the south across a
twenty-mile plain to the foot of Ararat, Europe's loftiest summit,
whose mighty, single snow-covered cone is reminiscent of Japan's
Fugiyama.

Armenia lay very low in 1917. Never large, its territory had been
reduced by its oppressors to the size of Belgium. Its population in
1939 was 722,000, its present population reaches one and a half million
people and rapidly increases. An essentially progressive people with
an ancient civilisation, it has persistently developed a vigorous and
individual life, whenever, under any tolerant rule, afforded the chance
to advance. Old irrigation tracks, entirely obliterated on the ground,
but rediscovered by aerial photography, bear witness to a former

prosperity: 2,740 years ago Armenian engineers planned and dug a forty-six mile canal.

Before the reign of Darius in 521 B.C., the present race of Armenians had arrived, a long-headed, dark-haired, narrow-faced people. Advanced in culture they sent their sons for education first to Greece and then later to Rome by whose armed forces, however, in 72 B.C. the Armenians suffered conquest.

Architectural remains and innumerable manuscripts still bear witness to Armenia's illustrious past. Most remarkable are the monuments we saw at Vagharchapat, in the sweltering heat of midsummer's day, driven there in a fine Zeiss car by an Armenian chauffeur who became our firm friend and was an excellent specimen of the lively Armenian. Dressed in red shirt with riding breeches and long, soft Russian boots up to his knees, he was gloriously picturesque. He had a happy humour, and the irresponsibility of a soldier newly returned from war. Once, swinging round a precipitous mountainside on a hairpin bend, he turned to speak to us who sat on the back seats. To our mild suggestion of impending peril he replied with an engaging smile: "I drove a tank at Stalingrad."

On the road we passed several companies of German prisoners excavating the new roadway which, linking up with a lofty viaduct, is planned to save the age-long climb up either side of the steep ravine of the Zanga river. Strong, bronzed, and stripped to the waist, the Germans looked decidedly well. There was neither undue fraternising nor any sign of hostility. Armenians, like the Russians, seem incapable of nursing hatred.

Mounting the far side of the ravine we passed a camel and an ass straining up the steep cobbled way and were soon amongst green vineyards and passing through the village of Parakar with its typical eastern mud-roofed, one-storied houses. By a tarmac road and over hump-backed bridges we reached the plain of Vagharchapat on whose fringe stands the ancient ruin of Zvartnotz.

We paused to examine a large vineyard farm, one of the branches of the Wine Trust of Ararat and made acquaintance with its managers and workers. The farm of 310 hectares is owned by 100 workers, a model farm, and planned as such to provide inspiration and impart approved methods to a wide range of other farms.

Midsummer noon in Armenia can be exceedingly hot and we were glad to rest awhile in the collective farm's cool clubhouse with its hall of 450 tip-up seats, and rather over-elaborated ornamentation. Cooler still were the wine cellars in which were barrelled annually, in casks made on the estate, some 200,000 hectolitres of choicest wines made from 1,200 tons of grapes.

In an inner cellar, perfectly plain and painted bluish white, stood a deal table covered with a neat cloth and adorned with a sprig of cherries in a flask. Sitting on seats carved out of barrels, which neatly supported the back, we began a fragrant meal of cool, white goat's milk cheese eaten with wheaten bread baked like pancakes, flat, moist and soft. Red French beans followed: cooked, steamed, dried and sprinkled with aniseed and other chopped green herbs. As Armenian pancake bread is torn not cut and as the beans are ladled out directly as needed onto the bread and eaten rolled up, as sausages are eaten in pastry here, one common spoon and one common dish sufficed for all. More formidable, however, was the wine tasting, and we were pressed to sample more than a dozen wines of choicest brands. Though a sip sufficed, each glass was filled to the brim, the remainder poured recklessly away into a common flask. The head man ate and drank with us, and others stood in groups around and listened to friendly banter and then to serious talk on politics and world affairs.

After careful study of this farm typical of the many farms constantly expanding in numbers and excellence as the fringe of irrigated water spreads further and further out, we drove to the ruins of Zvartnotz situated just on the edge of the irrigated fringe and there passed a lazy hour reclining on cushions, my head propped up at his own insistence on the faithful Stalingrader's tunic, lulled by the hum of innumerable insects, brushing away occasional ants and looking now through the hot desert haze at Ararat or again at the young Kolkhoz girls in long, white aprons climbing the trees in their hour's respite for the green sour apples which they enjoyed and I didn't.

We examined the stately ruins. Solitary, rising utterly alone from arid soil, it was hard to conjure up a picture of the gay scene enacted there long ago when sovereigns and princes of the Church and State thronged the Church and its adjacent halls. Built by Nersia Taietzi between A.D. 640 and 660 the Church remained intact till with the sway of power it fell into disuse in the tenth century. Of noble proportions and simple design, typical of much Armenian ecclesiastical architecture, the Church was circular within and polygonal without, one window and circular arch between each of its thirty-two angles. Above the circular ground floor rose a second circular clerestory of lesser diameter, supporting another clerestory of still smaller diameter, and itself crowned with a many-angled conical roof.

All now lay in ruins: huge slabs of masonry, some finely moulded, mingled with richly carved capitals scattered and piled on ground too parched even for weeds.

Such and such-like was the story of Armenia's illustrious past as told in stone. In manuscripts the story is more amply told.

One day by accident we stumbled across the tomb of Mesrop, the creator of Armenian script. After the long, hot service of Enthronement of the new Catholicos, for which I had specially visited Armenia, I sought my friends who were resting where the Zanga river flowed through a deep ravine in the low foothills. On the road thither, the car resting to cool an overheated engine, some sturdy young girls with heavy packs on their backs passed by. They saw and kissed my crucifix. Leaning over the noble old bridge which spanned the river was a handsome peasant boy. We spoke to him and I drew attention to a slender gold chain hanging about his neck beneath his loose-fitting unbuttoned shirt. He pulled the chain and showed a small medallion of the Virgin and Child.

We bathed where the village boys were wont to bathe in a shallow sluice above the mill, the Stalingrader keeping guard over the entrance. Returning to the car, we were surrounded by eager children, and after lively talk we found refuge in the garden of a well-to-do peasant proprietress, and sat with her and her family on a rug beneath a mulberry bush eating its golden fruit. Our hostess, nicely dressed, was adorned with lovely gold jewellery, her youngest son of three sitting silent by the basket, stolidly stuffing in berry after berry.

It seemed to be a Festal day and above us on the high plateau a crowd appeared as if anticipating some arrival. We had stumbled across the village which housed the tomb of Mesrop and it was Mesrop's anniversary day and the crowd were awaiting the arrival of the delegates come from the far ends of the earth for the Enthronement. The length of the proceedings had prevented their arrival and it was we who received the ovation instead, and, led through dense crowds by two old deacons in cassocks, we visited the crypt, and standing beside a small square stone lit up by a candle which a young girl had stuck in some carving above, it, paid homage to the Saint who gave Armenia an alphabet and a written script round about the year 412 B.C.

(B) *Cultural Life*

Yerevan can boast of good museums in which I spent many profitable hours. A morning in the Manuscript Museum was all too short to do justice to the rich storehouse of Armenia's literary past. Scientifically guarded in air-conditioned rooms are 20,000 MSS.— 9,000 of them large—with 200,000 supplementary papers and documents concerning the history of the East in general and Persia, with which Armenian history has many contacts, in particular.

Naturally the earlier MSS. dating from the beginning of the fifth century made the widest appeal. MSS. earlier than 412 A.D. were written in Greek. A philosophical MS. of the fifth century, one on mathematics from the seventh century, in which century also we find MSS. relating to chemistry and astronomy. The mathematical treatise was of especial interest, pre-dating Arabian influence, which did not penetrate till the twelfth century. Predating also any known mathematical MSS. in the rest of Europe, where they first occur in the twelfth century.

Medical treatises appear in the eleventh and twelfth centuries, amongst them a thesis on the structure of the eye and other organs. An eleventh century MS. gives a translation of Euclid, the thirteenth century a musical book and also a novel and short story. The renaissance began in Armenia two centuries earlier than in the rest of Europe, with studies in history and science.

An ivory backed book dates from the fifth century, a copy of a gospel appears in 887 A.D. Coloured and pictorial MSS. are especially interesting. One illustration of the fourteenth century shows a conflict between Persian troops on elephants and Armenians on horses.

The library of general literature is large, twice as large as before the revolution. During the war 450,000 volumes were taken to Mongolia for safety.

Armenia's literary remains are treated with reverential care; every page of MS. has been docketed by young Soviet scientists. The whole are to be housed in a magnificent new building, placed in a commanding position at the head of a stately avenue facing Ararat, and at the foot of the steep grassy slopes beyond the city's northern boundaries. The library, which will take four years to build, will be approached by a noble flight of steps, down each side of which waters will descend in great cascades.

(c) *Yerevan and Sevan: Civic Life, Agriculture, Industry*

The city of Yerevan itself, focusing and registering as it does the new agricultural and industrial prosperity of Armenia, is already a standing proof of Soviet national achievement. Mr. Mark Grigorian, the senior city architect, spent an afternoon with us, explaining with the aid of plans, as we drove in his car from point to point, the state in which he had found the city, the genesis of the early plans, the extent of the present achievement and the vision of the future. When he began his work, some twenty-two years ago, Yerevan was but a big village of 27,000 inhabitants, with mud-roofed houses, cobbled streets and primitive sanitation. Infant mortality reached shocking proportions.

The small electrical power plant of 1924, led to swift development of factories and public cultural buildings. Houses followed more tardily. Housing accommodation here, as everywhere in the rapidly expanding population of the Soviet Union, constitutes a vital and always present problem, aggravated in Yerevan by local opposition to the large, sanitary flats, splendidly situated in their own squares away from the traffic, provided for the people as alternatives to their present homes. Many in Armenia, as in England, prefer small self-contained units, especially those who live on sunny slopes with their own small gardens and mud-roofed, single-storied houses, and Mr. Grigorian admitted that mud roofs, cool in summer and warm in winter, have much to be said for them, especially where building space is ample.

But building space in the rapidly growing Yerevan is not ample, and the flats are proceeding.

Yerevan grows at astonishing pace, far outstripping all original estimates. New plans were needed and prepared by Tamarian, the academician, for a city of 150,000 persons. The population, however, already exceeds a quarter of a million, it still grows and further plans for a city of 450,000 persons constitutes the basis of present building operations.

It was these plans which we studied as, after winding up the hair-pin bends of the great trunk road which leads from the city to the highlands on the northern side, and standing on the summit of the hill and on the edge of the upper plain with cool winds sweeping around us, we viewed the panorama of the city. The wisdom of preserving these northern heights as open city parklands was obvious, the heights south-eastwards with equal propriety being devoted to homes and sanatoria for delicate children.

The trees of this parkland, already six years old, make, with the semi-circle of steep grassy slopes which now cover what were once unsightly mud banks, a notable show and spread like a green curtain along the whole northern wall of the city. Daily deluged through with water from the upper river, its grass keeps fresh and green in the hottest weather. Green slopes to the north and snowy Ararat to the south form a notable setting for any great city.

The plan, already partially executed, and not wholly interrupted by the war, provides for one central axis, which, with other main roads, utilises aesthetically to the full this superb setting.

Modelled on our own British theory of the green belt, industry is located, as I have already said, mainly to the south, away from the prevailing northern winds. The lower slopes of the hills which form the southern lip of the basin are pierced by a large tunnel which diverts the western traffic away from the heart of the city, and carries it, by a fine and recently completed stone viaduct, across the deep gorge of the Zanga river, making exit from the city swift and easy. Trees abound in the city and give cool shade from the blazing sun; they are planned to abound still more, part of that modern principle which encourages town invasion by country: parks and green spaces lie interspersed along the main axis and elsewhere throughout the city.

Yerevan bans skyscrapers. No great commercial units rising far up into the sky cause traffic congestion, overshadow the street and dwarf the cultural and social buildings. Yerevan's huge opera house already completed and in full and frequent use is, and will remain, a dominant feature of the city's profile. Yerevan's local tuffa stone—a pleasing warm ochre in colour, easy to work and durable—provides excellent building material ready to hand.

As industry congregates in the south, so professional life, universities, colleges, institutes, libraries, hospitals, congregate at the foot of the grassy slopes in the north, with great handsome flats for the professional workers.

Delegates for the election of the new Catholicos assembled on the day of our arrival and we joined them on an excursion to examine the beauties and engineering significance of Lake Sevan. Two or three of us ventured to swim in the cold clear water, from a spit of shingle left high and dry on the volcanic island in the north-west corner of the lake as the water of the lake recedes. A sun bath followed, then lunch of lake trout, salads of varied and scented herbs, fresh fruit and sweet preserves prepared by the hotel cook and staff who accompanied our numerous party and thoroughly enjoyed the day's outing. These large trout, two or three pounds in weight, cooked in rows on spits above an open-air fire of drift-wood lit on the high beach, made a feast for a king, with Armenian wines and toasts to round the banquet off.

After lunch we climbed up the steep flower-strewn meadows to the twelfth century church of an ancient monastery, a small, square building with typical pointed tower, disused now but kept in excellent repair. Sevan is Mecca to Armenians and men and women from many lands, who formed our party, could be seen reverently bearing away pressed flowers and pebbles as links in exile with the land they so passionately love.

Chugging back on the rough lake steamer our party, all Armenians, but each stamped with the hall-marks of the land of their exile, staged a concert, with a programme which varied from the yodelling of the countryside to the superb notes of a famous Parisian operatic tenor.

The beauty and romance of this vast highland lake, which we saw in brilliant sunshine and clear skies, and later in the afternoon in a deluge of rain as black thunder-clouds came rolling up from the mountains and burst overhead, in itself made a memorable day; my main interest, however, lay in the lake itself, in its practical aspect, in its extent and volume and high altitude, in its promise of illimitable hydro-electric power for the creation of a varied industrial life, in its irrigating power to bring into the glow of flowers and fruit an ever-increasing area of arid desert fifty miles away. I saw this huge lake as an agent in process of wise and scientific employment for release of the pent-up energies and cultural gifts of a virile race.

For Lake Sevan, one of the biggest mountain lakes in the world, lying 6,500 feet above sea level, about 300 feet deep and fed by twenty-six mountain streams, has immense potentialities. Its waters, issuing in the single river Zanga, flow down to Yerevan 3,000 feet lower than the lake and fifty miles away. The waters of the Zanga, already partially harnessed, are to carry a chain of hydro-electric stations, the earliest link being forged in 1924 by the small station in Yerevan, supplying the then existing capital with abundant light and power. The next link has been the construction of a larger station above Yerevan, which supplies power for an extensive aluminium plant already planned and soon to be in operation.

The present Five-Year Plan, however, proceeds in detail with the more efficient scheme visualised by Soviet engineers than the mere utilisation in successive leaps of the present Zanga river itself and consists, paradoxically enough, mainly of lowering the level and therefore the volume of the lake, with the provision of vastly greater power from its waters. The principle is simple. Lowering the level of a lake confined by mountain sides reduces the area of its surface without reducing the volume of its intake. That, in a hot climate. reduces the amount of evaporation and increases the volume at the outlet. Every gallon of evaporated water robs the turbine chain of power. Sevan receives 2,600 million cubic metres of water, only 5 per cent enters the Zanga river. Reduction of evaporation increases available power.

Hence the lake is to be drained in part. Its level will fall 100 feet, drainage is being effected by lowering the outlet of the present Zanga river to an equivalent depth. That has involved a new outlet tunnelled for six miles through the mountain side and joining the Zanga river at a lower level. The power station will operate within the mountain.

During the fifty years needed for the fall of the water power will increase continually, to be tapped in stages down the river towards Yerevan by eight hydro-electric stations, each fed by waters from successive turbine stations higher up the valley.

Another and obvious consequence of this vast saving of water is the extension of irrigation beyond Yerevan. The volume of the Zanga will increase year by year, and with it the surplus water available for irrigation. Three hundred thousand acres of new orchards, vineyards and cotton plantations are to arise in the Ararat valley.

High up above the ravine where the Zanga river swings round Yerevan, tower the gaunt, castellated walls of the headquarters of the Wine Trust of Ararat, which carries on under Soviet auspices an ancient industry, founded, you are locally assured, immediately after the flood by Noah, who descended from his Ark on Ararat. Huge cellars lead one ever downwards, seven stories deep, into the cool recesses of the rocks. Oval casks as big as small cottages built out of seasoned oak and containing thousands of gallons of wine stand in imposing ranks and battalions along the corridors, maturing the several vintages before they are bottled and sent to Moscow, Leningrad and every town and village of the Soviet Union. Brandies as well, distilled and bottled and kept ripe in special storage rooms and by special processes.

The picture of Ararat, the trade mark of the great Wine Trust, appearing on the bottles of the Trust, will always recall the dark, cold, ancient arched cellar, where, clad in overcoats after the blazing sunlight outside, we sat around a circular table making and receiving speeches and pressed to sample a dozen or a score of various wines and vintages. Other crops, besides the vine, wheat and cereals and especially fruit, give a balanced agriculture.

Passing one day through a village whose huge and highly prosperous collective farm was devoted entirely to fruit culture, peaches, pears, apricots, tomatoes . . . we were invited by a prosperous farmer into his orchard to eat our meal beneath his trees. He and his family brought out lovely eastern rugs, cushions, fruit, wine, herbs, cakes and coffee, and we had a feast where ripe cherries hung low on the branches above us.

Our host in a fine silk-embroidered shirt open at the neck and gathered in by a belt at the waist, his feet and legs hidden in soft black high Russian boots, was a splendid specimen of mankind. So were his wife and children. Munching great rolls of the pancake bread after covering them on the flat with white cheese and fresh-picked herbs, he dandled his naked son of eight or nine months on his knee. Then taking another child by the hand he led me around his own large garden under the trees to the precipitous side of the river to enjoy the view of Ararat lit up by the setting sun. It was superb. A still night and a cloudless, luminous sky.

The various fruits from this and other farms when harvested go to Yerevan, to be bottled and canned in the great factory which we visited, and where we were entertained to a feast guaranteed to test the stiffest digestions. Peas and beans, soft and tender as if gathered in early spring, excellent soups, pickles and ketchups. Bread fruits, well stuffed, served like cutlets and tasting like beefsteaks and onions came next, with tomato drinks and soups which comprise 25 per cent of output.

Cherries, white and red, pears, apricots, another primary product, blackberries from the "hedgehog trees," candied walnuts and other sweetmeats appeared in fascinating array together with raspberries, mulberries, rose-petals and I know not what besides: our hosts insisted that we should taste all and sent us from the feast with huge bales of jars and cans, which we distributed right and left in Moscow and finally amongst our friends in Prague on our homeward flight.

The manageress in charge of the factory was a fair-haired Ukrainian woman, one of those Russians who came years ago to instruct Armenian peasantry in the technique of bottling fruit and to set the pace for the new industry. The factory employs 800 persons, 90 per cent of whom are women, who produce 18 million bottles of fruit a year. Thus, with its vineyards and orchards, does the countryside of Armenia contribute to the industry of the town and together with a copper smelting works using local ore, an aluminium industry made possible by local electrical power, and synthetic rubber works utilising the local calcium carbide, build up a varied and balanced economy.

(D) *Cultural Life*

Industry and agriculture, created and regenerated by the Soviet Union, gave progressive provision for the means of life in Armenia and made possible the noble features of Yerevan its capital. But what of life itself, life, physical, cultural, spiritual? What of the quality of individual life, the final test of worth.

I began my examination as usual with the child, as one may observe him or her in street, school, playground, conservatory; on parade as it were, and also off guard.

In Yerevan I saw few children that could not be described as physically fit. Not so round and rosy as in northern climates, more swarthy, perhaps more lithe, certainly as fit. No diseased eyes as I saw in Bagdad, no signs of underfeeding, even after years of war. No child obviously ill-clad. Shepherd children in the high mountains were often ragged, but neither ill-fed nor lacking warmth of clothing.

I sought the older parts of the town, the quarter still retaining the more squalid homes. I was astonished to see that the children born and bred in these one-storied mud-roofed houses, consisting apparently of little beyond a single room, were obviously well nourished, many of them prettily dressed.

Pleasantly mannered, too. Once, for example, I encountered a lively group of children playing ball in the middle of a street, free from traffic, for it was Sunday. They paused in their play to look in curiosity at the passing strangers. They caught sight of the blue crown of my crucifix protruding from my girdle. To satisfy their curiosity I pulled forth the whole cross. The sunlight flashed on the diamonds. The children gave a gasp of admiration. Then the eldest lad stepped up to me, raised the cross gently in his hand and kissed the form of Christ. Each child followed suit. Finally with smiles and salutes they turned to their games again.

One of my new-found Armenian clerical friends questioned many children and young people privately, asking:

"Do you know anything of God?"

"Of course we do, and pray to Him always," was the reply, and some added, "and we go to church, too."

"How can that be so if you never hear of Him at school or have even been told by some that He does not exist?"

"Mother and father taught us at home," was the reply.

Visiting a large and typical girls' school also in one of the older areas we found 800 girls of all grades taught and controlled by a staff of forty teachers. Owing to war-time exigencies classes have grown in size; never did they reach the numbers of the school adjoining my Canterbury Deanery: they range from forty in the lower classes to a lesser number in the higher. Pupils per class are now planned for a rapid decrease.

End of term examinations were in process in one classroom as we passed and entering quietly we sat and watched the procedure. Each child received a list of questions from which to choose. A name was called and a child stepped out and facing the class delivered a short talk upon the subject chosen and then answered relevant questions, a method which develops courage and confidence. Speech was easy and ready and the replies in general prompt.

Glass cases around the walls contained interesting exhibits, and apparatus somewhat unusual in a girls' school. The physics class, for instance, possessed machinery of many types, with sectional models of steam engines and internal combustion motors, with electrical household appliances also of many kinds that girls as well as boys might become acquainted with their nature and use; as too, with theodolites and instruments of measurement in general.

Models and graphically realistic illustrations of the human body filled the cases and covered the walls of the girls' physiological class-room, with many an excellently executed section of bodily organs. The whole process of human growth from its earliest prenatal stages was illustrated by means of excellent models of the developing human embryo. And beside these cases stood the skeleton of a baby and another of a man. An endless selection of large-scale paintings, botanical, physiological, mechanical, hanging by hooks on movable rods were ready as needed for lecture demonstration. Only girls from the age of ten and upwards make use of the physiological room.

Of outstanding excellence is the musical training of Armenian children, and we spent four hours one evening, from 8 p.m. to 12 at the large but temporary conservatory, listening to a concert given, before a crowded and distinguished audience, by school children of Yerevan. Bishops, Archbishops and delegates of the Armenian Church sat in the front row and received demonstrations as they entered.

Before a friendly and obviously intelligent audience an astonishingly talented and artistic performance was given. Beginning with Beethoven's *Minuet* and Moussorgski's *Thinking* played sensitively by Seda Zakarian, a child of eight, it passed on to various recitals by child after child, in gradually increasing ages. An eleven-year-old boy—Henrik Genossian—from the fourth class of a ten-years' musical school played Berlioz' *Concerto part II* and Schubert's *Bee*. Zonke Sarksiom, twelve years old, played Vanyaski's *Romance* and Egiazarian's *Dance*.

One brilliant performance followed another, raising the audience to high enthusiasm, which culminated when a boy of twelve or thirteen who had played solo on the violin like a master, led as first violin an orchestra of twenty-four boys and girls of all ages from eight to fifteen with superb dash and exquisite rhythm through Vivaldi's *Concerto part I*. There was a roar of applause and spontaneous exclamations "that children's orchestra would take London, New York or Chicago by storm."

The second half of the programme after the juniors had retired, was marked with equal brilliance and concluded with a duet composed by two boys of seventeen and eighteen and played with characteristic energy and dash. Equally impressive was the spirit and appreciation of the large audience of everyday, workaday Yerevan life, educated to understand and appreciate this high form of artistic culture.

Among the delegates who thronged the small steamer on Yerevan my attention was arrested repeatedly by a short man with highly intellectual face and strongly marked mobile features. I met him several times subsequently. I observed him in the crowd which

N

thronged the sides of the processional path when the new Catholicos was consecrated. I saw him among the privileged few who kissed the hands of their newly elected and newly consecrated religious leader.

The man was Aroyan Aramanian, a "believer," a Shakespearean actor of high repute, with fame far beyond the borders of his native land and the chief agent in building up and fostering the new dramatic culture of Armenia. Meeting Aramanian one evening at the opera house I learned much of his own past and also of the development of the drama in Armenia. In his youth Aramanian had travelled widely. At an early age he had shown a passion for the stage. He came in contact with Sarah Bernhardt, and later joined her company in Brussels. Recognising his powers and seeing that he would go far in his art, the great actress had befriended him and he went at her advice for further study to Paris.

At the time when Henry Irving was at the height of his fame the young Aramanian made a journey to England to see him. Arriving at Dover and learning that Irving was ill, he returned at once. "Alas, in consequence," he said, "I never saw London."

At the outbreak of the revolution Aramanian was in Persia. Eager to return to his native land, he could do so only by travelling right around the world and entering from another quarter. He immediately began with Government aid to organise the first theatre in Armenia, or rather the first after very many centuries, for the theatrical history of Armenia began when *Euripedes* was played there 2,000 years ago.

Aramanian's whole family is devoted to the stage. His wife acts and of his five children two have achieved dramatic distinction. Too old now for more than occasional parts, Aramanian devotes himself to training youth and consolidating Armenian drama.

Aroyan Aramanian was bound in any event to achieve distinction. It was the revolution, however, which enabled him to carry art to such high distinction in Armenia itself. Art in the Soviet Union as we saw earlier is not a pursuit for a small and rather precious coterie. Art is for the people. It is State supported. An approved Russian or Armenian artist has no financial worry. And by approved, I do not mean one who has achieved a public name or fame. I mean approved by the heads of the artistic world as a competent craftsman, just as a doctor here is approved by the medical schools of his profession, and has his name admitted to the medical roll.

Art for the people, State-supported art, is enabling this artistic people to blossom forth anew, and contribute its own national contribution to world art in general. Rooted deeply in its own past and steeped in its own national tradition, it has much to give.

Armenian dramatic art is, as all dramatic art should be, part of a whole, which includes painting, drama, sculpture and literature. The peculiar problem before Armenia is perhaps how best to preserve and develop her natural sense of warmth and colour—particularly of colour—shown repeatedly throughout her long history.

A land that had no theatres now boasts of twenty-eight, eight of them in Yerevan, one being a mobile theatre planned to visit at least twice a year the various country settlements and collective farms of the neighbourhood. It is calculated that upwards of 1,400,000 spectators per annum see theatrical performances.

Each theatre has its own company, its own house, its own scenery, its own equipment. Of the twenty-eight theatres in Armenia, twenty-four are Armenian, two Russian, one Azerbaijan, and one Kurdish.

I saw, in company with heads of the Armenian Church, a play entitled *For Honour's Sake:* obviously an old morality play adapted for the present day. A rich man and his brother-in-law connived at robbing a nephew, whom they and the rich man's ne'er-do-well and drunken son and extravagant elder daughter dislike. A younger daughter has documents of inheritance entrusted to her by the nephew with whom she is in love, and which the rich man imagines had been destroyed. She pleads with her father and tells him of the documents. He is accused by conscience and prays but fails to act. His belief in God has no influence upon his action.

The elder son, who has hitherto held aloof, joins his sister in remonstrating with the father. This son is interested in industry and wants to build a factory, one of the many signs of readaptation. In a hot scene he says to his father: "I am not religious, I don't believe in God; but something within me tells me that your whole action and spirit is rotten and corrupt." Another touch of readaptation of an old play to the modern setting.

The father, though moved by his children's plea, never changes his design, and at length seizes the documents and flings them into an open stove. They burn.

The nephew enters and demands the documents. The daughter, to shield her father's honour, tells the assembled family that it was she who had burnt the documents. She then leaves the room. A shot rings out. She dies by her own hand in the passage. The father collapses and the play ends.

The futility of prayer and religion coupled with no corresponding action, the perfidy of the wealth-seekers, the new order as represented by the elder son with his deep moral sense and his earnest desire for construction, coupled with a disbelief in God which was only due to his father's futile belief: the tragic ending and its cause made it an interesting and illuminating play.

I attended also an excellent performance of national opera in the magnificent opera house which had been built just before the war for 31 million roubles, twenty-seven of them provided by the State and four by the city.

Four hundred workers run the opera at an annual cost of 4 million roubles, provided partly by the State and partly by box-office receipts. Theatre and opera in Yerevan develop without financial fear or risk. Five new theatres have been added even in the years of war, so great is belief in the cultural value of drama.

A flourishing philharmonic society deals not only with serious classical music, Russian, Armenian, and foreign, but also with lighter folk songs and dances. It is controlled by an ensemble of ninety artists, all chosen by the people. It is in process of creating its own symphony orchestra, employing native instruments as well as string quartettes.

The philharmonic gave us another memorable evening of folk songs and dances. Exquisite dances executed mainly with hands and arms. Northern races dance from the waist downwards: southern from the waist upwards. The grace and supple mobility of gesture of fingers and hands, arms, shoulders and head, must be seen to be understood, as must also the colour and form of Armenian dress both of men and women.

The men are handsome: the women lovely. The men—there were twenty of them—wear long cream-coloured coats falling below the knee and gathered in tightly at the waist. Big blue cuffs to the coat, with loose-fitting blue trousers tucked into close-fitting fawn-coloured boots with high uppers added one touch of colour—silk shirts, green at the neck and the sleeve, another. A dagger at the belt and fourteen cartridge cases, seven slanting inwards on one breast towards the waist facing a similar seven pointing inwards on the other breast, add the familiar cavalierish and fighting dash to the otherwise womanly graceful and colourful male attire, which matches admirably the light, lithe and almost womanly grace of their dance.

The women's dress defies description. Handsome, lovely; restrained in form, graceful in the long sweep of the skirt which falls down to the heels, smart in its well-tailored jacket over a looser blouse, in daring it mingles every contrasted colour with the abandon and faultlesss taste which makes a Persian miniature so charming. Heavy gold embroidery encrusting their small tight jackets, matches well the two or three-storied gold tiaras and golden earrings which adorn their heads. Veils partly hide and partly reveal their long black plaits of hair. These women carry themselves like queens and move on their soft-soled, tight-fitting, high-heeled shoes, heavily embroidered, like goddesses.

Some are exquisitely beautiful, all have finely chiselled features, with straight Grecian noses and well curved lips. Pointing out one even more than usually queenlike—more Nepheta-like than the rest—to my neighbour the Patriarch of Jerusalem, he said: "Yes, that is pure Armenian, rather rare in Yerevan, more common in the uplands, whither during and after the last war many of the pure-blooded Armenians fled."

Many of the dances, accompanied by national musical instruments, strings, light drum and flutes, are in general slow, subtle and sedate, though they rise at times to high dashing movements and breath-taking whirls. Generally they revolve round some simple rustic theme, as the young bride's fear of her mother-in-law or a maiden's play with the fine kerchief she had stolen from her lover, evading his efforts to recapture it till he produces another still finer and his quest is now exchanged for hers.

In the upper parade at the opera there hangs a striking portrait, painted obviously by a first-rate modern artist with fine insight and masterly technique. On inquiry I found he was "Peoples' Artist" Mastiros Sarian. Later, in the foyer, I met him and we spoke. A handsome old man, with a shaggy mass of dark hair, resting as he walked on the arms of two younger men. He had exhibited in London in 1910.

I urged this artist, with obvious flare for colour, to paint the ravishing and delicate colourings of the Cathedral Ceremony at Echmiadzin, which I shall shortly describe. He contemplates doing so.

I attended an exhibition of Armenian art and was introduced to many of the painters, some surprisingly young; one a sculptor who explained to me with pleasure how he could follow his own creative bent in art: assured of an income, he could work without producing "pot-boilers."

Speaking of youthful artists, I saw one day an adolescent boy in shabby war-worn clothes with a notebook in his hand at the Zoo, sketching as he stood. I sought permission to see his book, expecting a schoolboy effort. Actually it was highly competent work by a close observer of animal form and movement which he depicted with skill and flare.

(E) *Institutional Religion in Armenia*

The religious situation in Armenia, interesting at any time, was of particular interest at a moment when the whole country was stirred by the visit of some 124 delegates from fifteen major countries of the world, who, accompanied by several high dignitaries of the Armenian Church, had assembled in their homeland to elect and consecrate their new Catholicos, as the head of the Armenian Church is called.

This, one of the oldest living branches of the Christian Church, was evangelised in the second century, and ever since then Armenian religion has been bound up intimately with Armenian national art, literature and life. An objective study of the religious situation in Armenia at a crucial moment in national history was of high importance and I seized eagerly the opportunity afforded me for such study in the ceremony which took place in June and in all that led up to it. The ceremony itself, intimate and delicately beautiful, impressive but not pompous, intrigued artist and archæologist and stirred the Christian Churchman. Christendom owes much to a Church which had always been tenacious of tradition; and more to a Church which never showed intolerance.

The interest taken by the central Soviet authorities in the whole occasion; in the invitation to the delegates and in the ceremony itself—which was carefully filmed for wide publicity—had, of course, its own significance. Owing to delays, the delegates, some 124 in all, failed to arrive at the date first indicated and that gave me the advantage of a prolonged stay and wider opportunities for study.

It had been necessary in accordance with Armenian ecclesiastical law that the delegates of the whole Armenian Church be present at any election of its Catholicos, hence the delegates came from Europe, Asia, Africa, and America whither they had been scattered by Turkish persecution. Laity shared prominently in the election, indeed the vast majority of the delegates were lay.

The election itself took place in Echmiadzin and the consecration in Echmiadzin's Cathedral, whose foundation dates back to 303 A.D. when Armenia had adopted Christianity as the State religion, two decades before the Roman Empire did the same. By the end of the fourth century the Armenian Church had declared its complete independence from outside control. It has remained autonomous ever since. Alike in its physical resistance to assault from every quarter, Arabs, Persians, Kurds, Mongolians, and Turks; and in its religious resistance to the Orthodox Church and to the Church of Rome, Echmiadzin is peculiarly sacred ground to Christians of Armenian faith.

Echmiadzin Cathedral, enshrined in its own modest ecclesiastical buildings—monk's dormitory, library, theological academy, residence of Catholicos and various other subsidiary offices—stands back from the main thoroughfare of the quiet country town in which it is situated.

The only building of outstanding merit is the Cathedral itself, not large, but massive, austere and impressive, a prototype of Gothic architecture.

Erected sixteen centuries ago, its carved stone walls, highly durable in texture and richly warm in their golden-brown colour, stand out clean and fresh and will so stand for centuries to come. Cruciform in plan, the building was designed to withstand earthquake or siege and has survived both. Its walls are a fortress. Its cellars ample for food storage. Cold sparkling waters still rise in a well in the centre of the building. Every precaution has guarded the place against siege, even to underground drains designed to carry foul water a mile away.

Despite the ravages of successive invaders—Persians, Arabs, Genghiz Khan, Tamerlane and the Turks, the old church still possesses priceless treasures. Two keys, one in possession of the Archimandrite and the other entrusted to the Dean, are required to open the door into the treasure vaults. Staffs, vestments, fourth-century silver engravings, an old silver model of Echmiadzin and specimens of Armenian embroidery dating from nineteen centuries past would in themselves make Echmiadzin a place worthy of pilgrimage. The Church furniture is ancient in character and lovely in a simple way. The colour charming: on the great day of the consecration ravishing. One altar is silver, wrought in traditional Armenian workmanship. Another is marble with a covering of heavy woven cloth, the 260-years-old panels painted with pigments of a lost formula.

The Cathedral possesses two thrones, one of the seventeenth century of carved wood and another, very splendid, of the eighteenth century in silver and mother-of-pearl. The building itself and the furniture in it preserves resemblance to old Christian churches before the Council of Chalcedon in the fifth century, save for a few pictures of the late Italian school. Very tenacious of its past, Armenian churches have resisted innovations and rejected the Church furniture as well as Church doctrines introduced into Greek and Roman churches since Chalcedon.

My first visit to Echmiadzin was to attend the meeting of the delegates and to join in a memorial service for the late Catholicos.

We arrived early and met the high clergy in the garden of the Episcopal residence. The old residence was simple and attractive, a lovely, long, bow-windowed and restful house, with quiet, symmetrical, early Victorian stairways of plain rails leading to the main entrance on the second and only upper floor.

Very English in character, the house was whitewashed with faint blue architectural lines. It overlooked an enticing garden, formal only in its paths among fruit trees and vegetables and in the rivulets which formed a useful irrigation network. In the centre, a large, cool, vine-covered pergola provided a pleasant arbour where we sat and drank lemonade while we talked to the Archbishop of Beyrut, who might have been Ashur-ban-i-pal, the Assyrian monarch. Tall, extremely dignified, and with the same long beard, formally curling hair, noble nose and massive features, one always associates with Assyrian sculpture: one of the most imposing ecclesiastics I ever saw. Here, too, we were introduced to the Very Rev. Terenig Paladian, who had come to Cilicia with his Catholicos from New York five months ago.

The Armenian Church has two Catholicates, not through schism, but in order that it may never be without a man who can act as administrative head should, as so frequently has happened, persecution overwhelm it. The meeting of the delegates took place in the assembly hall, the *locum tenens* presided, and the Catholicos of Cilicia together with the Archbishops of Beyrut and Jerusalem sat on either side. Complimentary speeches were made, decisions to refound the library and seminary formulated, photographic films duly recording the occasion.

Archbishop Gevork Chovekchian, who was elected, has been acting-head of the Armenian Church since the death of the 141st Catholicos in 1938, a striking figure, with a striking career. Son of a peasant he was born on the Don and graduated in the High Theological Academy in Echmiadzin. In religion he is conservative, in politics a patriot. His popularity grew during the war. He threw the whole strength of the Church into the Anti-Fascist cause. He has been decorated with the Defence of the Caucasus Medal.

Studying theology in Berlin, Chovekchian is also a graduate in music: one of the few adornments of his simple residence is a grand piano.

Nersoyan, author of an able book on Christianity and Communism, till recently stationed in London, and a speaker for the B.B.C., and now holding high office in America, introduced me to the delegates, who gave me a cordial welcome. The meeting was followed by a Requiem for the late Catholicos. The high altar stands on a raised marble railless platform at the east end of the Cathedral, carpeted and approached by steps from either side. A canopy encloses the altar itself and a large golden curtain on runners hides the whole sanctuary from the congregation during the consecration prayers. The high altar of silver and blue is surmounted by tiers of shelves with ornaments. A picture of the Virgin and Child, which here as well as in all Armenian churches, occupies a prominent place behind the altar, is only varied at Easter and the Feast of the Holy Cross, when appropriate pictures replace it. Dignitaries also wear a pectoral enamelled medallion of the Virgin and Child in place of cross or crucifix. Austerity amidst beauty, and a colourful restraint formed a vivid contrast to glitter of gilt and complicated ironwork of the less restrained Russian Church.

When all available delegates were assembled the election of Archbishop Gevork as the new Catholicos took place. His consecration followed on the next Sunday, and we all assembled for it in bright hot sunshine in the garden of his house. I walked beside the canopy carried on four staves in front of the Archbishop by delegates of various important countries. The canopy, about five feet square, shaped like the top of a Chinese pagoda, was made of silk, and delicately embroidered. In front of the canopy and held at the four corners by two priests at an inclined angle so that the Catholicos could gaze upon it as he walked was a yard-square piece of white satin brocade with golden rays radiating from a picture of the Lamb of God. In front of this again walked cross-bearers and others carrying various essential and interesting objects. The cross was silver, with silver-embroidered velvet, shaped like a closed umbrella which fell over and hid the hands of the bearer. Boys of various ages in robes of a rich golden yellow, bordered on skirt and shoulder with green, fulfilled their several functions. Yellow, indeed, was the predominant colour amongst the various robes, a rich golden daffodil yellow, flowered when worn as copes by priests.

Curious silver plaques, called Kshots, the size of dinner plates, fastened vertically on hexagonal poles inlaid with mother-of-pearl, and hung around their circumference with silver bells, tinkled when quivered by the bearers. Kshot means "driver," its function is to drive flies away from the "Host." Incense bearers swung their censors, the incense to replenish them being carried in an exquisite model of the Cathedral.

When all were assembled the Bishops, Patriarchs, Archbishops and the Catholicos of Cilicia descended from the steps and formed in procession behind the canopy and the newly elected Catholicos. The copes were exquisite, more lovely than in all my travels I ever saw elsewhere, and less barbarically splendid than the copes of Zargorsk: more subtle, more delicate, and designed with vivid imagination. Wrought on a foundation of purple brocade, the designs, varied and bold, were executed in rich pure colours, wrought in finest needlework. Bishops wore the pallium, with a wide band of material thrown over the shoulders and hanging down back and front nearly to the ground; the head was thrust through the centre. Rich embroidery reaches its climax in the pallium where it breaks out into a variety of designs of scriptural scenes. The collar of the cope is stiff and heavy and standing three or four inches high often consists of a dozen or more gilt plaques of saints. The mitres, not confined in the Armenian Church to Bishops, are very large, Latin in shape and covered with embroidered designs. Each Bishop carries in his hand a small metal cross, its four arms stretching out from a circle of rays. It is an empty cross, containing no picture of the crucified Christ. Fitted with a metal handle for holding, it is clothed in similar form to the large crosses with something akin to a small embroidered handkerchief. Bishops wear the episcopal ring on their little finger, the Catholicos alone wears it on the ring finger. Copes and mitres have that subtle beauty always associated with China or Persia, indeed the cope of the Catholicos was in fact made in China and was itself a piece of sumptuous Chinese tapestry. The whole body of another cope in rich colour was elaborately designed as a picture or model of the Cathedral of Echmiadzin with its hexagonal pointed towers, in whose niches stand various saints and around whose walls blue-winged or red-winged cherubs fly.

The pallium of the Catholicos depicts Jacob's ladder on the back with Abraham's attempted offering of Isaac in front. His mitre depicts the crucifixion with attendant figures.

The lesser clergy assembled in front, deacons, priests, arch-priests, archimandrites and doctors.

The procession moved off, preceded by the cross: after it followed a banner in the form of a large gilded metal plate or plaque.

Along the hot, sunsplashed, stone-flagged paths between the green sward we passed—devout crowds lining the route, Aramanian the actor, among them—into the main porch of the Church. Bells clanged triumphantly, government cinema operators and camera men darted about. Inside the cathedral the Catholicos was lit up wherever he went with a blaze of light. It was obviously the Government's desire to obtain and show a full record of the splendid scene.

The Bishops, each with his own staff in his hand, mounted the platform and took their place on chairs allotted to their office. The Catholicos himself knelt in front of the altar. Two priests held his mitre upright behind him. Clergy in yellow robes grouped themselves in front of the platform, Mr. Polianski, the Government representative and his Armenian opposite number behind them, and then the delegates, who on this occasion were provided with chairs. Normally all stand. The Catholicos arrives. The Service commences. The music, supplied by a small choir and antiphonally sung between clergy and people, is curious, and in parts hauntingly beautiful and accom-

panied by a single monotonous low note like the distant booming of
a soft-toned bell.

Prior to the consecration of the elements the yellow curtain is drawn
right across the sanctuary and completely hides the altar and platform
from the nave and is only withdrawn when the consecration is complete. Mampre, the Patriarch of Egypt, who walked about in the hotel
with well-cut lay clothes and a golden-headed stick, took charge of
the elaborate ceremonial at the altar.

The Catholicos taking the oath in a husky, tired voice, kneels
straight upright on a cushion with no lateral or frontal support. He
faced the congregation and endured a blaze of cinema light only a
few feet from his face. On either side knelt two young priests. The three
knelt there an unconsciously long time, and I wished repeatedly
that the two young priests would let the old man—he is seventy-six—
rest on their arms. I wished also that the several Bishops could have
read their liturgy of prayer on his behalf in unison instead of
individually in succession.

The Catholicos made a striking and noble figure. Michael Angelo's
Moses sprang to my mind. Patient under the blazing lights, great beads
of perspiration gathered on his brow. From time to time he wiped his
face and brushed away the flies with a towel which only he, as
Catholicos, is entitled to carry. Half an hour passed and more, as the
monotonous chanting of each Bishop proceeded. From time to time
the Catholicos closed his eyes. His lips moved as if in prayer. He
endured without flinching. At the appropriate moment a veil was
placed on his head and he became the bride of the Church.

More and prolonged reading and then the Patriarch of Jerusalem
advanced with the consecrating oil which he poured from the beak
of a golden dove onto the thick, long greyish hair of the new Catholicos.
All the Bishops then placed their hands on the head of the Catholicos
to rub the oil in. Then followed the prayer that the Holy Spirit would
descend upon the Catholicos and fit him for his new tasks. Afterwards
his mitre was placed over the veil and the Catholicos of Cilicia kissed
his cheek, each Bishop in turn kissing hand and cheeks.

The Service closed and the 143rd Catholicos began his rule,
another in a long chain unbroken for 1,800 years or more. After the
ceremony the clergy returned to the Palace through crowds so dense,
as each pressed forward for a blessing, that there was fear of catastrophe.

Led by the New York delegate half a dozen of us joined hands,
and made a circle around the highest hierarchy in one of the oldest
churches of Christendom saving them and their tired frail Catholicos
from the surge.

The Catholicos received the delegates in the old reception chamber, where the public and even the lesser clergy seldom, or never, entered. Chovekchian himself had never entered it for thirty years, until he became Archbishop.

The favoured few, after the hierarchy had done homage, advanced and kneeling, kissed the old man's hand. As he kissed me warmly on the face I wondered if ever before had a member of the Anglican Church shared in any similar Service of Consecration in that same cathedral church.

BOOK VIII

GEORGIA

By air from Tbilisi to Yerevan one hour, by rail sixteen. Landscape and airscape differ widely and are complementary. I enjoyed both, but prefer the train, the wayside station, and the close-up view of mountain and stream, of plain, meadow and forest and the ever-shifting panorama of human life seen at close range.

It was hot when, by the midnight train, we left Yerevan. The "Stalingrader," accompanied by his wife—married to him at sixteen and a young woman of marked literary taste—took us to the station and waited, sad and downcast at our departure. To his immeasurable delight, and because he had treated me from first to last as a son to a father, I stooped to kiss his cheek, as the guard's flag waved us away.

Disobeying strict instructions to keep the window of my sleeping cabin shut I flung it open wide and soon was enjoying the cooler air of the uplands. The night was bright and a full moon threw sharp shadows of the coaches on the sheeplands as we sped along. Suddenly I saw the shadow of a figure creeping along the roof, then another and another. At wayside stations or when labouring up steep slopes, the train, crammed to the last inch by legitimate passengers—for transport after war is more difficult in Russia than here—is often subsequently invaded on footboards, between carriages and even on the roof.

I understood as I saw the crawling figures the significance of the guard's injunction: "keep your window closed." On the station at Yerevan and all along the line I saw troops returning, Armenian boys and Georgian boys, lean and supple, smallish, like Generalissimo Stalin himself, and with the same clean-cut regular features. Yerevan as we left it eagerly awaited the arrival of one of her famous regiments and the mile-long route from station to civic centre was, as a mark of affection and honour, to be spread with oriental carpets, loaned by grateful citizens.

I slept little that night that I might observe the more, upland plains, mountains, mists, scattered hamlets of rough, low, windowless stone houses, shepherds and herdsmen and children.

Hours of slow descent carried us through forests and gorges to widening valleys and fertile lands, rich with fields of thrusting maize and wheat, flowering potatoes, swelling walnuts, and cherry trees hanging red with ripened fruit. Peasants were richer in the lower valleys and better clad, and the stations a medley of would-be passengers mingled with pedlars pressing their merchandise. Garments of every description made the scene gay, women with swarthy heads bound up in purple wraps, men hidden beneath immense fur hats. One small young mother in fantastically bright native clothing, with a fat babe of two tied by a yellow sash on her back, fought desperately but vainly for clinging room on the carriage steps.

Wider valleys and richer lands brought us at last to Tbilisi, the capital of Georgia, where we prolonged our stay.

Tbilisi differs widely from Yerevan. The capital of Armenia had sprung at one bound from ill-kept village to imposing city. Tbilisi was already a modern city with fine streets and handsome buildings—Cathedral, mosques and churches and a population of 400,000 people—before the Revolution took place. Soviet progress in Armenia is focused in Yerevan, in Georgia outside the capital, which still retains, as in any considerable European city, its blend of old and new; broad streets, swift cars, pavements gay with flower-beds, and shaded by trees long matured in the modern quarter; the crowded hurly-burly of houses and people in the mediæval nucleus from which the city had sprung, clustering at Tbilisi round a swift curve of the river and dominated by the old castle.

Like Armenia, Georgia has enjoyed a long and distinguished cultural past, recalled and recorded with scientific thoroughness in a large museum of better finish than is common in Russia, primitive weapons and elaborate early drainage system with telescopic pipes and catchpools for sediment, relics of the early civilisation which led to a greater history, and relics of Queen Tamara, the twelfth-century Georgian counterpart of our Elizabeth.

Georgia early became important and in 1400 A.D. an Arabic manuscript records that, in gold francs, the wealth of France was estimated at three million, England four million, but Georgia ten million of the standard unit of currency.

Early MSS. of fifth and sixth centuries are preserved as binding paper for twelfth-century writings. Other treasures are a Gospel of 936 A.D., a twelfth-century MS. in original covers of tapestry on boards, once the property of Tamara, and decorated with elephants and tigers, a Psalter of the fourteenth century with realistic paintings of the human body.

More interesting and more moving to me than all these were treasures from the tombs at Samtavro, some fifteen miles west of Tbilisi, and till lately hidden beneath a peasant village by the riverside. There for centuries, two or three feet below the rooms where

men ate and slept and sat, lay an extensive cemetery in which, en-
cased in massive slabs of stone, successive generations of Governors of
the province of Southern Georgia were entombed. A handsome signet
ring in one tomb was beautifully chased on one side with heads on
a ruby-red stone and with names in minute lettering on the reverse.
Nearby was the tomb of the daughter of the Governor who owned the
ring, with her necklace, her mirror and her slender buckled spurs.
Most moving and most lovely of all was a heavily jewelled locket
the size of a crown with a pendant hanging by a chain beneath it,
the back, held in place by ingenious clips, revealed a child's tooth,
treasured by a mother as her small son or daughter passed to maturity.

Samtavro lies near Ntsheta, which was the capital of Western
Georgia in early times and contains an ancient and massive Cathedral,
standing in its own grassy cloisters and built in the eleventh century.
Its large, refreshingly plain exterior walls are ornamented in certain
parts by carvings in low relief and a lovely red in tone, sharp, simple
and clean-cut, reminiscent of Eric Gill at his best. At the east end
two angels, like Epstein's figures, hover in stone around the high
altar within. Precipitous east end walls and eaves above are plastered
with swallows' nests. Great lines of finely chiselled masonry run from
roof to ground on walls built of various coloured stones all blended
beautifully to one harmonious whole.

A distinguished architect and his wife who accompanied us
listened in nightly, they told me, to the chiming of Big Ben, and to the
English broadcast news which followed.

Invited to meet members of the Georgian Academy we spent a
profitable morning with its several professors, who described their
various tasks and answered our questions. The President being absent
in Moscow, Academician Yanaskia, Vice-President and Professor of
History, took the chair. Academician Ketshove helped us with
botanical inquiries, Mr. Tsereteli with sociological questions,
Chubinishvile with the history of Georgia.

Of outstanding interest was the work of Academician Cornelius
Cecelidze, Professor of the history of Georgian literature and of
Church history. Formerly a priest, he had discarded his orders during
the revolutionary days. He became a professor and his standard work
on the Georgian Church and Georgian literature, a copy of which in
two volumes he gave me, is an outstanding achievement. His lectures
on Church history are popular. This I learned from our young Georgian
guide, Cecily Dolenjashvili, a pretty, gay and intelligent girl of
eighteen, still at the university as a post-graduate student. The daughter
of George Hlvis Beri-Gdcha, a mathematician, her grandfather is a
priest, to whose country home in holiday time, and at the great festivals

the children—a doctor, an artist, the mathematician and others—
and the grandchildren assemble, Cecily among them.

Cecily loves her grandfather, his home and his library, though
he forbids, she says, his books going with her to Tbilisi lest they should
never return. Georgian men, Cecily says, object to women working.
As the war ends Georgian women return to their homes. They dislike
military duties, hence the Russian girls at the traffic points.

Cecily took me round the spacious university buildings and showed
me the athletic centre where 600 students were preparing for the annual
excursion to take part in the All-Union Sports-week in Moscow
and where they will meet young men and women from every quarter
of the Soviet Union's sixth of the world, a matter of wider significance
than many realise.

The jolt of the revolution has not been so great in Georgia as in
Russia, and in Cecily and her interesting family there has obviously
been less break than elsewhere between the old order and the new.
Her membership of the Communist Party does not prevent a keen
interest, for example, in religion. She attends the Church history lectures
of Professor Cecelidze, the one-time priest, and naively remarks
that something besides history comes across as he lectures, something
which made many of the students, Cecily amongst them, wish to visit
the Cathedral and hear the thoughtful and scholarly old Archbishop
and the eloquent young curate. "They sit and listen in deep silence
and are much interested," she added.

Being anxious to meet the Archbishop, who as Patriarch is head
of the Georgian Church, we visited the Cathedral, a compact building
in the old quarter of the town near the castle and immediately above
the deep rocky gorge where the river swirls far below. Morning Service was sung as we entered. We stood to listen. Two voices only were
heard in powerful and beautiful chant. Some twenty or thirty people
at a time wandered in from time to time pausing for a moment in
prayer.

Cecily asked the curate, who was dressed as a layman in a white
duck suit, if we could see the Archbishop. The curate departing,
shortly returned and led us to a small romantic house on the rocky
edge of the river where, on the verandah, among geraniums, the old
Archbishop met us with courtly grace, and warm cordiality. Short,
but dignified, dressed in cassock, with large medallion of the Madonna
and Child hanging by a gold chain around his neck, his long white
beard and hair formed a crown to a very handsome face.

"Very small lodgings," he apologised, as he led us into a sitting-
room. An old serving lady brought wine and sweetmeats. "Village
wine and harmless," said the old man, as he filled our glasses and drank

to our health. Ready to answer all our questions, he said he had been educated at Kiev, and though too old now to travel much had yet represented his autonomous Church at the recent consecration of Alexei in Moscow.

"Would this Church welcome the suggestion of an œcumenical movement uniting all Christian Churches in common conference and joint action?" I asked.

"I see nothing to hinder union between the English and the Georgian Churches," he replied, and drank a toast to our Church and to the good relationships between our respective peoples.

Of his curate, who lives with him and tends him like a son, and who is dressed in lay clothes, he said, "he dresses thus because he likes to mingle amongst the people, not too conspicuous." The curate attends the theatre and the opera and is on excellent terms with modern youth.

Cecily and Inna were particularly happy in this friendly, informal gathering, and carried on with us a long and interesting talk with both men. The old man spoke of Inna as a girl. "But I am a married woman with two children," she said. "Far too young to be a mother," he replied, and added: "Then may your daughters ever be like sisters to you, my child."

After drinking Inna's and Cecily's health, he said, "and now one more for the curate," to whom, turning, he added, "and may you always be faithful to the Church."

Mildly suggesting that many toasts ill suited my health, he added: "Then only one more; we always conclude with a toast to 'Our Lady'," and drinking to "Our Lady," we broke up a memorable party.

Several times we visited the immense and popular restaurant standing on the edge of a precipitous slope six or seven hundred feet sheer above the town and reached by a funicular railway. A peculiarly pleasant building with slender columns ending in carved capitals and supporting the glass roof which covers the whole. Three stories high, spacious verandahs enable one to sit and eat and enjoy to the full the exquisite views of the town spreading out beneath us along the winding bends of the river, with the Caucasian hills and mountains beyond. Extensive hilltop gardens surround the restaurant, bands play and for a copper or two parents can leave the heated streets and spend the evening with their children in chat or dance or quiet walk. A small girl of six sat opposite us in the descent. She had a sleeping infant in her arms and was shepherding another child of four, all returning from their afternoon on the terraces.

Not infrequently and for a change we attended theatre or opera where one night we watched a famous old Georgian morality play depicting the struggle between love and duty, considered topically useful in times of war.

The theme was simple. A beautiful rich girl rescued from bandits of a neighbouring village, begs her rescuers to conceal her identity lest her misfortunes should defile her name. Shooting the bandit, one of the rescuers falls in love with the girl, and is loved in return. Later he discovers that she is affianced to his friend. He is compelled by his father to attend the wedding ceremony. The husband, being disappointed at the discovery that his wife loves another, he leaves home and betrays his country which is at war. The lover having confessed to the shooting of the bandit and called to account therefore by the Duke, is ordered by his father, who is head man of the village, to occupy a very dangerous post on the flank of the enemy's line. Dallying with the girl he neglects his duty and the enemy breaks through. Furious with anger and shame the father slays his son. The other youth who had betrayed his country shot himself. This morality play, enforcing the truth that when love replaces duty, tragedy follows, was well acted and gave great scope for the display of ancient customs and costumes. The music was local and unique. The manager who entertained us afterwards described it as over-tonal, owing something to Byzantium and something to peasant yodelling.

At the opera on another night the tenor sang to us again in the staff room, where we were entertained by the management, and handed us a magnificent bouquet of flowers given to him by an admirer. He has deserted medicine for the stage on account of his splendid voice.

The legend of Jason and his Argonauts, who sought the Golden Fleece at any rate hints at the very early activity in this part of the world, and also at its connection with Greece and the West. The legend of Prometheus who brought to mankind the magic of fire is traced in its origin to Georgia, and may have some connection perhaps with the oil resources of Baku.

Georgia running for several hundred miles along the Turkish border, contains a mixed population of 3,700,000 people. Converted to Christianity in 345 A.D., it remained semi-feudal till 1917. Sub-tropical agriculture is highly developed along the Black Sea coast. Vast quantities of Tunga-oil, used for varnishes, tea, tobacco, and fruits of all kinds, particularly grapes and citrus fruits, are cultivated. Through Batumi pass by rail and pipeline two-thirds of all the Baku oil supplies. For its size Georgia possesses higher hydro-electric potential than any other area in the Soviet Union, and develops her water-power resources with great speed. Four new hydro-electric stations with an aggregate capacity of 169,000 kilowatts are to be built and put into operation by 1950. By 1950, the number of schools is to reach 4,333 with an attendance of 642,000 children. Hospital beds will increase to 17,900. The total volume of capital investments in Georgia in 1946-48 is to be 4,130 million roubles. And we must remember that all this is for a people whose total population in 1939 was only 2,475,729, with an urban population of 1,066,560.

The industrial production had already by 1935 increased from 43 million roubles to 640.9 million roubles.

Another index to Soviet change is seen in the number of doctors—351 in 1913; 4,670 in 1940.

BOOK IX

ASIA

1 . INTRODUCTION: GEOGRAPHY AND
HISTORY

T H E Asian Republics lie in a world by themselves. A world where
water, flowing from the eternal snows of vast mountain ranges, is
captured and utilized by the life it supports ere it is lost again in the
vast encirclement of parched lands and desert sands, blistered by
scorching suns of summer and stiffened by bitter blasts of winter.

We flew by air from Stalingrad to Uzbekistan, the queen of Asiatic
Republics; a long flight from 7.45 a.m. to 4.20 p.m., with but one short
break for fuel. At a height of 6,000 or 8,000 feet we crossed the "Caspian
depression," a brown, hungry land, intersected at rare intervals by
dried-up river beds. Two hours without sighting a single tree. Then one
only, poor, stunted, and standing entirely alone. Fuelling at a desert
station on the Tashkent-Moscow railway, we rose again and, flying
higher than previously, looked down for hundreds of miles on utterly
lifeless wastes. No tree. No blade of grass. No vestige of life. Sand,
desert, salty depressions, with a loneliness rendered even more stark
still, when for a brief moment we struck the Moscow-Tashkent railway track, a minute silver filament running stark and straight through
endless desolation into invisibility on the horizon.

The pilots of our planes were men of distinction, who had piloted
Molotov to San Francisco. Acquainted with England by a brief
stay, they had returned with a story grossly misrepresenting English
life in wartime. A girl, accosting the younger man in Hyde Park, had
assured him that for two days she had tasted no food, hunger compelled
her to sell her honour. The man seeing other girls wandering on
similar intent in the Park believed it. No young woman in wartime
London, we insisted, lacked either work or food. The girl had lied.
Similar stories culled from girls in Leicester Square found their way
into America, where returning soldiers will at times confidently
assure their friends that 50 per cent of English girls are pregnant
before marriage. Similar stories have been told to our soldiers by the
same class of girls in Berlin concerning their prior treatment at Russian
hands.

Eight hours' monotonous flight, then faint and dim on the eastern
horizon appeared a line of hills, outposts of the mighty Pamirs. Touches

of green appeared, frontiers of the well-watered central Asian lands. Forty miles more, and the plane swept low across the large, well-planned modern city of Tashkent, the capital of Uzbekistan. We circled, descended and drove to our destination through the city.

A large town; the pre-war population of Tashkent of over 700,000 has been swollen by war-time evacuees, mainly from Belo-Russia, one of the sixteen Union Republics, to a million souls. Noble streets, shaded by stately poplars or limes intersect the town in various major directions; strips of brightly coloured gardens with small fountains perpetually at play, dividing the brown pavements from the broader highways and making the city gay. Tashkent wears the aspect of a high-class southern European town.

Our home was a "dacha," a moderate-sized country house, approached from the highway by a narrow lane and surrounded by its own gardens and orchards. A swimming pool added to its amenities.

The gardens glowed with summer flowers, the orchard with summer fruit—pears and peaches, plums, apples and grapes, growing on trees, tumbling on the grass or loading our dishes at every meal.

The house itself, ground floor only, with a great common room, wall-less on two sides and shaded with soft, white curtains, recalled the country houses of wealthy Americans. The Russian lady who managed the "dacha," presided as hostess, mother and adviser all rolled in one. She managed with distinction the great dinner party we gave to scholars, scientists, administrators and dancers, she doctored our minor ailments. She sent our clothes to be pressed or our boots to be mended. She bade her staff of young maids brush the dust off our shoes when we entered from the dusty lane, or carry cushions to the verandah, or sprinkle water on the verandah floor for coolness, when we sought siestas. She ran the "dacha," as smoothly as well-regulated English country houses are run, and her thoughtfulness followed us even after our departure. Carelessly I had left an unnoticed shoe behind, but she found means to return it, and four months later it arrived at the Deanery via the London Soviet Embassy.

Though midsummer, the climate was lovely and healthy. Hot by day, it was never oppressive, and the nights deliciously cool with air from the Pamirs. Tashkent differs utterly from the general run of oriental towns. It is clean, it is flyless. I slept with no sting from mosquitoes beneath the orchard trees; the rippling of the stream and the soft thud of an over-ripe peach the only sounds that broke the stillness of the southern night. A dim figure squatting on the ground, motionless throughout the night, was an Uzbek soldier set there to guard me.

With much to see in Uzbekistan, we lost no time in starting our rounds and after a meal and a wash we drove to see a film depicting in dramatic form, the digging of the Fergana Canal, a great Asian achievement.

The scenario, written by a friend of Inna's—a young and "intolerably lazy," part composer of the new National Anthem—began with the legend of the prince who loved a lady. Piercing the mountain to release the needed water was the price of her hand. He failed. But where the prince failed, the common Soviet people succeeded, and the film recorded the steps in their achievement. An army of peasants cut the canal which makes the desert blossom as the rose.

A prelude to our visit, this film emphasised something primary in central Asian life, the importance of water. By water alone can Asian communities live and Soviet Asia utilises water with scientific thoroughness and with full appreciation of its economic potentialities.

In Uzbekistan we met a wide range of people, farmers, artisans and managers of factories, teachers and children, professors, scientists, historians, archaeologists, artists, actors, writers and dramatists, religious leaders, and governors in city and State. We met the Prime Minister, and the Iman, the religious head of the Eastern Moslem world.

This enabled us better to study the geography and the history of this fascinating land together with its present scientific aims, its agricultural, industrial, educational and cultural activities, its civic life and the whole political set-up of Uzbekistan and its four neighbours who together form the central Asian group of nations with a total population of twenty-one millions.

The Asiatic portion of the Soviet Union comprises seven-eighths of the mighty whole and extends eastwards from the Ural mountains, the Ural river and the Caspian Sea. Central Asia is that smaller portion of the greater whole which lies immediately to the north of the vast mountain ranges dividing the Soviet Union from Iran, Afghanistan, India and China. Waters from these central Alps, create, when intelligently used, astonishing fertility. Under men like Genghis Khan and Tamarlane in the thirteenth and fourteenth centuries the cities of Central Asia blossomed out into Holy Bokhara and Golden Samarkand, which even in decay are ablaze with mosques, minarets and domes of gold and azure blue. Under the Soviets these ancient cities rise afresh, every worthy ancient monument restored and cleaned, the old preserved with care and understanding and blended with skill into the pattern of the new.

Scientific use of water provides power, extends irrigation and together with drought-resistance trees as shields against the drifting sands, thrusts back the desert, supports virile populations and shares its newly acquired wealth with other Soviet lands.

Central Asia consists of a group of five nations—Tajikistan, Kazakstan, Kirghizia, Turkmenia, and Uzbekistan. The last four of Turkish, Tajikistan of Persian origin. Consider Central Asia geographically and historically first.

Tajikistan, bordering on India and China is a land of peaks, glaciers, deep valleys and steep, sloping foothills. Not unlike Switzerland and four times its size, its people are tall, blue-eyed and straight-nosed, ethnologically akin to present-day Iranians.

This once powerful and widespread people sank lower and lower through a thousand years. To-day as a nation they are driven to mountain passes; as individuals they scatter far and wide through Central Asia. Despite their fine physique and handsome features the Tajiks are hewers of wood and drawers of water for other peoples. The wealthy Aga Khan, as head of a Mohammedan clan, drew large sums from these poverty-stricken mountaineers. Under the Tsars only 0.5 per cent of the Tajiks could read, their food was in the main a poor cake made of ground mulberries.

Cut off from ancient trade routes, one of which ran through Alma Ata, another through India, Iran and the Caucasus, and a third through the Red Sea, Tajikistan lost touch with the outer world: losing ancient culture and acquiring nothing new, she preserves interesting fragments of earlier associations. Many regard the Tajiks as the most ancient of all peoples, the fount and origin of our race.

Between Tajikistan and China arise the gigantic Pamirs, the Roof of the World. Stalin Peak is 24,590 feet high; Everest for comparison is 29,141 feet.

Science finds rich material and wide scope among the Pamirs, whose lower valleys are 13,000 feet above sea level. Archæological and ethnological discoveries are made, rare and precious substances found and cosmic rays explored.

Kazakstan, stretching from the Volga 1,600 miles eastwards to the borders of China and southwards for another 1,000 miles from the Trans-Siberian railway to the borders of Uzbekistan—which itself touches Afghanistan on the south—is one million square miles in area, equal to one-third of the U.S.A. The Kazaks, some six and a half million in all, are herdsmen in the main, their seats are saddles, their clothing skins, their religion Mohammedan and their food precarious.

Rich in minerals, however, containing more than half the Soviet Union's known deposits of cooper, lead and zinc and possessing at Karaganda, Russia's third largest coal basin and in the Steppes some of the Soviet's most fertile soil, Kazakstan confronts a glowing future. Alma Ata, "Father of Apples," the capital of this wide-spreading land, is beautifully situated with snowy peaks to crown its vast panorama. Through Alma Ata—whose population has increased seven times in two decades—and partly along a road through inner China, which I visited in 1932 with Major Todd, the American engineer who built it, have flowed food, munitions, medical supplies and other equipment to aid China in her war with Japan.

The "Turksib" rail line running north and south through Alma Ata and linking Tashkent as well as Kazakstan with the Trans-Siberian railway, is the pride of the once primitive tribesmen who built it.

Kirghizia, the small mountainous country lying eastwards in Central Asia, borders on China's vast mountain ranges. Its population of one and a half millions was formerly nomadic, poor, dirty, sickly—a people living in black bell tents. To-day the Kirghiz are adopting a stable, agricultural life. New canals have extended the area of culti-vation by 75 per cent. Collective farming increases the yield of cotton and sugar-beet. Industrial development expands. Coal is mined. Rare metals, valuable for manufacture of light, strong alloys occur in rich deposits. Engineers carry the great Kirghizian highway over the large Alps and into China. Scientists have discovered in Kok-sagyz a natural rubber, a valuable alternative to the rubber plant itself. Ten acres of Kok-sagyz yield one ton of rubber. Millions of acres are devoted to its growth.

This most backward of all the Central Asian peoples possessed no alphabet until the Soviets gave them one.

The westernmost and southernmost area of Central Asia, running along the northern front of Iran is Turkmenia, the land of the far-famed dark red carpets, with a population of 1,300,000; a dry and blistering land: 80 per cent of its area swallowed up by the black sands of Kara Kum. In no area of Central Asia does the water problem press more urgently than in Turkmenia, where in some towns water from the salty Caspian Sea itself must be distilled for cooking and drinking.

Soviet Scientists never rest from the attack on the problems of these dry lands: they turn to industrial use some of the natural salt deposits, they experiment in rain production by sprinkling chemicals on passing clouds and sometimes succeed.

Uzbekistan, finally, exceeds all its neighbours in importance. Situated in the centre, south of Kazakstan and north of Turkmenia, its area of 160,000 square miles is larger than that of Britain, its population of 6,600,000 slightly smaller than that of Sweden.

Uzbekistan illustrates, best of all the Soviet Republics, Russia's colonial policy and activities. Hot and dry, but furnished with ample irrigation water from the Pamirs, Uzbekistan is admirably adapted for cotton culture. Cotton was the white gold which enriched Emirs and feudal lords. Modern science enriching the soil, selecting plants and utilising for power and irrigation the great rivers on their journey to the desert has increased fourfold the cotton yield.

The origin of Uzbekistan and its relation to the whole of Central Asia and to the outer world makes an interesting story. The Tajiks are Persian in origin. The other four peoples, Kazaks, Kirghiz, Turkmen and Uzbeks are Turkish, not to be confused with the present Turks of Asia Minor. A nomadic people who came from Asia between the tenth and fifteenth centuries, these Asiatic Turks appear first in history as a servile tribe in China.

Rapidly spreading south and west they reached their first high peak in the period A.D. 546-582. By 567 they made trade treaties with the Romans and co-operated with the Greeks against the Persians. Their forward surge at this period carried one stream to China: I met Turkish elements in Kansu in 1932. Another stream went south and west. Spreading out over southern Asia, reaching the Bosphorous at Constantinople and invading the Caucasus and Azerbaijan, they provided the human bridge to Europe.

Two events of outstanding importance in the record of these invading peoples left deep impress on Central Asia—the descent of Ghengis Khan and the rise of Tamarlane his grandson.

Ghengis Khan, a contemporary of Francis of Assisi, sweeping down from the north early in the thirteenth century left destruction as his legacy: Timur, the lame, or Tamarlane, his grandson, left in the glories of Samarkand a nobler and more lasting memorial. Carrying his conquests west to the Caucasus and south to Africa and India, decimating the male population as far west as the Caucasus he spared the artisans, the pick of whom he placed in Samarkand to erect buildings whose glories stamp it still as the jewel of Asia.

Great though cruel, Timur left a powerful empire. Rivals were removed, order was restored. Trade flourished. But it was a one-man kingdom and lacking national or economic ties it collapsed, illustrating Tallayrand's words, "you can do everything with bayonets except sit on them."

From the ruins of Tamerlane's kingdom Uzbekistan arose, with its centres Samarkand, Bokhara and Merv.

The siege of Constantinople by the Turks in 1453 brought grievous repercussions on Central Asia, severing land connections east and west and ending a brilliant period in politics and art. Money, always needed by the ruling class, and which trade now ceased to yield, was exacted by taxation from the common people. Middle-class and proletarians grew relatively weak. Culture faded; the empire disintegrated into several states, foremost amongst these were Kogand in the beautiful Fergana Valley, Bokhara the centre of Moslem learning, and Merv the trade junction of the south, all socially reactionary and all at constant war with one another.

Such was the situation when the Russian drive, south and south-eastward began. Peter the Great in the early eighteenth century sought trade contacts with India, Afghanistan and China. Central Asia, through which his emissaries passed, came into the limelight. From 1835 onwards Russian influence increased in consequence as the power of the divided kingdoms waned. At length Central Asia itself was absorbed into the Russian Empire.

It was customary in early Soviet days to regard Tsarist imperial expansion with hostility, and look upon it as inimical to the people. Later Soviet historians, obviously encouraged to do so, glorify the unification. The younger people grasp the point and defend the policy even though due to Tsarist policy.

Bonderevsky, a young Jewish refugee from Odessa with us throughout our stay in Asia, and one of the ablest of the younger men we met in the Soviet Union, defended with vigorous argument this Tsarist unification, though hostile, naturally, to Tsarist aims and economy.

The economic advantage to Central Asia of Tsarist centralised dominance was, of course, the provision of a ready market for Asian cotton, the nucleus of factories and the skeleton of a railway system. From the Soviet Socialist point of view the factories were crucial: they were the secd plots for revolt by the creation of a factory proletariat.

It would have been worse by far, Bonderevsky argued, had Central Asia fallen into the hands of Persia or Afghanistan.

The October Revolution had speedy effect in Central Asia. Bokhara fell to the Bolsheviks, other places, too. The whole area was at first organised as the Republic of Turkestan, but as each several part of that whole had its own distinctive culture, the Soviet Government wisely decided to provide for each its own opportunity of growth. Five Republics instead of one was the final method of organisation.

2. INDUSTRY AND BALANCED ECONOMY

In a spacious room in the large new civic central building of Tashkent we had a long and interesting interview with the Uzbek Prime

Minister, a youngish man and handsome. His Foreign Minister joined us and we discussed many matters, the operation of the February 1944 decree granting increased autonomy in matters relating to Army and foreign relations, new plans for agriculture and industry; development of electrical power resources and matters on the cultural front.

The Premier assured us that the 1944 decree was no dead letter. Wide scope for its operation is offered, especially in relation to Persia, these two countries having much in common economically and culturally. More especially still in relation to Afghanistan whose northern territory borders Uzbekistan with immediate effects upon trade, industry, culture and politics. The Army here is for obvious reasons less concerned at present with the exercise of its enlarged powers.

We next spoke of agriculture and industry. New industries, machine building, aircraft factories and the like are planned: wolfram, molybdenum, iron and coal, recently discovered, are scheduled for speedy exploitation. The quest for gas and oil will proceed: the presence of gas being suspected near Tashkent.

Water power to the last ounce is to be utilised for power: the runaway water to be spread out frugally in irrigation. One large hydroelectric station was begun and completed during the war; another is in process of preparation at Farkand on the Syr river and will shortly become the centre of new chemical industries.

The Premier emphasised the importance of balanced industry. Uzbekistan needs wheat and tractors. Russia needs cotton goods. There lies the basis of mutual exchange and therein, too, the danger. Uzbekistan supplies half Russia with cotton and silk, receiving in exchange, wheat and tractors: Uzbekistan deliberately avoids an isolated economy.

At the same time, warned by the fate of Cuba, which tied up her whole economy to specialised production of sugar, suffering severely when her sugar markets were invaded, Uzbekistan plans a safer balance, growing and manufacturing, in addition to cotton, many commodities for her own internal consumption, with consequential transport economy as an additional incentive.

Tashkent formerly sent all her raw cotton a long journey to Moscow, awaiting the return of the finished goods for home consumption. To-day, Uzbekistan cotton is woven in Uzbekistan mills.

Leaving the Prime Minister we examined forthwith the cotton mills of Tashkent, and traced the whole series of operations whereby raw cotton became finished woven and printed goods.

Uzbekistan cotton mills have little to learn from the U.S.A. and less from Lancashire. Scientific dispositions of parts and processes, together with scientific administration of the whole is apparent through-out, and goes hand in hand with cleanliness, neatness, and due regard to beauty and amenities. The country invades the factory, weaving and spinning sheds open straight on to shaded gardens, so grateful in a hot land. Irrigation streams murmur amongst flowers which bloom beneath a smokeless sky.

Sheds built on the most approved designs of twelve years ago are already outmoded. Modern shops, cooler and more airy, rise up beside them as the industry expands. In Moscow I met the man who planned these mills. In one thing, alas, Tashkent shows no improvement on Manchester: the roar of the spindles and looms is deafening. Happily high organisation and keen co-operation between workers and manage-ment is greatly limiting the number of workers hired for this task. One girl tends an incredible number of looms and spindles.

In another department I examined a plant supplied by a noted Lancashire firm a dozen years ago to dye cloth. It takes three days in the process. Beside it stood a plant of Soviet invention performing the same process in three hours.

During an instructive interview with the management in a spacious board-room, I sat at a table spread with well-thumbed, but up-to-date magazines of the cotton industry culled from every land. It is sometimes, and even officially, alleged in England, that advertising in Russia is futile because industrial managements have no choice of purchase: all goods being selected and ordered from one centre in Moscow. Certainly ordering is centralised, but the units have a wide choice in the selection. Advertising in the Soviet Union is there-fore of greater importance, nor should we neglect it.

We motored far up the Syr river to where a hydro-electric station provides the power to operate a huge chemical works producing ammonia and nitrates; works uncanny in their minimum of human element owing to labour-saving machinery.

Uzbekistan shares in the new Five-Year Plan, which provides for the all-round development of her productive forces with further advancement of the standard of living of her population. This can best be done by considering the place Uzbekistan occupies in the economy of the whole.

Supplying Russia with two-thirds of its cotton needs during the war, it now aims at a still greater increase. Scientific farming on the one hand, with the basic productive processes mechanised to a higher degree than before the war by large-scale introduction of cotton-picking machinery effecting great saving in labour power; and on the other hand, an increase of cultivated area, especially in the Ferghana Valley, the Zeravshan watershed and the Bokhara and

Khovezm oases arc designed to achieve this aim. About 40 per cent of all Uzbek capital investments, with the exception of industry and the All-Union requirements, is scheduled for irrigation under the Five-Year programme.

Industrial development will aim primarily at providing the requisites in agricultural machinery—cotton-picking machines amongst them—a Soviet-designed model being even now ready for immediate mass production.

The first steel mill was a war-time achievement; the first rolling mill will be the achievement of the new Five-Year Plan.

One of the U.S.S.R.'s biggest copper smelting installations and refineries will be built together with large aluminium works, and the expansion of mining for rare metals. Electrification of both town and country is one of the salient features of Uzbekistan's forthcoming Five-Year Plan. Other features are plants to process agricultural bye-products, a glass factory, and food industry enterprises. Consumers goods are to be increased, together with housing.

3 . AGRICULTURE IN ASIA: COTTON

N o w h e r e had the work of Michurin deeper significance for the Soviets than in the central selection station of the All-Union Cotton Institute at Tashkent. Into that Institute come cotton seeds from every cotton-growing land, especially from Egypt and the United States. Out of that institute, which covers a large acreage of experimental ground, issue wholly new varieties of cotton: disease-resisting cottons; early-ripening cottons; long-fibred cottons easy to weave.

Most interesting of all to me, and perhaps to the cotton world in general, were the new natural-coloured cottons, with a range from brown to green. For here are fast and natural hues, eliminating artificial dyeing. Of almost equal interest were the cottons which approach the texture and possess many of the qualities of wool. In a fascinating pattern-book of coloured cottons I saw, already produced, a blanket of a greyish-green colour, woven out of undyed cotton evolved at the Institute, and now in production on many farms of Asia.

We spent a whole morning at the Cotton Institute under the skilled guidance of its director, Mr. Sergei Kanash. It was a hot day and the drive to the Institute from Tashkent was over a dusty and viciously bumpy road. But the Institute was cool and pleasant: the cotton plantation around it green and refreshing with promise of an excellent crop.

We explored each laboratory with its own specialist. We discussed the coloured cotton with Mr. Strumal, its producer.

Mr. Kanash was dressed in a white tropical suit. Mr. Strumal wore the beautiful Ukrainian embroidered white shirt. Cotton garments predominated.

The morning's study began in the way usual in the Soviet Union, with a formal description of the work of the Institute. After what proved in this case to be an extremely valuable lecture, questions were asked, followed by detailed investigation of laboratories, fields, and processes. The several specialists were eager to help.

The object of the Institute is to produce the raw cotton for fabrics of better quality, wider variety, and greater cheapness. It is naturally located in Tashkent, the capital of Asian Uzbekistan, which produces 70 per cent of all the cotton used in the U.S.S.R. Ninety per cent of all cotton seed used in cotton cultivation issues from this Institute, which keeps in closest touch with every Russian cotton-growing farm.

So close, indeed, is contact between Institute and farm that each new and valuable variety discovered spreads with commendable speed throughout all the Asian cotton-growing world. The past twenty years, for example, have seen three complete changes in the seeds issued, responsive to successive better types.

Until 1927 only local seeds were grown. These gave poor crops and short fibres. By 1932, through successful work with North American and particularly with Egyptian, seeds, crossed with local seeds, new varieties with the long fibres of the Egyptian cotton, but with the local qualities which Egyptian cotton grown in Asia lacks, issued to the farms. During 1940 intensive work began for the production of cottons with longer filaments, for varieties more suited to technical processes, for disease-proof varieties, especially resistant to fungoid diseases, and also for cotton substitutes for wool.

The war quickened the process. In 1932 only 2.3 per cent of the cotton was of the long-fibre variety. In 1943 this percentage increased to 90. In 1932 the average length of fibre was one inch: in 1945 one and a quarter inches: in many special cases much longer. The reduction of waste through the development also of waste-resisting qualities has saved 80,000 tons of cotton a year.

Changes are effected through hybridisation of seeds, through the effect of soil, of nourishment, of light and heat and different modes of irrigation. A high-yielding, long-fibred variety from abroad may be tough and disease-resistant whilst retaining all its good qualities by crossing it with a low-yielding but hardy local variety. New non-wilting varieties of Gos Hirsutum that have been developed greatly reduced the prevalence of verticilliose diseases in the cotton belt.

New varieties of Gos Barladense have been developed that are early ripening, have big bolls, and are impervious to fusarium wilt. This latter variety was obtained by a long and complicated process of crossing Egyptian varieties with plants obtained from Peru.

It was in the hybridisation of seed that Mr. Strumal made his sensational discoveries. Mr. Strumal is a fair-haired, modest man, who looks northern rather than southern. In his laboratory whole bushes, with the coloured bolls still on them, stand in rows on the benches. Fluffy coloured balls in addition, the size of footballs, enable one to feel texture as well as see colours.

It should be emphasised that the coloured cotton of Central Asia is in no way connected with Peruvian or Ecuador cottons. The Kanash variety, named after the Director himself, with a brown staple, was obtained by crossing poor quality Gos Hirsutum cottons that were of no commercial value with the best varieties developed by selection in the Soviet Union.

Green, blue, and other shades of cotton were developed by means of what the Russians term "distant hybridisation," i.e., crossing of different species—Gos Barladense, Gos Hirsutum, and Gos Purpuracens. Cotton obtained from these varieties and used for the final crossing of white staple was work begun only eight or nine years ago. Much yet remains to be done.

The selections stations belonging to the Tashkent Cotton Research Institute are now growing hybrid lines with green, dark green, blue, pink, ash-grey and dark blue staples. No cotton of a pure black colour has yet been developed.

Progress proceeds in producing cotton hybrids of fast colour and necessary technical qualities for ready weaving. And a number of selection lines already developed of a fast dark green and dark blue colour possess the adequate textile strength of five grammes and higher.

The planting of naturally coloured cotton of brown, dark green and khaki shades is proceeding in this year, 1947, in the Uzbek and Turkmenian Republics on 30,000 acres. Other varieties of coloured cotton—blue, light green, pink and orange—are being cultivated on experimental plots.

Uzbekistan agriculture is by no means confined to cotton. Nor is the cotton station the only station in Tashkent for the study of scientific agriculture. We inspected, for example, the Shroedder Government horticultural station for experiments in the culture of fruit, berries and sub-tropical plants. The station covering 183 hectares is managed by forty specialists with 200 supplementary workers. We examined the grapes, apples, figs, pomegranates and other fruits in process of cultivation: thirty-six varieties of wine grapes; forty varieties of desert grapes for example.

Apples are a staple crop in Uzbekistan and where formerly the country possessed only two varieties which ripened as early as June, there are now fourteen, with seventy other varieties ripening in July. We saw trees, thirteen years old, which will live to sixty years and yield on an average half a ton per annum: some trees yield one ton. One hectare of two acres and a half yields about 100 tons of apples per annum. With heavy fruitage the question of branch support becomes important and we examined nine modes in process of trial. In large orchards many considerations must be weighed: supports must be efficient, cheap, of accessible materials and permissive of close ploughing by tractors near to the trunk of trees. Experimentation has resulted in sixty good varieties of figs, some capable of yielding 100 kilograms a year. Cultivated on the bend, in winter they are hidden for protection against the bitter cold under deep layers of snow.

Small plants of new and approved varieties are sent broadcast for cultivation on Uzbek farms: 70,000 were thus distributed in 1941.

Visiting a collective farm, a sample of the many we passed daily on the road, we were met at the entrance by the chief herdsman; a short, stocky, strong man, with dark olive complexion and close-cropped black hair beneath his gold-embroidered cap. He wore medals for achievement in his craft.

Before a walk round the farm we were entertained for a typical feast at a low fruit-laden table, sitting in an open-sided booth on a dais spread with silk quilts so lovely that I instinctively proceeded to remove my dusty shoes till I was prevented by our host with a "no need" gesture. The fruit was delicious, especially the melons. Wine accompanied the rural feast but as in China, in tiny glasses and in reasonable quantities. Speeches were made with singing and dancing while we ate and talked. Men sang, women sang. These farmers, as I saw them everywhere, are a powerful, healthy group. The women with dark multi-plaited hair, wore heavy golden earrings and as often as not had gold crowned teeth. They sang and accompanied their song with dancing, gestures of fingers, hands and arms, the local guests encouraging the singing and dancing with loud ejaculations.

We examined the stud horses, magnificent creatures with six fine English stallions granted to the farm by the Soviet Government on account of its outstanding achievements. We spoke to two shy boys, one of thirteen and another of nine, who both rode as jockeys in the races: the youngest had ridden his splendid horse to victory in an All-Asian contest.

This was a perfect specimen of a farm and beautiful, too. A field of seeding onions waist deep and running on to the far horizon, a rhythm of grey-green balls growing smaller and smaller until they became a hazy mist, was a sight I shall never forget. Would that Van Gogh had lived here to paint them. The rhythm of the cotton fields is lovely, too, with bushes 20 inches high in rows like potatoes, creating superb patterns drawing great lines of colour and form as they rolled on across the undulating hills.

The Government had lately exchanged with this Kolkhoz 1,000 tons of wheat for equivalent value of cotton. As a war-time gift the Kolkhoz had presented to the Government amongst many other things, ninety-six horses, thirty-six of them of English breed, together with 1,800,000 roubles.

In pre-war days, the staff numbered 850 workers, reduced during the war to 550, with however, an actual increase of 50 per cent owing to women's work and greater mechanical aid. Many neighbours intercepted us on the road home, with invitations to attend similar feasts. At a night performance of *Othello* at the opera that same evening, we recognised and spoke to our Kolkhoz friends.

4. CULTURAL LIFE IN UZBEKISTAN

WITH great determination Uzbekistan is eliminating illiteracy.

We visited a school for 554 girls, divided into twenty-two classes and served by thirty-two teachers. I saw older girls at examination and younger ones at play with round games, not dissimilar from ours. An interesting talk with one group at play, revealed the mixed nature of the class, Uzbeks, Tajiks, Tartars, with a wide sprinkling of children evacuated from Kiev, Odessa, and Belo-Russia.

Native Tashkent children, of course, predominated, and I spoke to a child of twelve with dark hair woven into thirty-two small tight plaits, very neat are these and they need attention, I was told, only once a week. One rather diminutive child, still bearing traces of starvation, came from Leningrad. Another, six years old, from Odessa, which she left when three years of age; she could not remember the famous steps. A lively pretty girl of twelve from Kiev told us that her father and mother were both doctors, her father serving in the Army, her mother practising in Tashkent. She and her mother lived with another Russian family, rather crowded but happy: the child looked happy, and all these small strangers mingled on friendly terms with their hosts, nor have they apparently suffered from the change of climate, rather the reverse.

Elementary education rapidly approaches completion and the

P

largest item of the present Five-Year Plan is 4,740 schools by 1950, with an attendance of 1,085,000 children out of a population of upwards of six millions.

Elimination of illiteracy is, however, only a preliminary stage, and Uzbekistan aims at the complementary task of introducing a universal standard of positive knowledge combined with a scientific world view. Children must understand the entire organisation of production and distribution in their country. In the words of Leonard Barnes "they must grasp the social process as a whole and know how it works. Responsible citizenship is impossible for anyone who lacks this understanding. The main arterial roads leading to it are books, the press, the films, the radio, the stage, supplemented by study and discussion circles, correspondence courses, evening classes, and the like."

The advance along these lines can be estimated in several ways. In 1936, 11.2 million copies of books of 1,213 titles were published in the Uzbek vernacular. The public was served by 222 newspapers.

Before the revolution Uzbekistan possessed no theatres. By 1936 she could boast of thirty-seven and 564 cinemas. After barely a dozen years from its first theatre or operas, crowded audiences now follow closely plays by Schiller, Molière or Shakespeare, who is a universal favourite. Crowds of young men and women will follow closely and tensely the long dialogue of *Othello*, for instance, for four hours and a half in its unabbreviated form.

At the Opera House we saw a fine performance of a play which took for its theme the story of Uleg-beg, an Uzbek monarch—contemporary of our Queen Elizabeth—who, as a distinguished scientist and astronomer, was bitterly opposed and at length assassinated by the reactionary Moslem priesthood.

I sat next to the composer's wife, who told me much about the theatrical world of Asia, amongst other things the amusing story of the first night when *Othello* was acted. Swept away by the tragedy and in passionate hatred of treachery, the crowd interrupted Iago with vehement cries to Othello: "Don't believe him, don't believe him: he lies."

The opera was a vivid feast of colour. Moslem art, with traditional avoidance on religious grounds of portraying the human figure, has spread itself in colour and form. The drop curtain with its gorgeous white horses of satin stitched to open network introduced us act by act in the Opera House to a grand display of ancient Uzbekian robes in masterly compositions. Finest amongst these perhaps was a superb tableau which introduced Uleg-beg's Chinese wife, a queenly palefaced woman sitting on her silver throne: Chinese restraint in vivid contrast to hot Asian colour and quick ecstatic motion.

The Uzbek government has loaned to the Opera for the purpose of this play, the ancient garments, treasured still in Bokhara, and thus fostered and augmented the legitimate pride of race and tradition enhancing still further the national content within the Socialist form.

The new Opera House was in process of construction and was to be completed within four months, as fine a building in its way as any in Moscow or London and following traditional oriental lines of architecture.

5 · SAMARKAND

T H I S pride in race and tradition was to be seen at its height in the development of Samarkand, 220 miles to the south-west of Tashkent, whither we flew, our pilot landing with exquisite skill in a blustering wind on a tiny airfield amidst meadows fissured with deep ancient waterways.

The golden Samarkand of romance lives up to its name. Beneath the brilliant Asian sky, its rose-pink bricks, its emerald-green and turquoise-blue tiles clothing the minarets and bulb-shaped domes, here and there broken by the glittering flash of gold, are breath-taking in their beauty.

An ancient city on this site had been destroyed long ago by Alexander the Great. The Moslems again reduced its successor to ashes in 711. On its site they founded a brilliant seat of Arabic learning, which Genghis Khan destroyed in 1221. The glory that survives and is now cherished with peculiar care began when Tamerlane made Samarkand his residence in 1369. Glorious mosques and gilded domes were falling into ruin in Tsarist days through sad neglect: Samarkand as an ancient seat of learning had lost its influence at a much earlier period. The Soviet Order arrived just in time to preserve what was left. With scrupulous care and archæological understanding restoration of the old proceeds side by side with rapid industrial and general cultural advance.

The Righistan, or central square, is the city's high spot. The three noble colleges of Uleg-beg, Sin-dan and Tilla-kari surround it, an immense doorway decorating the front of each with high, deep-pointed arches reaching nearly to the top of the lofty façades of smaller arches and elegant towers—all decorated with tiles, rose-pink, blue, green and gold of strange designs and exquisite harmony. Art in the Moslem world runs to colour and geometrical form.

The smallest of these colleges was built by Uleg-beg, grandson of Timur in the fifteenth century, and was justly famed for its school of mathematics and astronomy.

Rising above a larger square to the north-east lies the summer palace of Timur and near it the grave of Shah-Ziudeh his companion. Built in the fourteenth century, this shrine, with its gorgeous internal decorations, stands on a terrace reached by forty steps.

Perhaps, and certainly from my angle, the summit of all this loveliness was reached when we came to the tomb of Timur, its chapel crowned by an immense and exquisite dome and covered inside with turquoise arabesques and inscriptions in gold. Lovely in form, too, were the simple memorial stones themselves, long, low and restrained. I measured one, 5 feet by 13 inches by 13 inches, which was of dark green Nephrite, a low marble fretted balustrade surrounding it.

Tamerlane's tomb was equally small, and reproduced in exquisite lines the Moslem pointed arch.

Tamerlane was buried, contrary to Moslem custom, in a coffin: he had died abroad and his bones were thus brought back. This coffin was opened in 1942 and Gerassimov has, with physiological skill, made a reproduction of his features.

Two days before visiting Samarkand, Inna had a dream which she related to us at the time. Her head, she said, was cut off and she held it in her hand whilst still alive. As we stood by the tomb of Uleg-beg's son, called the "Living King"—held still to be alive—and were told the story, new to us, that he cut off his own head so as to prevent it falling into Christian possession, holding it in his own hands whilst he disappeared, we recollected Inna's dream, and were led on naturally to a discussion of Dunn's theory and Priestley's play based upon it—with both of which our young Soviet friends were familiar.

In the grounds of a large mosque which Timur had built in 1407 stands a huge marble support on which a copy of the Koran, many square feet in surface area, could rest, three quarters open, whilst the Mullahs read aloud from its pages.

A delightful expedition into the country to see the open air observatory of Uleg-beg was interrupted for a while on the roadside until a damaged car caught us up. We rested whilst we waited in the grounds of a little Tchaikhana or tea-house, beside which flowed a stream, in whose cool waters, the day being scorchingly hot, Inna and I paddled. "She must be a virgin," whispered the countrymen, "no married woman would bare her legs to paddle." The observatory was most impressive. A great and delicately and accurately carved marble segment of a circle sweeping down deep into the earth and up again not quite so high on the other side carried a bronze rail on which traversed the astronomical instruments, the astronomer walking beside them on the accompanying stairway.

Here were calculated the astronomical tables which made Uleg-beg's name famous. English travellers came in Queen Elizabeth's day and perhaps from her Court, to examine Uleg-beg's observatory. Doubly a hero in these days of scientific enthusiasm, Uleg-beg's memory is honourably recorded: plays are written around his life and tragic death.

I could well have lingered on in this lovely old town and in the comfortable "dacha," entered from the high whitewashed-walled old dusty lane where we lunched and rested from the midday heat. The old-fashioned gardens, the swimming pool, the great arbour—vine-walled on the hot sunny side and open to the cooler airs of the north, where we retired from the midday heat—fitted in exactly with one's picture of Samarkand: there we ate our fruit, rested, smoked and chatted at our leisure. Our hostess took me to the still cooler shade of an inner room, reminiscent of the wide cool seaside rooms of my extreme youth, both in its furniture, in the green venetian blinds, and the snowy-sheeted mattress on a Victorian brass and iron bedstead, where I rested in great comfort for the half hour before departing. It was a leisurely Victorian interlude between the noble and exhilarating records of earlier centuries, and in the midst of the throbbing newer life of the Soviet industrial and agricultural world. For the grip and purpose of Soviet life is on Samarkand, restoring the old with archæological skill, animated with a modern and fierce faith in the power of science, with a purpose for the masses of the people unknown before in these oriental lands, and with a belief in life and destiny which set all the young people around me eager to talk and discuss on a hundred different themes whilst we paused for a moment before we followed our pilot back again to the plane, and to Tashkent.

6. INSTITUTIONAL RELIGION IN ASIA

To pass from Russia into Asia was to pass from a world with Christian roots to a world with Islamic roots.

The Islamic faith practised still in Asia dominates 200 millions of mankind, spreading its influence through China, Asia, India, Arabia and Africa—beltwise across two continents, from the Pacific in the east to the Atlantic in the West.

Beginning as an Arabian nationalist movement, Islam—for such we should call it and not Mohammedanism—spread out far and wide, though remaining still at heart a heat-belt religion, making few conversions where climate is temperate, effecting no permanent foothold in Spain, Sicily, Malta, or Greece and maintaining even in Turkey but a precarious foothold.

Islam, though still spreading in Malaya and Central Africa, proves more vulnerable than Christianity to the modern spirit, losing ground rapidly among the youth. Not, however, before serving mankind in various ways.

For that mysterious Arab, its founder, living obscurely till his fortieth year in Mecca, six centuries after Christ, and then, like Joan of Arc, hearing voices, some early, some late, and founding a faith on the voices he heard and heeded, struck deep chords somewhere in human hearts.

The earlier and later voices differ, the later permitting Mohammed to have fourteen wives—most of them indeed the elderly widows of his friends—and calling him to expand his faith through fire and sword, register the degeneration due to age and power. His earlier voices, speaking in nobler tones, enabled him to extend a broader, cleaner, fresher and more rigorous political and social ideal than that then prevalent in the decadent Byzantine Empire.

As a "gradualist," Mohammed effected no radical social reform, though the abolition of infanticide and cruelty to animals are no mean social achievement, neither was the abstinence from alcohol, inculcated at first that man might concentrate on worship, and only later becoming an absolute direction.

Mohammed's contribution to social science is best illustrated by his final recorded utterance: "Ye people! hearken to my speech and comprehend the same. Know that every Moslem is the brother of every other Moslem. All of you are of the same equality."

On the religious side Mohammed's outstanding contribution, terrible and dangerous in its one-sided emphasis, lay in the austerity which corrects weaker and more sentimental conceptions of God. To Mohammed, God is strength personified. The word Allah means "the strong," or "the mighty one." This belief in transcendent power, stark, sheer, absolute and arbitrary, taken at its best produces a dignified and restrained type of character not unlike that of Scottish Calvinistic Christians. At its worst, it makes for non-moral fanaticism.

The conception of deity as absolute transcendent power where will is arbitrary and can be changed at pleasure in contrary directions, leaves no room for fixed moral standards at all. You may do one thing to-day, and its precise opposite to-morrow. The sole obligation of man is submission, the very word Moslem means submission.

With Moslem fanaticism the Soviet regime was forced to cross swords. The tension is largely resolved to-day: it was great at first.

The Soviet authorities made no frontal attack, even on what might be called abuses. The Imam, for instance, still has more wives than one. The Soviet authorities, however, insisting on a wide standard of modern education along scientific lines for all its citizens, compels the religion of Islam to operate not in a vacuum, but amongst critical men and women. Islam will survive only if it appeals to a community rapidly becoming educated. This in itself will profoundly affect the Moslem attitude towards morality in general and towards the Koran in particular. Evil elements are doomed to die.

From one angle certainly Moslems have cause for gratitude to the U.S.S.R. and know it. Moslems enjoy civil liberty as citizens and religious liberty as believers. Formerly and under the all-dominant Orthodox Church backed by Tsarist power they lacked both

Naturally anxious as far as was possible to make direct contact with this Moslem world, I lost no time in doing so, and spent the first Friday, the Moslem sacred day, with the Imam, the head of all Asiatic Moslems, first at a general reception before worship in the mosque, and subsequently at a long and quiet afternoon in his country house.

We met, and were formally received, at the headquarters of the Joint Council of Church and State, approached by a hot, narrow, dusty, but otherwise cleanly street, lined with mud-walled windowless houses.

The Imam, an old man of eighty-two, with thin, darkish face, and straggling beard, clothed in a rich blue silk gown, met us at the entrance and led us with oriental dignity to a narrow room fitted along its entire length with a twelve-inch-high table, loaded for our entertainment with endless fruits, candies and sweetmeats. Silk quilts, exquisite in colour, and luxuriously soft, spread out upon the ground, served as seats.

Two ancient Mullahs with long white beards, one a Kirzhiz, the other a Kazak, plied us ceaselessly with cups of fresh-brewed tea poured from gay pots into shallow dishes of superbly delicate painted china; no beer, wines, or spirits, happily for me, ever invade a Moslem feast.

The Imam, whose visit to Mecca in 1914 gave him the right to wear the green turban, and qualified him for high office, is a man of few words. To eat with him was restful. To be silent was not discourteous. Conversation was intermittent. Every now and then he would press me to eat and load my plate with fruit and my cup with large crystals of sugar candy, and then ask questions:

"Is it hot in England?"

"Neither so hot nor so cold as here."

"Have you food in England?"

"Enough for health, but too little for such a feast as this," was the appropriately polite and smiling reply.

We spoke of children, whose physical fitness here and elsewhere in the Soviet Union contrasted vividly with children in other Asiatic towns such as Cairo or Baghdad: no flies, no squalor, no diseased eyes.

Life too, is valued in Tashkent, child life especially.

"Children," I suggested, recalling these facts, "are the real wealth of a country demanding supreme care physically and psychologically in their training."

"God aids life," was his laconic reply.

The Imam is learned in the Moslem way. He converses easily in several Asiatic languages and of course, knows Arabic, the language of Koran and prayer.

Feast and talk lasted an hour. Then we adjourned to the Mosque. Walking slowly through the hot, narrow streets—the Imam never drives to Mosque—we passed the 600-year-old seminary where Mullahs are trained. We entered the enclosure which surrounds the 200-year-old Mosque.

Though controlling fifty or sixty such mosques in Tashkent, some larger and more imposing than this, the Imam expressed his preference for this smaller place of worship.

"Here I learned to pray," he said, "and here my father, too, learned to pray. My heart is here. I worship here for choice."

The Mosque was smallish, holding perhaps 500 or 600 worshippers. On the low stone balustrades of the portico, cool and raised above the crowd by a flight of steps, covered the day of our visit with cushions, we sat down and looked out on the crowds within and on the crowds, in orderly ranks, standing outside, each before his own personal mat. It was a spectacle impressive in its simplicity and sincerity.

The whole atmosphere of the place on that hot, still July morning, together with the slow walk along the quiet street with its waiting crowds, silent and reverent, followed by a service, itself so utterly simple, recalled the austere sabbaths and austere worship I knew and loved as I recollect it on hot, still August and September days in the Scottish Isle of Arran in my youth.

Of music, imagery, ritual, there was none. Just man, face to face with invisible, inscrutable God. Directions for worship were given in a loud, clear chanting voice by the Imam's son, an alert and pleasant Mullah, clad in bright yellow robes. The prayers took dual form: time was allotted both for individual and collective petitions. When moved to individual prayer, a man, standing in orderly fashion by his own mat, and with the corner of his turban hanging down as is done in prayer, would suddenly draw his hand downwards across his

face as in the motion of washing—and then bow himself lower and
lower till at the culminating point of some seven postures of worship
his forehead touched the earth in the attitude of complete submission.

Collective prayers for country, army or other corporate needs
were from time to time, and as directed by the Mullah, offered by all.
Then all fell prostrate in unison. Such collective prayer was offered
for England. All prostrated and as the crowd arose one impulsive old
man covered my hand with fervent kisses.

All visible worshippers were male and adult. Neither women nor
boys under thirteen years of age may enter the body of a mosque.
Women are confined to a secluded and screened gallery.

After service, we drove to the Imam's "country house," adjacent
to the town on one side and entered thence from the narrow lanes.
On the other side it bordered open country.

It was refreshing to step from the hot streets into the cool courtyard, the size of a tennis court with a large surround. Low, whitewashed, mud-roofed buildings enclosed it on every side. A pool, fed
by running water, and surrounded by pathways, occupied one half
of the court, a large dais and a smaller one, each respectively about the
size of a large and small room, occupied the other part with a couple
of beds beyond for sleeping in the lovely night air, uninfested by
mosquitoes by night, as it was free from flies by day.

A third dais stood against an outer wall in a gap in the range of
rooms. Against the outer wall hung patterned carpets, whose rather
garish sparkling colours added a note of gaiety to a very happy scene.
The dais spread with soft covered silk quilts on which we sat, and the
low table laden with upwards of a hundred dishes, added other sparkling notes. Trees, with sparse but ample foliage, shaded us from the heat
without any sense of darkness. Fretted and tempered sunlight fell
softly through motionless leaves on to pool and table.

It was a striking scene, quietly gay, but very restful. The conversation, though a score of people sat around and talked, was low
and intermittent and mingled harmoniously with the murmur of the
brook. The two serving Mullahs and those who bore in the cooked
dishes walked about on soft felt shoes. An occasional child, bare-footed,
would glide now and then rather than walk on the more distant
paths. Nothing broke the quiet harmony of the afternoon, and it was
a long afternoon. We sat five hours at a feast which shifted its quarters
as the sun moved, leaving one dais and passing across to another.

A significant but simple ceremony introduced the eating. After
we were all seated the Imam took some round slabs of bread, the size
of saucers, broke them in two and handed the halves to each guest.

Breaking of bread is important. It is a religious act. A symbol.

A sacrament. An outward and visible sign of inward and spiritual meaning. We were guests at our host's table. We were more. We had entered the family circle. We were friends, brothers. We were admitted to the closest communion with our host. He was sharing with us, as brothers do.

This sense of community is probably the earliest element in all religious observances: it persists in various forms throughout many religions right on to this day. That is the truth in the saying that religion begins in community, fellowship, friendship. The breaking of bread and all that it signifies may be regarded as the religious complement of the organisation of Socialism, the spiritual augmentation of life, the creation of friendship and affection. Whatever does that is religion. Hence the significance of this simple act of breaking of bread—none the less significant, even if its full implications are often unperceived by those who perform the act.

This element in religion is a marked characteristic of the eastern world, perhaps for that very reason Socialism and Communism find there more appropriate soil for the extension of the same principle in its scientific form.

The meal pursued its even course. Incessant importunity to eat the only interruption. So far the food had been mainly fruit. Then came meat, bits of mutton on silver skewers, one for each.

After three hours I whispered to Inna: "Perhaps we may go now?"

"Certainly not yet," she replied.

Then the Imam's grandson, a fine, tall youth with smiling face and close-cropped hair, entered the garden leading a large black sheep by a rope. I prepared to admire the family pet, when I was bidden to pronounce a blessing over it: the formula being "For God and the guests."

I said the formula and thereby sealed the fate of the poor beast. It was led out, slaughtered and dressed: within an hour and a half it returned on a huge platter served up with dumplings, the concluding dish of the feast.

In the meantime, happily the Imam had said to me: "Guests should rest after a meal," and took me to one of the surrounding bedrooms: his own, plain but comfortable, its mud-walls colour-washed and stencilled. On the snowy sheets of a high, iron-framed bed I slept for a space, then hearing low voices in the courtyard went outside. An open door tempted me and I passed out into a wide garden with open fields beyond.

At the end of a path I spied the Imam's son in his brilliant yellow robe, talking to his wife who held their babe in her arms. He beckoned to me to approach. This I did, and won the unusual privilege of seeing one of the women of the household. For women do not appear at a feast. The Imam has two wives living, his third wife having died. I saw neither of the others. The young Mullah, however, belongs to a newer generation. Change and further change in these matters is inevitable.

Back at the feast again on the second dais because of the sun we ate the famous dish called Plov, made of rice, grated carrots and mutton, a good dish, but greasy. Politely I used my fingers as my host did his, he offering me choice bits with his own hands. We wiped our fingers on a towel.

Spoons had been provided for those who wished to use them, beautiful spoons, wooden and painted, archaic and lying in odd juxtaposition to the colourless plastic spectacles—the last word in modernity—on the Imam's nose. After the final dish we departed, but not before the Imam had said that if we would stay the week he would kill a sheep every day, and not before the Imam's youngest grandson was brought to us in the arms of his nurse. We asked that we might see and speak to the other grandchildren, two small boys and a small girl: the old man was pleased and the children came.

Little Emir Said, the youngest grandson, made friends at once, toying with my wristwatch. He enters a world differing widely from that his grandfather entered eighty-two years ago.

As we prepared to depart the Imam's son produced his father's presents to us, magnificent silk robes and caps with flowers and aromatic herbs.

This Moslem community, as the Imam explained to me, has received civil liberty and religious liberty from the Soviet Union, in return they have as a community and in the emergency of war, contributed a large sum of money to the Soviet war effort and as much foodstuffs as a hard-pressed transport service could carry.

BOOK X

THE SOVIET UNION AND HER NEIGHBOURS

1. SOVIET FOREIGN POLICY

Is the Soviet Union a force for peace? The question of Soviet strength is settled, the only outstanding problem is the way she will use her strength: Is she aggressive, expansive, imperialistic? *What is Soviet foreign policy?*

Let Stalin's historic speech of March 1939, give the answer: "The Foreign Policy of the Soviet Union is clear and explicit:

1. "We stand for peace and strengthening of business relations with all countries. That is our position, and we shall adhere to this position as long as these countries maintain like relations with the Soviet Union and as long as they make no attempt to trespass on the interests of our country.

2. "We stand for peaceful, close and friendly relations with all the neighbouring countries which have common frontiers with the U.S.S.R. That is our position and we shall adhere to this position so long as these countries maintain like relations with the Soviet Union.

3. "We stand for the support of all nations which are the victims of aggression and are fighting for the independence of their country.

4. "We are not afraid of the threats of aggression and we are ready to deal two blows for every blow delivered by instigators of war who attempt to violate the Soviet borders. Such is the Foreign Policy of the Soviet Union."

Nothing could be clearer. There is no mystery about Soviet Foreign Policy, nor ever has been.

From first to last Soviet Russia declares for peace, but never ceases to add that "peace is indivisible"—her own invented phrase—and that no security exists save collective security.

Russia has ample motives for desiring peace and for urging that no country gains by war, not even the victor, and she ought to know. Twice within thirty years has she suffered from devastating war and twice emerged victorious. Five years of war, forced upon her at the outset of Soviet history, cost her millions of lives and billions of property. Hitler's treacherous attack cost her fifteen million lives and two-thirds of the hard-won wealth of two Five-Year Plans.

Russia has also positive, in addition to negative, reasons for pursuit of peace. Only in peace can she carry to its logical conclusion her new society which, in internal affairs, substitutes, in principle, peace for strife, co-operation for competition and has no such compulsion as Hitler experienced for external war to screen internal dissension.

Soviet Russia's actions from first to last lend support to her peaceful asseverations. Soviet Russia took immediate steps to reverse Tsarist imperial policy. Soviet Russia led the way in giving up territorial rights in China; relinquished all Russian dreams of annexing Constantinople; made non-aggression pacts with eleven bordering states; signed the Kellog-Briand Pact for outlawing war and entered the League of Nations with full determination to honour her League obligations both in letter and spirit.

From first to last also has Russia championed collective security, calling persistently on all peace-loving nations to unite in resisting aggression—if necessary, by force. She urged it when Japan attacked Manchuria, when Mussolini invaded Abyssinia; she urged it in defence of Spain, Austria, China and Czechoslovakia. Russia alone expressed her willingness to act: other League members refused. Single-handed and on her own initiative she fulfilled her League obligations to China and Spain.

Again, when Czechoslovakia was threatened, the Soviet Union, in accordance with the Soviet-Czechoslovakian pact stood willing to give immediate aid. She also urged a meeting of the great Powers of Europe to devise means for maintaining Czechoslovakian territorial integrity. Whitehall made no reply. And later, when Poland and Rumania were threatened, Mr. Chamberlain turned down Russia's second proposal for a conference as premature. Every Soviet effort towards collective security was rebuffed. Herself agreeing to the League Covenant's stipulation that members should afford passage to fellow members co-operating in protection of the Covenant of the League, she sought passage for Soviet troops in their march against the Nazis. Poland refused passage facilities: England and France supported Poland's refusal.

This led in the summer of 1939 to the breakdown of British–Soviet negotiations. Collective security collapsed and the fiasco foreseen by Stalin broke over Europe. In the German–Soviet non-aggression pact Russia saw her only alternative, securing, as it did, a brief respite in which to hasten on with her own defences. The pact had the effect of revealing that the real motive of the "appeasers" was to turn the war, if war there must be, against Soviet Socialism.

Lord Lloyd in his book *The British Case*, which had the blessing of Lord Halifax, at that time Britain's Foreign Secretary, said of the German-Soviet Pact: "This is Hitler's final apostasy. It was the betrayal of Europe." Germany had been permitted to rearm in the belief that she would stand as Europe's bulwark against "Bolshevism." Hence the expression, "Hitler's apostasy."

Collective security collapsed: the fiasco foreseen by Stalin broke over Europe. The Soviet Union in self-defence signed the non-aggression pact with Germany. It was no alliance, simply Hitler's promise not to attack the Soviet Union if the Soviet Union promised not to attack Germany.

Russia, back in the jungle, was bound to take all precautions for self-defence, chiefly to secure the removal of the Finnish frontier to seventy-five miles, instead of twenty miles, eastwards from Leningrad, her second largest industrial area. The generous treatment of Finland in 1940 and 1945, show clearly that the motive was security and not aggression. The White Russian and Ukrainian sections of Poland and the Baltic States voted to become once again part of the Soviet Union from which they had been torn at the time of the first World War.

Thus did Russia not only forestall the Nazi Coup, but actually pinned down, as Hitler later admitted, a million German troops and vast stores of equipment otherwise available against Britain.

Never for a moment, not even in the crisis forced upon her, or since, has the Soviet Union been disloyal to the cause of world peace, and collective security as its permanent foundation stone. Her statement that peace can be achieved only through respect for international law, based on collective armed force of all the allied States, appears in the Polish-Soviet agreement of December 1941: the same thought reappears in the Twenty-Year British-Soviet Pact of May 1942, and was endorsed by the Four Nations Moscow Declaration.

Another item in Soviet Russia's programme, illustrative of her attitude to the outside world in general and to her immediate neighbours, is her doctrine of the self-determination of peoples. As early as November 1917, Lenin and Stalin signed a Soviet decree granting to the former subject peoples the right to secede. The present constitution upholds this principle. Any constituent nation not entirely enclosed in the Soviet Union may secede. Finland, in 1917, was permitted to secede. "Russia," said Mr. Henry A. Wallace, in his address to the Congress of Anglo-Soviet Friendship in 1942, "has probably gone further than any other nation in the world in practising ethnic democracy."

This then, in general, is the Soviet Union's attitude towards external nations, towards world peace, collective security and self-determination of peoples.

And it is against this general attitude as background that we must approach her particular attitude towards her immediate neighbours, recollecting at the same time two other factors of supreme importance. The first is the acknowledged hostility and suspicions of the western world during the period between the two world wars. The other is the fact that from the west and the south, and through the lands in question, Russia has suffered repeated attacks: from Gustavus Adolphus, the Swede; from Napoleon of France; from Kaiser Wilhelm of Germany; from nine allied nations of the West plus Japan after World War I and from Hitler in World War II. It is hardly surprising that Russia seeks security on her western frontiers against any repetition of the horrors of the two recent wars.

Of Russia's attitude to Poland and Czechoslovakia which I visited in person, I shall write later. Of her attitude to her neighbours in South-Eastern Europe I cannot improve upon the words of Mr. Taplin who in a recent broadcast on "World Affairs," said:

"Don't make the mistake of thinking that Russian policy there is particularly complicated—it's really pretty simple. In the first place, Russia is interested in the Balkan States as near neighbours, just as we're interested in our neighbours—France, Belgium and Holland. Secondly, Russia is particularly concerned about the economic life of these countries—as you might suspect of a country whose whole development in the last twenty years has centred around an economic revolution. And finally, the Russians regard the Balkan countries as owing something for their sacrifice in driving back the Germans, and they're going to see that they pay what they owe."

It should hardly be necessary, when one considers the facts, to meet the charge that Russia is expansionist, were the charge less persistent. These are the facts. During the war, and largely through military necessity, the Baltic States, a small part of Finland, Bessarabia, the country east of the "Curzon Line," and a small fragment of East Prussia have been incorporated. With the exception of the last small item all this was part of Russia at the time of the Revolution and with the exception of the Baltic peoples all were of Russian, Ukranian or near-Russian stock.

Compare with this the U.S.A. acquisition. The German islands in the Pacific, opposed by our peoples at UNO. Air basis in Iceland against the Icelandic Government's wish. Endeavours to force Denmark to accept joint defence of Greenland. Air bases in Saude Arabia. Military and Police Advisor in Teheran. Active support to Greece and Turkey—the latter on the Soviet frontier—with military equipment. The supply of arms to Chiang Kai Shek and the training of his picked men; playing also an important role against the Communists in the Chinese Civil War. Directly or indirectly the U.S.A. controls threequarters of the world and from that direction at least charges against the Soviet Union of expansionism or undue influence could meet with justifiable rebound.

The Soviet Union has never sought isolation. She does not seek it now. She is more determined than ever to prevent the rest of the world from falling into what she considers to be the errors of the past. She may not be skilled in diplomacy, but she will learn and she is strong; she knows what she wants, she has vital interests in her immediate neighbours and she still believes that peace is indivisible. That she desires co-operation may be gathered from many signs; she is educating youth as a priority and as a long-term policy for foreign service both in the diplomatic and economic fields; the teaching of English is compulsory in the schools; school text-books have been freed from remarks derogatory to Britain and America. The U.S.S.R. is now, for the first time, in diplomatic relations with most of the countries of the world. Stalin in his speech of February 1946, goes out of his way to assign the allied share in the war its due place, making it clear we were in it before the Russians were. Stalin added that war in general might perhaps be avoided if raw materials and markets could be redistributed periodically among the countries in accordance with their economic weight by co-ordinated and peaceful decisions. Here is an open door for world co-operation.

2. POLAND

(A) *During the Liberation*

ONE of the most remarkable women whom I met frequently in Russia, both before the war and since, is Anna Louise Strong, an American woman by birth and still retaining her U.S.A. passport, though married to a Russian editor. She has moved between Russia and the U.S.A. ever since she first entered the Soviet Union in 1921, and has stayed with me more than once in Canterbury.

From Anna Strong I learned much of the New Poland before my visit there in May 1945. My friend D'Eye and I were the first Britishers to enter Liberated Poland: she was the first American writer or correspondent to enter the Council Chamber at the birth of the New Polish Government.

Miss Strong's fascinating career deserves a chapter to itself did space permit. Taking a degree in philosophy she awoke to serious and vigorous life only when social consciousness dawned. Then followed an adventurous and probing career which carried her at length to Russia in 1921. In 1930 she married a Russian editor and journalist who has since died, but she keeps her maiden name. A voluminous writer herself, she organised the English edition of the *Moscow News*. Once a matter of dispute concerning the paper was laid before Mr. Stalin; Miss Strong admired the clear way in which he quietly sorted out the tangle and gave her a free hand for her work. Her knowledge of Russia—its strength and its weak points—is profound, and long comparison of her statements with subsequent knowledge of facts and unfolding events made me rely much—as I found so many Moscow foreign correspondents also relied on her knowledge and judgment.

Anna Strong is an acute observer and an intrepid explorer, fearing no danger and shirking no hardship: her forceful presence, her linguistic skill and her obvious sincerity and moral depth gain her audiences and entrances granted to but few. I knew her story would be of high value and that I could check it up later at leisure and carry it forward from personal observation. Here, then, is the substance of what she said and read to me in her flat at the National Hotel in May, 1945.

On New Year's Eve, in a yellow-columned hall in Lublin, Miss Strong saw the birth of a new government. The National Council, or Rada, of Poland, attended by ninety-eight deputies—those from occupied Poland coming secretly and to express the desires of the occupied areas—voted unanimously to form a provisional government to hold power until all Poland was free and a new government could be formed by formal election.

Naturally regular governmental forms could not be observed in their completeness: half the deputies were elected by trades unions, cultural societies or village councils, men who had carried on underground operations throughout the occupation.

It is of great importance to observe that the new Government was formed of men, and elected by men, who at infinite cost and peril to their own lives had remained in Poland fighting back ceaselessly against the Nazi. These were the real leaders, the real soul of the nation. It was they who were trusted to carry on the task of leadership after the liberation because it was they who had never left off or departed during the occupation.

The reason given by representatives of four political parties at this formal and solemn Council Meeting for their decision to set up a Provisional Government was that the Rada contained leaders from all sections of the Polish people and had substantial public backing.

Eight weeks tour had enabled Miss Strong to verify this statement: she gave two instances. Spychalski, chief of the city planning in Warsaw before the war, had gone underground after assisting the

Q

Warsaw resistance in 1939, organising the first group of partisans who later became the People's Army. It was he who handled the technical organisation of the secret meeting of the Rada, which one year earlier, and in Warsaw during the occupation, had launched the organisation now constituting the Government. At the liberation he became Mayor of Warsaw.

Father Borovets, again chief of the legislative government of a fair-sized state, who had taken an important part in the organisation of the peasants before the war, had also helped the underground movemoent during the war; during the organisation of the land reform after the liberation he had paid personal visits to each village, superintended the new land distribution, and seen that it was carried out with order and common-sense.

These and many such-like strong personalities made up the National Rada.

Boleslaw Bierut—quiet, reserved, chief thinker of the Government, prominent, formerly in the co-operative movement and in the Polish Workers' Party—was elected President of the new Provisional Government, of which Edward Osubka-Morawski—accessible, friendly, and always at home with workers and peasants, member of the Socialist Party—was elected Premier, and presided over a cabinet of eighteen members: five Socialists; five Peasant Party; four Workers' Party; one Democrat, and two non-party men including General Rola Zymierski, the Commander-in-Chief.

The Congress was held on New Year's Eve—anniversary of the Warsaw underground Rada and a day of jubilation at the new liberation. The air was charged high with popular hopes.

To Miss Strong the normal questions, "Does the Government maintain order?" "Is it independent or a Soviet puppet State?" sounded odd and unreal, returning as she did from a country where a national government was in process of birth, where its problem was the creation of order out of Nazi-produced chaos and its immediate task was the quest or leaders and organisers and their incorporation into a government. It was, most emphatically, the local Poles who did the job and solved the problems unaided.

The new Government functioned. That was the major fact. The peasants gave their harvest quota without military compulsion. Hence the Government could feed the civil servants, the army and the industrial workers, and thus establish a stable routine of work. The people accepted Government-printed money as payment for food and goods; young men accepted mobilisation into the army, and locally elected committees of peasants parcelled out the land. The Government came into being while German armies still occupied two-thirds of Poland

and with the Red Army confronting the Germans on a bitterly contested line. The Polish Government intended to act in independence: the Russians in word and deed supported the intention.

In the spectacular blitz which followed, millions of underfed Poles emerged from cellars to create the new Polish Army and rebuild the daily life.

The Germans had sought methodically to destroy all civilian activities. The Russians forestalled them by a carefully prepared terrific break-through, carrying their armies deep into the German rear, thence to reattack the Germans from the West. In this way they saved many Polish cities, Cracow, for example; the partisans preventing destruction in the final moments of demoralisation. Warsaw might thus have been saved had not the Polish General Bor on advice from the London Poles, made a premature attack which cost Poland half a million lives and handed Warsaw over to unutterable destruction.

Local government was the primary need: to stop looting, to bury the dead, to fight epidemics, to provide food and housing were the task of local people: no London government could cope with this, only men on the spot who could co-operate with the liberating government could do it. During the latter half of 1944 Mikolajczyk was urged repeatedly to return as Prime Minister of Poland. As he declined to come the government was organised without him. Far-sighted, patriotic Poles foresaw the local needs and organised for them a year before the Nazis were overthrown. The dynamic Sphychalski called together the National Council of Poland on New Year's Eve, 1943, under the very nose of the Nazis and in Warsaw, Poland's capital, a thrilling story of skill and daring.

When the pre-war Polish government fled to London—taking with them the Polish gold reserves—the Polish political parties, the trade unions and various cultural organisations remained and continued to function underground. Groups gradually developed, and seeing in the Red Army's victories hope for Poland's freedom, they parted company with the London Poles whose hostility to the Soviet had never, and has never, ceased. Division based on differing attitudes to the Soviet Union marks the dividing line down to this very day.

When the Red Army marched into Poland in late June, the underground Rada emerged and formed an open and legal Polish Committee of National Liberation from leading Poles in the various spheres of the government.

The Red Army never set up any military government, a civilian government in the hands of Poles being already in existence and recognised by the Soviet Government as the administrative power in the liberated areas. In every liberated town or village the Committee called together the leading citizens to form local councils; they called on parents and teachers to assemble schools, not waiting for desks and other equipment, nor even for regular school buildings. Polish terrorists claiming allegiance to London formed the greatest hindrance to the new order: fifty representatives of the Polish Council of Liberation were assassinated.

Food was a primary need. The peasants assisted in collecting the quota for the Committee, which had freed the poorest peasants from any delivery, reduced the medium peasants quota to three-quarters of the German levy, but demanded the entire harvest of the landlords, many of whom I discovered later had departed with the Germans or fled at the outbreak of war.

Out of chaos order slowly emerged. Men were chosen for ministers rather casually, just as likely persons happened to arrive. One of these arrivals, for instance, was the Polish engineer Osenski with whom I stayed and of whom I shall say more later. He was chief road engineer in Afghanistan, and gave up all to return to Poland. After wandering at a loose end for a week around Lublin, he was suddenly made Vice-Commissioner of roads and waterways for all Poland. Living and working in one hotel room with six others he remarked: "I am so happy that I can work for Poland now at this turning-point in our history for a thousand years: we always ruined ourselves fighting the Russians; now we are going to be friends." In that sentence Osenski struck the keynote of future Polish policy.

I have related the substance of Miss Strong's graphic story of the genesis of the new Polish Government at some length—it has subsequently been published in full, in fine pamphlet form by the National Council of American-Soviet Friendship—because it shows with convincing clearness what I speedily discovered myself on entry into Poland, that neither the Polish Committee of National Liberation not the Polish Provisional Government were in any sense puppet governments.

They were formed in Poland, not in Moscow. Their origin was from the Polish underground movement, developed through five bitter years of struggle. All the help that Russia gave, besides the supreme gift of Liberation, was arms and equipment for the Polish underground army; some materials and machines for industry, and certain short-term credits repayable in goods. Nothing more. As Beirut said: "We did not even ask for loans or money to start our Government, expecting to live from taxes and food collection." The Government printed a small number of notes for immediate needs.

(B) *Warsaw, Cracow and Danzig*

Receiving an invitation from the Polish Commission for inquiry into German crimes, to visit Poland and see the facts for myself, I flew with Mr. D'Eye and another, a Russian friend, to Poland on 26th May, 1945, and thus made direct contact with one of those border-line countries which form the western fringe between Socialist Russia and the Western capitalist world. We were the first English observers to enter and saw, in its earliest creative stages, what has become one of the crucial workshops of the newly emerging world order.

Similarly, a month later we saw Czechoslovakia at first-hand, and in its own earliest post-war stages. These two visits were not unimportant episodes. They provided a spring-board for the study of Russia and her neighbours, the raw material for judgment. We saw in miniature then what all begin to see writ large now.

We visited in succession Warsaw, Cracow, and Danzig as centres, talking with many people officially and unofficially, in country and town, with priests, artists, novelists, peasants, and artisans. We visited the countryside, we spent a day at Auschwitz.

We met official Polish personages, Mr. Swiatkowski, the Minister of Justice; Mr. Sawicki, the Public Prosecutor; Mr. Kurylowicz, a Deputy; Mr. Berman, representing the Jewish community; Mr. Osenski, Governor of Dantzig Province; Mr. Kotus-Jawkowski, President of Danzig City; Dr. Alfred Fiderkiewicz, President of Cracow, and many more.

We concluded our vist with an hour's intimate and interesting conversation with Mr. Beirut, the President.

Warsaw was a terrible sight; with devilish ingenuity and at great cost, the Germans before they left had spent some three months in destroying every building of note, every block of shops, every block of flats. Every street presented the picture of a pile of rubble.

To reconstruct Warsaw, even to clear away the rubble, presented a Herculean task. Yet at that moment, within two months of the departure of the Germans, life stirred again. Stalls arose in the streets in place of shops. Long farm carts drawn by horses took the place of trams and in the Art Gallery, reserved by the Germans for destruction to the last because of its use to their forces, and then escaping in the final over-throw—though with its treasures barbarously and deliberately ruined—was an exhibition illustrating on the one hand the ruin and barbarity, and on the other the design for the new Warsaw which is to arise from the ashes.

It was a marvellous and moving exhibition displaying once more

Polish skill and artistry, by interlacing of Polish flags and eagles, by the symbolic illumination on the walls, by the arrangement of the photographs and exhibits—charred timbers, ashes of books, broken statues, the polite and begging letters of Dr. Frey, the German archæologist, set side by side with the broken skulls and mutilated relics of Poland's past history which with his own hand he had smashed, depicting the horrors of the occupation. And then the pictures of the new Warsaw as it is already planned, painted on glass in tinted background, a plan as ingenious, scientific and imaginative in conception, as was the skilled, the graphic mode of depicting it in such a way that every simple visitor could see at a glance what was proposed and receive courage and determination to work for its fulfilment.

Crowds, bravely or artistically dressed—Polish artistry in dress is great—in fragments of clothing they had rescued from the blitz, circulated the exhibition and the streets on that fine Sunday afternoon in May. The Poles are a proud people and they were now free. We spent a Sunday morning in Warsaw attending churches and in the afternoon sitting in conference with ministers and officials of the new Government.

After Warsaw, Cracow, an hour's flight, brought great refreshment and delight. Cracow, an old mid-European town, was and is the very model of what a town should be, not too big or too small, traditional, cleanly, comely, enriched with lovely and dignified buildings and parks and boulevards and trees. Cracow was untouched, unharmed; undespoiled, save for some treasures removed from churches and from the Castle.

Cracow was Frank's headquarters. The Russians with their fine strategy had approached from the West and Frank had fled precipitately, leaving even his soup untouched on the table. Cracow was saved.

And so Cracow, breathing again, looks as any lovely mid-European town looked before the war. Its boulevards filled at midday with sauntering crowds in a dinner-hour promenade, nursemaids with babes, Russian soldiers strolling quietly with Polish friends, church bells ringing and churches filled with worshippers, markets where country folks spread out their wares, trams running and cars, and theatres open at night. . . . Food was apparently carefully and equally rationed. Manufacturers wisely controlled, and life in general well organised and full of hopeful expectation. Hardship undoubtedly existed and it pressed particularly and naturally on the upper classes, especially upon the professional classes who had settled not uneasily under the German yoke. I got glimpses of it in occasional surreptitious talks. Acts of violence were not unknown, and ruthless deeds were still perpetrated—I occasionally heard gunshots at night in Cracow, though returning late from theatres and cafés I saw no signs of trouble.

We visited the concentration camp at Auschwitz, accompanied by the Mayor of Cracow, who told us the story as he himself, a victim, experienced it.

On Corpus Christi Day after attending an early and crowded Mass in Cracow, we flew from south to north and visited Danzig, arriving in time for lunch and for Corpus Christi evening celebration at a grand old church which in Zappot had escaped destruction.

Danzig has suffered as Warsaw has suffered. The loss to civilisation perhaps exceeds the loss at Warsaw. For Danzig was unique, one of the very few surviving Hanseatic League cities, a mediæval seaport, full of rich and irreplaceable treasures. All gone. Fire bombs still smouldered amongst the ashes of the port.

We stayed in a quiet villa at Zappot with Mr. Oksenski, visiting the wrecked docks and, most horrible of all, the factory where soap— scented soap—was made from human bodies. We passed German citizens in the streets—the bulk were Germans. Russian Red Army men were vigorously helping life to revolve again. Danzig lacked a native male population as yet. Russian Red Army men built bridges, lent machinery and helped with the spring sowing.

Four outstanding studies occupied our minds in Poland—the concentration camps, to see which was our primary mission; the personnel of the new order; the religious situation, the new social and economic set-up, with the day to day life of the people. I must speak briefly of each.

(c) *The Grim Square Mile*

Auschwitz—Oswiecim the Poles call it—contains the world's grimmest square mile; methodical destruction of so many millions puts Oswiecim in a class by itself. It demanded the fullest investigation and the fullest documentation, and this was proceeding whilst we were there.

On a strip of malarial land, in a camp designed for 50,000 or 60,000 persons, and always crammed to capacity, 4,000,000 human beings were done to death with German thoroughness, caught in a net from which few ever escaped alive.

Of those few I met some. Dr. Alfred Fiderkiewicz, the President of Cracow was one, with his No. 138,907 neatly tattooed on his arm. He had worked in the camp for a year as a labourer and then as hospital physician, escaping the final round-up by hiding among corpses. Dr. Fiderkiewicz's legs looked like sticks with starvation: "Musselman" he and suchlike were called with grim humour, and with reference to thin hinder legs. He took me round the camp. I saw other such limbs, the limbs for instance of Eva Muhad, a Jewish girl from Budapest, who with others in the hospital escaped in the final confusion. A photograph by her side taken the previous summer showed her as a lovely child in her late teens dangling shapely legs in the waters of a swimming pool. Her age is twenty: her weight sixty-six pounds.

Greta Rausch also, of pure German blood, from Gnadenburg, condemned to death camp through unavoidable absence from work for three days. She cannot survive. Her age is twenty-one, her weight sixty-four lbs.

These few had slipped through the final sieve. Millions had no such luck. Four million is an underestimate. The evidence—the careful dossiers, the camp itself, holding upwards of 50,000 always full to capacity, and fed by crowded trains up a special siding to the gas station and incinerator; the furnaces and their capacity; the long supplementary open pits for burning. . . .

Working all out the crematorium reached peak capacity of 24,000 in one day in July, 1944, and as reward the Commandant received a decoration "for distinguished services on the civil front" and a letter of thanks from Hitler: the operators extra vodka. The grim records are extant.

Dr. Fiderkiewicz's billet lying alongside the special siding, enabled him to see the daily tragedy. A train of 2,000 victims would arrive, selection would begin forthwith, some 300 of the strongest would be despatched to the labour camp to work till they dropped. Entering the camp under an archway bearing the bitter title "Arbeit macht frei," the vast majority found no freedom save in death—happy indeed if death came through sickness or exhaustion and not through the dark cell, the gallows, the shooting-wall.

Those cells will always haunt me to my dying day. Inscriptions abound, scratched with human nails on whitewashed walls: "Nothing to smoke; nothing to eat. It is dark. We sit here twenty-three days. Victor Carasov" or a woman's name: "Washa is here. Odessa 1944."

Into one cell whose only window was a hole $4\frac{1}{2}$ ins. square through a thick wall and which measured 12 feet by 7 feet and was 8 feet high, an immense number were shut in with no sanitation at all. That cell was found in an indescribable state of filth and stench.

There were death cells with the gallows and the shooting-walls—lined with cork to prevent bullets from rebounding at the executioners, just beside them. German prisoners watched our inspection; they had just endeavoured to obliterate evidence of the German crimes. For instance they had smashed the gallows. I suggested that they should be compelled to rebuild them as they had found them.

Those rejected in the first selection from the train, passed to a more speedy and methodic death. They were marched to the "chimney," as the crematorium was called. Mothers with young children had no chance. Very occasionally a strong young woman would hand her child over to a sickly woman or leave it in the crowd and escape to the labour camp.

Those condemned to die entered a large room, and were bidden to strip, preparatory to a bath, and "a new life." Then down a corridor, a mingling of women, children, babes and men, they walked or were pushed into a room the size of a narrow tennis court, packed tight with hundreds of victims; savage dogs set at their naked bodies to squeeze the mass still further in; then to the sound of terrifying cries and screams, doors slammed, gas was injected, and in twenty minutes merciful death came.

When all was still the corpses were dragged out in two lines past dentists who extracted gold teeth and plates, and barbers who shaved the hair and thence to the furnaces; two bodies on each metal shutter; four in each oven, or under pressure, five.

The total capacity of the ovens is known. Correspondence is extant in which the makers of the oven claimed and received additional percentage through exceeding the stipulated tale of destruction.

On piles of timber in supplementary trenches, corpses were flung when the pressure was too great. A huge grey dusty mound beside it with fragments of teeth and steel crowns protruding everywhere completed the horrible tale.

The dwellers in the camp could distinguish the burnings—camp victims created smoke, fresh victims from the trains created flames, they were fatter. The hospital charts showed sudden drops in numbers, the German doctors deciding when a batch of no further use should be sent to the "chimney."

Fresh camps were projected. I saw the plans—damning evidence that the mass murder was to be extended far beyond the 4,000,000 already recorded. In the meantime the work was speeded up. Incinerating trenches were dug and sometimes half-gassed bodies were thrown on to the flames.

Feeling sick, we passed to the vast storehouses, their cellars piled with hair—gold, brown, flaxen or grey, some already packed into tight neat bales ready to stuff pillows on which other heads would lie in Germany. In rooms above were mountains of boots, slippers and shoes; mountains of spectacles, brushes, combs and razor blades, parts of the periodic consignments to Germany. On the uppermost floor, garments in piles reached to the ceilings.

Our walk had by this time become a procession of mourners. Dr. Fiderkiewicz, Mr. D'Eye, an Austrian doctor, seven years in the camp, an Italian boy of noble family with a Jewish grandmother who had also been a victim, the stern-faced Polish Advocate who sifts the evidence of crime and criminals, Russian and Polish officers, and other local authorities.

The young Russian woman doctor now in charge of the hospital handed me a baby's small woolly vest. No words were needed to conjure up the scene when a mother's trembling hands had so recently drawn tiny limbs from the sleeves and pressing the babe's naked body to her own naked body had entered the death chamber amidst cries, groans, oaths, and screams and the barking of hounds, then the closed doors, the dark, the gas, and at last, death.

Silently now, and with a kind of ritual the doctor motioned me to take the garment home. With gulping throat I took it, and we passed down the stone stairs and paused beside a pile of white glazed soup dishes. The Advocate, more stern and pale than before, showed me the mark on the back, S.S. He handed it to me and indicated by a sign what I might do. Raising it high in the air I crashed it to the ground where it broke into a thousand fragments on the concrete floor. As the echoes died down we all stood in silence and then passed out into the bright sunshine of a late May day.

So may the echoes of hateful Nazi Fascism depart for ever from God's earth.

(D) *The Danzig Soap Laboratory*

In Zappot, a fair suburb of Danzig, now known by its Polish name— Gdansk, and situated among gardened villas, stands the German Institute of Hygiene, with its large demonstration theatre and special cellars beneath. Hidden away in those cellars is a spectacle of utter horror. We were the first Englishmen to see it.

It was raining, and as we descended the sodden steps a Polish Lieutenant turned to me and said: "You must be prepared for a sight which will hurt your heart." We entered cellars dimly lit from basement windows. As our eyes grew slowly accustomed to the light we found ourselves surrounded by ranges upon ranges of red-painted, travel-stained steel cases, 5 feet 6 inches long, 4 feet wide and 4 feet deep. Each case was fitted with headless, stiffened corpses, or mutilated fragments of corpses. Corpses rigid and moulded into the shape dictated by the pressure of the packing.

By their side smaller cases contained dried hairless human skulls. Bodies and heads of many races, European, Asiatic, Mongolian. The tattooed chest of a Red Navy man was discerned amongst the others.

These bodies numbered 340. Some were headless. Some cut into small pieces for convenient packing. Some had been slit open from neck to abdomen; the large pockets of fat removed, the incision sewn roughly up with string.

It puzzled me to know how objects so bulky and weighty could be carried down the steep stairs. But there they stood, surrounded by litter of papers and rubbish ready for their final journey to the soap factory. German soldiers had used the cellars for a shelter and eaten and slept on these very cases.

In the grounds of the Institute and cheek by jowl with the neighbouring villas, stands a long shed, with a chimney and a loft. The loft contains boxes of skulls and major bones. The shed is a soap refinery, installed with appropriate modern machinery.

It is a makeshift laboratory, though the machinery is new and modern, the vat and the boiler complete with glossy enamel and stainless steel clamps and handles and taps. In that range of rooms human bodies were rendered down by German scientists to make human soap for human needs. Scented soap.

These scientists had laid by a special store of soap for themselves, their families and friends. The vats were still filled with awful ingredients. A slab of white soap still stood on a bench in a disordered inner room, whence the Germans had so recently and so precipitately fled.

A case on the ground contained large strips and squares of stiff parchment-like substance wrinkled into fantastic shapes. This was human skin, tanned and prepared human leather for women's reticules and gloves. Nothing was wasted in that laboratory. What defied utilisation was burned. The furnace operated by night. The stench was too offensive by day.

We were several witnesses who saw and minutely examined this horrible place. The President of Gdansk City Council himself accompanied us; a man who had himself suffered severely and bore the marks of it upon his face. Fresh photographs were taken while we were there.

The whole thing was so recent, it had stopped working but yesterday as it were. Fires were still smouldering and waking into fitful blazes in the wreckage of Gdansk's riverside, while wisps of smoke still filtered from the smoke-bomb casks on the wharves at Gdynia. The war had only just swept by, leaving its usual trail of battle devastation—leaving in this case, the deliberate blowing up to destruction of every historic monument and all the lovely mediaeval buildings of one of Europe's most interesting and charming towns. But I doubt if ever before war has left it so revolting a memorial of human wreckage and depravity as is witnessed by this human soap factory, by these cases of stiffened corpses and by all this scientific machinery, on which German children still gazed down during our visit from an upper window next door. There was a devilish coldness and inhumanity about the whole thing. An utter disrespect for life or values of any kind which make it peculiarly revolting. And this human soap factory is only the final stage of one vast process of human murder, the end of the belt of mass destruction of human life and values. This laboratory must be seen in its context and its context lies in a network of murder camps, chief of which is the camp at Oswiecim, near Cracow, in the extreme south, as Danzig lies in the extreme north of Poland.

(e) *The Massacre of Jews*

Quite outstanding, of course, has been the German massacre of the Jews. Poland has become a Jewish cemetery. Jews had been brought to Poland by the million to be burned. Out of the 3,500,000 Jews in Poland before the German occupation, only 50,000 remain alive to-day. Two hundred thousand had fled to the Soviet Union; 98 per cent had been destroyed; 99 per cent of children had been murdered. Children had been killed in gas or high-pressure steam chambers.

We visited the Ghetto, or rather the pile of rubble far as the eyes could reach, which had once been the ghetto. Here destruction had been more thorough than anywhere else in the war areas. Only one chimney remained. The Jews had fought back before their extermination, 50,000 young men and women in Warsaw alone.

Our Polish interpreter, a young and attractive woman, who herself had suffered from the Gestapo—her thumbs had been crushed in thumb screws—told us a grim story of a Jewish girl. Daily led to their work from their concentration camp past the ruined ghetto, they observed one day an emaciated starved creature in a ruined hole: she had subsisted for months, as the sole Jewish survivor. They gave her daily scraps of food from their own starvation ration. At length the Gestapo discovered her. The German authorities expressed astonishment that anyone could survive so long and in such circumstances, and granted her her life: they fed her until she was well on the road to recovery. Then, the experiment of the rate and nature of recovery after such prolonged starvation completed, they shot her.

Mr. Berman, the leader of the Jews, from whom we gathered much information, sent greetings to the English Jews from the remnants of the Polish Jews. "Not even yet are we safe," he said. Reactionary elements still exist and murders of Jews are not isolated or casual. Several hundred Jews had been murdered in the last few months. For the rest, the Jews have complete freedom, socially, politically and religiously.

(F) *Religion in Post-War Poland*

Knowing that to my country the state of religion was a matter of foremost importance, and that much hostility to the Polish Government sprang from religious sources, I made an effort to understand the attitude of the Government towards religion, and the attitude of religious people, both clergy and laity, towards the Government. With that end in view, and also because of my natural desire to worship with the devout common people in Poland, as in any other country, I attended church services whenever and wherever I could. I had frequent opportunities.

In Warsaw, in Cracow, in Gdansk, I mingled with the worshippers and talked with priests, ministers, pastors and congregations of Catholic, Lutheran, Methodist, and Calvinist Churches. I also spent an afternoon with Mr. Swiatkowski, the Minister of Justice, an authority on the religious situation in the past, and entrusted by the Government with much say in the formulation of future policy.

For instance, on Sunday, 29th May, I attended Services in three of the four churches which were all that were left in Warsaw. First with a large congregation of soldiers on parade in the big city Church of St. Cross, and afterwards with the civilian congregation in the same Church, kneeling close beside the High Altar throughout the Mass.

St. Cross had survived utter destruction only because it had been used as a German stronghold in the struggle for the city. It was partially roofless. Spring sunshine filtered through the glassless windows and played on the altar and upon the richly carved old choir stalls. Small children who had spent all their early years underground and in terror of Nazi soldiery, now moved fearlessly, unconstrainedly and quietly among the worshippers.

It was a moving sight, and no less moving was the dense congregation listening to an eloquent sermon in a Crypt which was all that was left of the handsome baroque Church of St. Alexander. No less moving again was the smaller, but sorely stricken congregation, Lutheran and Calvinist combined, which mingled in front of the altar of the Calvinist Church and listened to Dr. Michelis, Pastor of the Lutheran Church. Bishop Burs of the same Church, together with his three sons and grandson, had been killed in a German concentration camp.

The stark simplicity of the Lutheran altar was outstandingly impressive. Plain bricks, piled sideways, supported plain boards. A neat white cloth covering the centre of the boards hung over the front. On the boards and on either side on the floor stood spring flowers in tall vases. Not glass vases. These were unprocurable. Just empty shell cases.

Behind the altar and on two charred timbers from the ruins hung an ancient crucifix: perfect symbol of the martyred city and the sacrificial heroism of men and women who died for their friends.

I talked with Father Neajeelah and Father Albert in the vestry of St. Cross, and with Dr. Michelis, the Lutheran pastor and others. All spoke of the generosity of the Government aid. None hinted at complaint. "The Government are rebuilding our roof as a first priority," said the priest. "The Government give us every aid in their power," said the pastor.

May 31st was the feast of Corpus Christi. It was observed in Cracow, where I spent the morning, as a holiday. All streets were deserted, save by children in their gay Polish holiday dress on their way to church.

I attended Mass in the beautiful baroque church opposite the Hotel de France, oriented so that the sun entered through western, not eastern windows. Sunlight streamed on the altar and the gorgeous banners which lined the nave. The church was a blaze of colour. A dense crowd thronged the church and overflowed into the street. The previous afternoon I had spent at tea with Father Mackai, Rector of the large gothic church of Santa Maria, occupying a similar position to that of a Dean of Manchester or Liverpool. His church is the chief church of the city, and his relationship with the city authorities and with the President or Mayor of Cracow was entirely cordial. I learned this from each of them independently; they have indeed, very much in common. Both are radicals. Both are enthusiastic supporters of Land Reform and both entertain cordial feelings towards the Soviet Union: Father Mackai is a member of the Polish Society for Cultural Relations with Russia.

Mackai's radicalism brought him into conflict with a minority but he was not only permitted to read a very radical address at a Church Assembly, but was appointed to his present responsible position by the Archbishop of Cracow after he had read it. Mackai by no means stands alone in his advocacy of Land Reform. Quite casually, whilst talking with the newly founded Self-Help Union at the village of Otczyzny, some thirty miles east of Cracow, I asked what attitude the parish priest took to the new activities. "He is a member of our Society," they said.

A noted priest in Warsaw had been one of the earliest agitators for Land Reform.

Here, at any rate, were some members of the Roman Catholic Church not hostile to the new Government. They may have been in a minority. The large number of country clergy were still hostile, as were many peasantry. But some of the clergy were friendly and bore witness to the value of land and other reforms.

In Cracow also, I met the Minister of the American Methodist Mission. I was able to set his mind at rest on a problem which was troubling him. He had solemnised so many marriages between British soldiers and Polish girls, and the Polish parents had been very anxious to learn whether in English law the marriages were legal. I was able to reassure him.

Attending a Service on Corpus Christi in the morning at Cracow as I have already said in the extreme south of Poland, I attended another Service in the afternoon at Zappot, in the extreme north. Such is the possibility of air travel. It was a crowded Service, and only perhaps in Beauvais have I seen a procession more simple and beautiful. Round a long wide-spreading Gothic church wound a singing procession led by tiny girls with chaplets of spring flowers on their heads. Against the whitewashed walls leaned an avenue of fresh-cut young birch trees.

The Mayor of Danzig joined us in the procession. The Governor of the Province, though not, I think, a Catholic, had attended an earlier service at the special request of an ardent young priest whom he had admired, and who was organising for him the Scout movement in the Province.

Religious liberty occupied a primary place in the Atlantic Charter. Pre-war Poland lacked religious liberty. Post-war Poland is bent on securing it.

The Minister of Justice, Mr. Swiatkowski, a lawyer by profession, explained to me that no Church save the Roman Catholic Church had the right of registering births, marriages and deaths.

Mr. Swiatkowski had spent the later pre-war years fighting the battle to secure freedom of like organisation and association for the non-Roman communions. The formal right, given by the Constitution of 1921, had become a dead letter. Poland, he argued, had possessed, like England and America, its great non-conforming traditions. He desires to revivify these healthy trends of the Reformation as a basis for a sane democracy. The Roman Catholic monopoly of religion was fundamentally undemocratic and morally unhealthy. Equality of all religions is the goal of the new Government in Poland. It is significant in this connection that the Minister of Public Instruction in the so-called London Polish Government was a Roman Catholic priest.

I have written elsewhere about Church property. In the south and west of Poland the Church owns large estates. These remain untouched, and will so remain until after an election which is to be free, equal, secret and on a proportional basis.

(G) *Builders of the New Poland*

We met outstanding men in Poland. Let me select four. The first is Dr. Mayer. Of him I shall say little. I mention him merely to salute him as one of the first to challenge Hitler, and quite the first to suffer Hitler's malice.

Dr. Mayer is not Polish. He is German. He was a member of the Reichstag, and was flung into a concentration camp thirteen years ago. He remained there till the Red Army released him recently.

Mayer is still youngish, bald-headed, but not grey. The years of his imprisonment span the years of the Fuehrer's mad career. The Fuehrer has gone. Mayer looks forward now to the day when he will take his share in rebuilding on a sounder basis the structure which Hitler destroyed ruthlessly so.

1. Outstanding among Polish clergy is Father Ferdinand Mackai, Rector of the magnificent Gothic Church of Santa Maria at Cracow, of whom I have already written. The Cathedral of Cracow stands remote from the city, perched on the high hill by the Royal Palace. Its Archbishop seems to show a certain tolerance towards the Government. The important and much more lovely church is that of Santa Maria in the city itself.

Mackai is big in every sense, tall, dark, powerfully built and of commanding presence. Politically he is Left Wing. He was an outspoken radical before the war. At a church gathering of clergy and laity, he told me, he had read a paper which had caused a storm of disapproval from a minority. In consequence, a titled land-owner had resigned his leading position in the church gathering.

Mackai's paper had, however, passed the censorship of the Archbishop and Bishop before he had read it himself. The authorities had no quarrel with his action and he himself had been appointed after his reading to his present important post.

Mackai is a keen supporter of the Government's planned reform policy, and otherwise co-operates with the authorities in important offices. He is a member of the Polish-Russian Society for Cultural Relations. As an ardent patriot he preached on Victory Day an outspoken sermon on Polish independence. It had been maliciously hinted that he had disappeared. But, as he said with a smile, "I did not even receive a hint from authority that my sermon was indiscreet."

2. A warm friend of Mackai is Dr. Fiderkiewiez, Mayor or President of Cracow. since then appointed Polish Ambassador to Canada, with whom I spent two strenuous days, one of them at Oswiecim camp. In order to accompany me to the camp he had flown straight back from Warsaw, where he had just been appointed head of the important Commission appointed to investigate the German crimes in Poland.

Dr. Fiderkiewiez is a Pole, trained and long resident in the U.S.A., and holding a Boston Doctor's degree. He returned to Poland and practised in Cracow, and remained at his post when the Germans came. On account of his liberal principles he was thrown into the murder camp at Oswiecim. The Germans had destined him to work for a period and then be killed. Fiderkiewiez, however, thought otherwise. "I am a confirmed optimist," he said. "I determined to escape the chimney," and he did escape, by the ruse of hiding under corpses as I have already mentioned. His wife, at first, failed to recognise him. He was a mere skeleton, as I said, his legs like match-stalks. Within five days of his release, however, he had been chosen as Mayor of Cracow.

Dr. Fiderkiewiez is small and spare, dressed in a dark-grey, well-fitting suit, he was the perfect picture of a Harley Street specialist, polished, alert, quick and confident. Cracow and its many activities were already flourishing under his jurisdiction. Municipal enterprises were already beginning to repay the Government's initial loan. Cultural activities abounded. Six theatres were operating. At one of them I attended an amusing old Polish play *The Broken Wall*, in which a ninety-two-year-old actor took part.

Cracow owes great things to its Mayor. "We may not have much," he said, "but what we have, we share all round."

By skill and in line with Government policy he brought down the price of bread and the price of utility goods. There was a certain charming naivete about Cracow's energetic "non-political" Mayor. "Poland," he said, "is to be neither Socialist nor Communist, but just democratic," and he explained to me some decidedly Socialistic activities he is undertaking at Cracow.

3. My third notability is Dr. Osenski, Governor at that time of

R

Danzig Province; an idealist, and a man of engaging simplicity. With the face of a saint, a smiling saint, he is good through and through. I had heard much of Osenski from my friends, and greatly desired to meet him. Incidentally we are brother engineers. I spent a long night with him in the small but beautiful house by the seaside, which he used as headquarters. We sat till morning enjoying Polish music and intimate talk. It was a cultivated home, presided over by a wife so young and beautiful I had mistaken her for the daughter of the house.

Osenski, like Fiderkiewiez, looked back on remarkable experiences. He was a civil engineer. Road transport was his speciality. He had prepared plans for road development and laid them before the pre-war Polish Government. The schemes met fierce and ignorant hostility. He was driven from the country. He worked awhile in China with Major Todd, the American engineer, with whom in 1932 I had penetrated into Tibet. Subsequently he built a network of roads and bridges in Afghanistan.

With the rout of the Germans, Osenski, like so many engineers and warm friends of the Soviet Union, returned through Russia to Poland, but not before the Afghan Prime Minister, having failed to induce him to stay, though he had offered to double his salary, and moved by the blazing patriotism which led this man to risk his all for love of his country, had embraced him warmly and called him "brother."

He reached Poland in bitter wintry weather, and then, when Danzig had been released two months previous to our visit, had been appointed the Governor of the Province, having previously been made Vice-Commissioner of Polish Roads.

Osenski is engagingly frank. He told me he hardly knew where to start. No food, no seed, no transport, no bridges, a dearth of workers and the spring advancing. But the idealist who had organised Afghan labourers to build Afghan roads was no man to be balked by Polish problems. He set to work at once. The Red Army built bridges and lent spring seed with Red Army men to do the sowing; it had also lent heavy machinery with the blunt remark that it was emergency help only—"Poland must accept her own responsibility and manage her own affairs." He could not have been more definite on that point; he could often have wished the Soviet authorities had given further help in the managing.

Osenski accepted the situation. He was working hard and hopefully. He was accessible to all who sought advice or aid. Like other important men in Poland he walked freely and unguarded wherever he would. He has found time to organise a flourishing Boy Scout movement, placing it in charge of an energetic young curate from the big church where I attended "Benediction," on Corpus Christi day.

A major problem lay with the German minority, and the temporary shortage of Polish workers. The Poles in Dantzig Province numbered at this time 10,000; the Germans 130,000, mostly the very old or the very young.

Seeing the situation on the spot, it was hard to avoid the conclusion that Poles and Germans could no longer continue to live side by side. The appalling story of the camp at Oswiecim; the smaller but even greater horror of those 350 bodies in iron cases in process of being manufactured into scented soap, openly in the very midst of the fashionable bourgeois suburb. All this seemed to make any mingling impossible. Osenski, the realist, saw this and acted upon it. Osenski, the saint and idealist, added, "One cannot be harsh or unkind to German children," and when I expressed the belief that with right environment and right training a German child could become a good world citizen —to think otherwise was purely to accept the German racial heresy— his eyes filled with tears, and he said "I believe it with all my heart."

Osenski was firm but kindly, realist and idealist combined. Able to organise and modest in seeking advice and above all, with a profoundly optimistic belief in man and man's future. The choice of Osenki for Gdansk, casual as it might be, appeared to be not unsuited to the time and occasion. This man, together with the others I met, was certainly no agent of the Soviet Union.

I was loath to leave Osenski. We parted at the aerodrome. Joining hands as the plane started up, I used words infrequent on my lips because of their oftentimes perfunctory connotation. I said "God bless you." Instantly his head bowed, his lips tightened and he said, "Thank you. May it indeed be so."

4. My last personality was Mr. Beirut, President of the new Poland. Medium size, stoutly built, with a fine face and abundant hair which from time to time he sweeps back with his hand, it is difficult to realise the hardships and sufferings through which he has passed. He at least was well guarded in his headquarters in Warsaw and was busy when we called with a long line of visitors.

Twice imprisoned before the war, the last time on a long sentence, Mr. Beirut had shared all the perils of the underground movement during the German occupation. His hardships had seriously affected his health, but had never prevented his output of work.

Beirut is a realist of iron will. The soft, almost effeminate hands, at which he looks as he talks, never lead one to suspect their iron grip. Nor from the fine, but firm face would you suspect a man of grim awareness, watchful patience, and stern persistence—a man who knows what he wants and how to get it.

Born in Lublin, Beirut had worked as a printer. He organised a co-operative movement in his home town, and came thence to Warsaw, where he built a series of fine co-operative dwelling-houses, coming into repeated conflict with the pre-war political Polish Government, and twice suffering imprisonment.

During the German occupation he remained in the underground movement in Warsaw, moving from one mean lodging to another to avoid capture, with permanent ill effects on his health. The Poles who remained, naturally love Beirut as the man who had shared their pains and struggles, the man also who had struck back ceaselessly and fearlessly. He asked me many questions. His own answers to my questions had an abrupt directness.

5. Mr. Swiatkowski, the Minister of Justice, is widely known as a specialist on religious affairs. He talked to me long and seriously about the religious situation in Poland, and outlined the plans of the new Government for granting real religious liberty. He has an acute, legal and highly trained mind. Religious liberty is his passion. It was not true, he said, that Poland had possessed religious liberty before the war. No religion was recognised by the State save the religion of the Roman Catholic Church. He had fought bitterly for religious freedom in Poland both as a lawyer and as a Socialist, and has had a training which makes him well fitted for the post of Minister of Justice. The three major religious bodies other than the Roman Catholic never possessed the right of registering births, marriages and deaths. They were, all of them, the Anglican included, treated as outsiders or heretics. The Minister's task during the last years before the war had been to secure for all the religious communities, freedom of life, organisation and association: to put them, in short, on a complete equality with the Roman Catholic Church. The Polish Constitution of 1921 had indeed ostensibly given full rights for all confessions. In real life these rights hitherto had no existence.

(2) POLITICAL AND SOCIAL SET-UP IN MAY, 1945

MY last evening in Poland was spent as I said, with Mr. Beirut. He asked for my impressions. I gave them to him. His concise and clear remarks and amplifications served further to crystallise my thoughts. Here, then, were my conclusions. Chiefly, I had noticed the continued but by no means obtrusive presence of the Red Army. I had observed also a correct attitude in Ministers of State, Governors of Provinces, Mayors of Cities and clergy towards an Army which had come as a deliverer and had remained in no sense as conqueror, but as an aid and as providing a base for further operations westwards. Foreign policy and national inclination were now firmly based upon Polish Soviet friendship, a natural sequel from many points of view, not least because Russia had saved Poland from Fascist barbarism.

Russia, I had also discovered, was aiding Poland effectively in her economic extremity. Russian engineers had built bridges across the Vistula. Russian soldiers had helped in the spring sowing. Russian technicians had repaired community centres, and helped also temporarily to make good the lack of craftsmen and technicians, many of whom had been slain, many had fled. Though Polish foreign policy was obviously based—as it was reasonably bound to be based—on Russian-Polish friendship, it was no exclusive friendship. Indeed, I perceived everywhere a keen desire for friendship with Britain and the United States of America. Agreeing with this, the President remarked: "The Poles are a Slav people; Russia is their natural ally."

Secondly I had perceived the presence of a strong national feeling, pride in Poland and determination in internal policy that Poland must be free, independent and democratic. It was emphatically true of all whom we had met, members of the Government, intelligentsia, priests and common people. We heard the same sentiment expressed in small villages as well as in great towns. We saw it visually expressed in posters on the walls.

I had observed also, that the Soviet Government obviously sympathised with this wish so long as it was coupled with and not antagonistic to the policy of Polish-Soviet friendship. The Governor of Danzig, I recalled, in acknowledging his debt to the Soviet authorities for material assistance in and after the war, had emphasised the persistency with which the Soviet authorities had constantly urged that Poland must stand on her own feet: "Poland is yours, you must govern it yourselves."

Undoubtedly the centuries-old fear of Russia had left its heritage behind. Many within Poland, particularly those of the upper classes who had settled down more or less comfortably with the German conquerors—and still more those outside Poland who had fled for security to other lands—desired a minimum of contact with Russia. Polish freedom was in any event, a matter of prime importance to patriotic Poles, and I was pleased to observe the apparently unrestricted liberty to express oneself strongly on this question.

I recalled Father Mackai's assertion that he had never even

received a hint from authority that he must act with greater circumspection after his outspoken sermon on Polish Independence on Victory Day.

Turning now to social policy the outstanding change was the new land policy of the Government: the division of the large estates among the peasants, with the retention of the forest areas for the Government. Such landowners as had accepted the new position were given somewhat larger holdings than others or had obtained Government or administrative positions.

How, I asked myself, had the change affected agricultural production? But little, so far as I could see. Driving considerable distances by car into the countryside, or observing fields and farms closely from our low-flying planes, I had observed no ill effects of the switch over. Buildings were being repaired and the land was well tilled. Everywhere I saw signs of a forthcoming good harvest. Difficulties undoubtedly existed, and inefficiency in many cases.

More particularly I inquired how far what appeared to me to be a major disadvantage of small ownership—its tendency to neglect new and experimental and scientific methods of agriculture, which could only be practised by those who possess ample margins of wealth and land—could be avoided. Even as I was asking the question we were taken to a nearby experimental station where the house and the immediately surrounding land of a landowner who had fled, had been already turned into a State experimental farm, where I saw rows of women diligently planting out experimental seedlings.

Church lands, especially in the south and west, were extensive: they had not been divided. The decision as to their future disposal, I was told, was to be left until a properly elected Government could express the will of the people on this problem. I also learned that many, and among them some of the leading clergy, like Father Mackai, had welcomed the land reforms as long overdue, though naturally many others resented it.

Great stress was being laid upon the proposed character of the new elections, they were to be free, equal, secret and proportional; without privileges, freedom for all parties except for Fascists.

The Minister of Justice, with whom we had long conversation, urged that there had never been a stronger Government than the existing Provisional Government, for its strength was based upon the combination of workers, peasants and intelligentsia, i.e., upon the majority of the nation, because of its immediate legitimate benefits to the people, e.g., in the land reform, because it had legitimatised workers' councils in factories, because it had given a share in control to industrial workers and because it had introduced free education from primary schools to universities.

In industry, I observed a desire to avoid unnecessary jolts. For example, in the furnishing trade, an estimate of national needs for furniture for the year having been made, a quota, calculated in bulk to meet this need, was allocated to each furniture-producing factory. After they had supplied their quota of utility goods at a State-fixed price, the factory was free to produce and sell different goods or luxury goods at what price they could command. There was apparently no rigid doctrinaire switch-over to Socialism.

Beirut and the London Government had differed, as in so many other respects, especially in their estimate of the possible result of the war. Russia and Germany, the latter thought, would wear one another out, and then there would arise a conflict between Britain and the U.S.S.R. That would be Poland's moment. Poland must conserve her strength. Beirut had disagreed with this design to stand back and let the major antagonists fight it out by themselves. "We must fight back now," he said. Hence the organisation and activities of the partisans as a striking force. They had hoped the London Government would aid them, but were disappointed. I understood, though not from Beirut himself, that though he knew that the London Poles had nothing to give—neither money nor experience—yet lest it be said that the Poles are always quarrelling it were better to keep in touch with them, and he would seek the return of the Mikolajczyk despite the fact that he was no real democrat; and that he feared the people. Though in agreement as to the necessity of land reform, Mikolajczyk disliked the Provisional Government's brand of reform; perhaps because it deprived his sails of wind. It was the U.S.S.R. which had helped the partisans, equipping their army, and then restoring industry and supplying the essential machinery, to be returned at length in kind.

My general feeling was that the Government had come to stay, and that the bulk of the workers who counted most were on their side.

Such was the Poland that I saw in 1945. Its early promise is being steadily and rapidly realised. Poland develops quicker than the world thought possible. Large-scale changes take place, Poland as the result of the war has shifted from east to west. The colonial policy forced on pre-war Poland has gone and a backward agricultural country develops efficient industry with a balanced economy. Manpower shifts from overcrowded country to town. Large-scale industry, now nationalised, strides ahead. Despite innumerable handicaps—ruthless exploitation, outworn machinery and lack of skilled staff—coal production shows phenomenal increase, due to splendid enthusiasm and scientific regrouping of mines. Mr. J. Cyrankiewicz, the Polish Prime Minister, in his speech at the June session of the Seim, reported that during the first half of 1947 output amounted to 27,169,000 tons, giving promise of exceeding the target of 50 to 60 million tons this year and enabling Poland to increase exports of coal to 20-22 million tons as against thirteen million tons shipped to other countries last year. Poland thus becomes one of Europe's chief coal exporters. Poland and Czechoslovakia, their former tensions resolved, are exchanging Polish coal for Czechoslovakian machinery. Similar advance takes place with textiles, electric power and the metal industries. Pre-war Poland possessed 10 motor-vehicles per 10,000 of population, against Denmark's 379. That is the measure of Poland's pre-war backwardness and the measure of Poland's task.

To raise the standard of living for the masses: that is the central aim of the Four-Years Plan, particularly in educational and cultural life. The rapidly realised goal for education of youth is school until 19 years of age for all boys and girls.

3. CZECHOSLOVAKIA

(A) *Prague, Lidice, Skoda. Leaders in Church and State*

CZECHOSLOVAKIA to-day is a key country on the border line between east and west; with an opportunity and a mission second to none, and after three months in Russia I gladly accepted a special invitation from the Czechoslovakian Government to visit their country and broke my journey homewards at Prague.

Flying in the special non-stop plane provided for us, the journey took eight hours from Moscow. Storm driving us down to tree-top height, we could study at close range the ravages of war, and the prospects of harvest. These latter promised well in Russia, Poland and Czechoslovakia. Also in Germany, over which at length we took our final homeward flight.

War damage was appalling in the Russian sector of our flight. My diary, written every few minutes, reads for hundreds of miles, as I quoted earlier, with monotonous regularity: "Tank trenches, wreckage, appalling wreckage; smashed houses, smashed bridges, immense shell holes. . . ."

The Polish sector had less to show: damage at least, was confined to special localities. Similarly in the short German sector.

Czechoslovakia along our route had almost entirely escaped, with the exception of some few bombs on Prague, which had also suffered by the last-minute efforts of the S.S. troops as the Russians broke in.

At the Skoda Works, which we visited before leaving Czechoslovakia, and which lie some hundred kilometres south-west of Prague, it was different. Here the magnificent modern plant had been pitifully wrecked by concentrated and scientific attack from American planes, eleven days before the war ended, a stunning blow to Czechoslovakia, which desperately needs the locomotives and other output from this her major engineering plant. Czechoslovaks made guarded but bitter remarks about an attitude which seemed to them wanton and from any military angle needless at that stage of the war.

Landing in Prague, we drove around the city. Built on the Vltava, dominated by the Cathedral and Castle—a long renaissance building—covering the heights, Prague, a city of towers and spires, of mediæval buildings and fascinating bridges, of fine streets, and riverside walks, has few peers among the capitals of the world.

That first evening we sat on a friendly balcony to watch a mass demonstration of 15,000 persons of Czechoslovakian origin, dressed in national costume, come to beg or demand incorporation in the Czechoslovakian republic; one of those pockets of peoples lying right within German territory.

The procession was picturesque and impressive. Native costume is varied, colourful and gay. Trades were represented—dramatically by butchers with gleaming theatrical axes, by sweeps in black suits, white hats and gay sashes, athletic clubs with red shirts for the men and red skirts for the girls. Occasionally Communist emblems appeared. One huge red banner with hammer and sickle in one corner and the flags of Czechoslovakia, Yugoslavia and other Slavonic peoples forming the border, was an outstanding feature and a portent.

From Dr. Bedenhark, a Professor of the Huss Faculty of Theology, we learned of the six years' German nightmare. The Gestapo had terrified all. Gestapo agents seemed omniscient, confronting victims with terrible knowledge of the past and present. A single false step, a single malicious word by housemaid or porter or local tobacconist might mean death. Happily the Professor survived.

This quiet, religious, scholarly man of seventy-five, once a student at New College, Edinburgh, and a professional lecturer in many lands on practical Christianity, is a Socialist. In his own country, he lectures and writes on Communism and Christianity with penetrating insight. His story and outlook are typical of the intelligentsia of Czechoslovakia.

Dr. Hnik, another clerical professor, lately returned from England, where he had spent the war years, took us to Masaryk's burial place and to the country home some dozen miles from Prague, which was his favourite retreat.

Masaryk's body and that of his wife lie beneath a raised grass mound, placed there by his own wish. We stood at the spot in silence. Hnik, with deep emotion, laid his hand reverently on the turf, and we moved away. Thus do the Czechoslovaks revere the great statesman who made Czechoslovakia once more a nation and welded it to a new unity. The same solemn reverence marks the country house where Masaryk lived and the room where he died, left exactly as on the day of his death.

Amongst the many books in English, German and Czech in Masaryk's country house—left exactly as on the day of his death— I pulled out one entitled *The Life of John Huss*, published, if I recollect aright, in 1929 in America. It concluded with these words: "As I prepare this little volume for printing I cherish the hope that it may arouse in the minds of its readers a hatred of every form of spiritual and secular tyranny whether it be theocratic or Jacobin." Whose words and whose book? Mussolini's!

We saw Lidice. Once a village, now a ploughed field. Its happy rural community of 600 souls murdered or scattered to other lands. Two hundred men shot at dawn. Women dragged to concentration camps. Children torn from parents' arms and dispatched to Germany. One mother, just returned from captivity, showed me the picture of her young husband beside the truck he drove. Of her child of three she has no trace.

Only one memorial stands. Perhaps the most moving I ever saw. On rising ground which once had been the head of the village street stands a rough pine pole 20 feet high. At the junction of a cross pole nailed to its upper end is a 5-foot iron hoop, wound with barbed wire strands. A cross and crown of thorns. And placed there by Red Army men and on their own initiative. May it always thus remain. No memorial more fitting for victims of a savage act. No memorial more fitting, too, for the village priest of seventy-five, who refused his freedom and has said: "for thirty-five years I have lived and prayed with my flock. I will pray with them still and die with them." "Died at his own request" is the laconic entry in the German dossier.

Is there tension with the Red Army of occupation? There is tension with any army of occupation. As Stalin explained to Benes: "Our men have fought through a thousand miles of terrible war. They feel themselves conquerors. All are not good. The bad will take advantage of their victory."

But as Benes added when he repeated Stalin's words: "Fortunately our people have humour, and no serious trouble arises." The people recognise from what the Red Army has freed them, and that and all the minor kindnesses, tell against the minor and major irritations—a petty theft here or a proportion of Czechoslovakian cattle driven off there to make good the outstanding loss of Russian cattle.

Many are the signs of friendly feeling. I saw a Russian army lorry pull up in silent reverence as a village funeral passed. I saw a Red Army soldier sitting by the roadside in deep and friendly talk with a group of Czechoslovakian boys and girls. I saw the cross at Lidice. Shop windows carry two large portraits interlaced: Benes and Stalin. The flower beds in the green opposite the Opera House bloomed in star-like shape with crimson flowers.

Prime Minister Keelering threw light for us on many problems; as for example, on the cession to Russia of Carpathia. Had the initiation of that cession come from Russia? we asked.

"Emphatically not. The offer was ours, and freely made. We always knew that the Carpathians were merely guests. Valued guests certainly, but guests, and as such must eventually leave."

"What about the demonstration, we had witnessed?" I asked.

"We sympathise with the demonstrators," he replied, "but we seek no added territory. Many amongst them have sympathy with Germany. Those who genuinely and passionately desire to join us can come. We now have in the Sudeten land vacant territory to receive them all."

As to the shrinkage of Germany's "living room," and the dangerous problems that some in England feared would ensue, Mr. Keelering said: "Germany has lost many millions of population." This is true, but German babies will remove the disparity in twenty years' time and his further remark was more convincing. "Modern science enables larger numbers to live in smaller areas." A true remark and doubly significant in view of the possibilities opened up by the "split atom."

At a complimentary civic lunch we met ministers and industrialists. In the middle of lunch, the Prime Minister, by whose side I sat, handed me on a piece of paper just received, the first results of the British General Election. "What does it mean?" he asked.

"A landslide," I said.

"Will the Labour Government proceed to nationalise the Banks?"

"The nationalisation of the Bank of England is in their programme."

A glint of pleasure lit his eyes. Nationalisation of banks is part of the Czechoslovakian programme and a clash with English financial interests had been their major fear.

Lunch over gave us opportunity for an interesting talk with Dr. Ydenek Nejedly, the Minister of Education, much dreaded in English circles as wildly revolutionary. How amusing, I thought, as I looked at this mild, elderly, diminutive professor, with good head and benign expression, and heard him outline his programme of educational reform. The Order of Lenin, the highest Soviet order, adorned his coat.

Dr. Nejedly, an authority on music and other matters, is an historian by profession, and after lecturing on Slavonic history in Moscow University throughout the war years, he had returned to Czechoslovakia as Minister of Education. "Our educational programme is more advanced than Russia's," he smilingly explained, as he outlined its features.

Education is to be free, compulsory, and equal to all up to the age of fifteen years. Education will continue thence till nineteen years of age; a fifteen years' school as against Russia's ten years' school. From fifteen onwards the courses for the subsequent four years vary, branching along lines technical, industrial, the humanities, or the arts. A tree with its strong trunk rising aloft and then dividing into several branches was his own simile. At nineteen the graduate course can begin for those who have capacity and desire it. Qualified children can proceed free of charge throughout the whole twelve years' course, free colleges being provided in addition for those whose home economy cannot afford their keep. Denominational schools will cease, two hours' provision for religious teaching in Government schools meeting the religious needs of the people.

The new Czechoslovakian church is also significant and interesting. I met the editor of the new Church magazine, who had spent the war years in German concentration camps: a man of outstanding courage, who had maintained unbroken the high spirit of the camp. He is a Communist with a rich wife, and both are devoted to the Church cause.

We spent a memorable evening with Dr. Hnik and Dr. Kovar, chief minister of the new Church, a very remarkable man, who when the election for the Patriarch is held—the office was suppressed during the German occupation—is almost certain to be the new Patriarch.

Dr. Kovar, a clean-shaven, smart-looking man who might be taken in England for a prosperous K.C., was in his youth a Roman priest. He and 3,000 more priests had petitioned Rome early in the century— at the time of Tyrrell and Loisy—for certain reforms; services in the vernacular, non-compulsory celibacy and the like. These requests being rejected the major part submitted to authority, but one hundred stood firm and on 8th June, 1920, the Czechoslovakian Church was formed.

This Church survives. It now numbers a million and a quarter adherents, distributed among 400 congregations. It now has eighty-nine candidates in training for the ministry. This new Church is modernist in spirit, maintaining continuity with the past, but with the forward, free, adventurous outlook akin to that which marks all scientific thinkers to-day. The Church's sympathies are strongly social. It avoids doles and seeks radical change. It recruits its members mainly from the lower social strata, the lower middle classes and the intelligentsia.

It has, I am convinced, a great future before it. Here is the spirit of Huss rising again in the twentieth century. Its theology both traditional and forward-looking is interesting. The Church architecture, modern and well thought out, is equally interesting. Its symbols and decoration are interesting. Chalices in place of crosses crown its towers and a chalice replaces a cross on its altars. Its columbarium where the cremated ashes of the first heroic founders of the Church are laid and where the names of its subsequent members are now recorded, is full of imaginative symbolism, and instinct with the feeling that death is but an incident in life.

The leaders of this new Church know well how to evaluate what Russia has achieved. It has a great future before it and will occupy an important place in directing the changes which are bound to take place in the Christian Church in the new world.

In which direction do these new changes point in Czechoslovakia?

That was the question which concerned us most vitally as we journeyed to Prague. For Czechoslovakia occupies a unique position in the post-war world.

Standing as a border state between Western Europe with its ancient traditions and highly prized liberties, and the Soviet Union with its newer forms of economic liberty, its new modes of life and its newly found strength, it is a matter of vital importance to west and east which way it turns and how it acts.

Will Czechoslovakia maintain her ancient western traditions or discard them? Will she seek to understand the Soviet Union or meet it with distrust and hostility? As a Slavonic people with western culture Czechoslovakia is well fitted for the role she has to play as buffer state or rather as an interpreter to each of two diverse modes of life, seeking to preserve the best of both.

Western culture has blossomed into some of its highest forms in Czechoslovakia. Prague, for instance, embodies many of the noblest elements of western civic culture. Few European towns surpass Prague for sheer loveliness. The Skoda works and the Bata boot factory provide outstanding examples of modern industrial equipment.

Kubelik, whose son we met at lunch, just before he went on a musical tour to the U.S.S.R., can speak for art.

I was glad, therefore, to be assured on every hand that Czechoslovakia is strong in her fidelity to western ideals, that she is and will remain free and independent. In that determination she has the sympathy and aid of the Soviet Union, whose constant expressed desire is to be surrounded on the west by strong, democratic and independent neighbours. I was glad, also, but not surprised to learn that Czechoslovakia was determined to maintain and strengthen her friendly relations to the Soviet Union. Czechoslovakia was progressive and had already outlined a programme of social reform, radical in spirit but not violent in form, in which policy she had the goodwill and encouragement of Russia.

I heard the same thing from the lips of Dr. Benes, the President himself, and all I have subsequently heard and learned bears out the theme.

(B) *President Benes Interprets Past Events and Outlines Future Policy*

I met Dr. Benes in his beautiful and dignified renaissance room in the castle, from whose wide-flung windows we looked out across a forest of mediaeval roofs and spires on either side of the Vltava, to the high ground beyond.

Benes spoke for an hour and a quarter, a chronological, ordered and emphatic discourse. He obviously had something to say and designed for more than private ears. It was something the world should know. After a masterly review of the past he summarised the present and projected the future.

From the first, he assured us, he had known that Lenin and his friends would succeed, he also knew why. Benes goes straight to the essentials of any situation. And the essential factor at the time of the revolution was the utter bankruptcy of Tsardom. The new order, if possessed of any promise whatsoever of progress and any nobility of aim was bound to succeed in its preliminary stage, a success which would strengthen the new Government to carry through its subsequent programme. Russia, he knew, would advance, as she did, from strength to strength. From 1922 and onwards Benes increasingly strove to bring Russia into the European community.

"By 1934," said Benes, concluding a long line of argument, in which he had enumerated his points on his left hand, forcing each finger successively down as he drove his point home. "By 1934 I *knew* that war was inevitable." He then bent every resource of his country to meet the blow. The Skoda works received new impetus. In 1935 he had discussed the progressively deteriorating situation with Stalin in a talk which lasted from 1 to 6 p.m. "Tell me all," said Stalin, who at that time alone of all the world's statesmen would give him a hearing. In 1934 Benes, as Chairman of the League of Nations, succeeded in bringing Russia into the League. In 1938 he believed that war would come within five or eight months: it came within eleven months and faced him with an appalling decision. Since Russia was willing to honour her pledge, should he with Russia's aid resist or should he yield? He yielded. He knew that to enter the war with Russia alone would split Europe in two. France and England might have sided with Germany: "In a war with Germany, it is a prime necessity that she should have to fight on two fronts."

In May 1939, Benes met and assured Roosevelt—"a clever man"— that Poland would crack, and crack soon, and that ultimately the United States as well as England would be drawn into the fight. When asked by Roosevelt what aid Czechoslovakia would need, he said: "Money, industrial and economic assistance, perhaps the fleet—I hope we shall not need your boys."

In vain, in May 1940, had Benes endeavoured to persuade Sikorski to align Poland with Czechoslovakia in friendship with Russia against Germany. Sikorski had believed that England and the United States could defeat Germany alone: "Miracles," Benes had replied, "do not happen twice."

"And the future?" I asked.

"Great changes are taking place in my country and throughout the world," said Benes. People were looking for radical change and the Czechoslovakian Government promised big instalments of change.

Mines were to be transferred to the State. Electricity undertakings and all sources of power were to be nationalised. Certain elements of heavy industry and the Skoda works were to be nationalised. Banks were to be nationalised. That last was crucial. Railways were already national property and the big landed estates had already been divided. Everybody working on the land must have their share in the owner- ship of the land. These changes were definite but to be effected at not revolutionary speed. The Social Assurance programme was similar to the Beveridge scheme in England.

In the political sphere Dr. Benes assured me that Czechoslovakia was determined to maintain political freedom, freedom of conscience, freedom of religion and press. Censorship was to go. A provisional Parliament representative of all four parties—Roman Catholic, Social Democratic, Communist and National Socialist was to meet in September: the general election would probably take place in November.

In the early ·stages of Czechoslovakia's release from German control, the Red Army must needs apply necessary military precautions. These were temporary war measures. They have now gone. In no sense have they been political measures, and Czechoslovakia was fast becoming one of the freest countries in Europe. Dr. Benes's final words were on State Planning. Already an important state organisation which undertakes the all-important planning work exists and operates.

What I had heard and learned in Czechoslovakia from many sources and what was clinched by the lucid dramatic speech of Benes satisfied me that the prized liberties of the western world were safe in the hands of this frontier State and that her pledged friendship with Russia was based on deep Slavonic sympathy and intellectual understanding of what the Soviet Union was and had done. These were powerful factors making for the future peace of Europe and the betterment of man.

The summer of 1947 sees in Czechoslovakia a country with a well-developed industry and high standard of living having achieved public ownership of the basic means of production and proceeding further with planned economic development. We can now trace by means of available statistical material the trend of production between the liberation and the launching of the Two-Year Plan.

Industrial enterprises employing more than 300-500 persons, together with all units large or small of key industries have been nationalised. It becomes apparent that wholesale nationalisation differs not only in quantity but in quality from nationalisation of certain industries only, especially when joint-stock banks and insurance companies become public property.

Another feature is worth noting. Public life and participation in power is barred to those who prior to the war were leaders in big industry and finance and who during the war were collaborators with the enemy.

Towards the end of 1946 basic production in Czechoslovakian industry had reached the average of the last three pre-war years: it exceeded the three year average in lignite and electrical power. Coal and steel approach the 1937 level. Output of locomotives, electrical motors, tractors and motor-cycles exceeds the best pre-war years, the progress all round being greater in the fully or predominently nationalised industries.

Despite the drop in the number of German workers from 230,000 to 60,000, the entrance of women and Slovenians into industry has actually increased the number of operatives and the quality of the new recruits rapidly improves.

Output per head, which is the key-factor, has also increased. The 50 per cent rise in production in the period September 1945 to November 1946, when industrial employment showed only a 10 per cent increase, is significant. A further average productivity increase of 10 per cent is planned for the end of 1948.

Bottle-necks appear and are mastered. Transport, for example, failed to meet the needs of coal increase and needed stimulation. These preliminary difficulties surmounted other and more differentiated bottlenecks appear, as in ball-bearings or rolled steel. The problems indeed grow in intensity but the bottle-necks themselves are proof of expanding industry; production of primary goods being no longer limited by the capacity of the market to consume goods economically unattainable by those who need them.

Czechoslovakia trades with her neighbours of a like economy. A million ton steel deal between Poland and Czechoslovakia is announced and in return for 200,000 tons of wheat, fodder, fertilizers and cotton, Czechoslovakia has booked orders with the Soviet Union for many years ahead for locomotives, railway equipment, pipes and electrical plant.

S

BOOK XI

CRITICS AND CRITICISM

T H E end of the war saw the rise of the critic. Newspapers first, then books, some few serious, mostly frivolous. Frankly hostile writings, many of them, finding a ready market with those whose ideological antipathy to Socialism had been smothered but never assuaged by Russian victories, grudgingly accepting Russian help in peril, disliking Russia the more because to it they owed their safety. Others, always on the quest for Utopia, with its easy quick solutions to life's problems, and having thought that paradise had descended ready-made from heaven in Russia, received these books more sadly for the bitter disillusionment they caused.

Arthur Koestler, stands first in the disillusioned class. Looking for Utopia in Russia he suffered violent reaction when, stumbling across the reality, he saw not angels carrying all before them with noble ease, but one-time economic serfs and spiritual helots slowly arising to their gallant task of building a new civilisation upon foundations of substantial economic equality and freedom, but sadly hampered by the defects of their inherited past, stumbling on a difficult road, committing blunders which made the critics scorn and the fastidious wince.

What Koestler and his followers failed to appreciate was the vastness of the achievement. The miracle had happened, a wholly new order tried and not found wanting; economic serfs growing to economic manhood, smashing Hitler even on his own stamping ground. Like Wilbur Wright's first heavier-than-air machine—the curious contraption of string and wire and wooden plates—the new bird had risen from the ground; it flew.

When Alexander Werth, living open-eyed through Russian years of struggle and blunder, travelled at length to Stockholm he wrote: "In a new world a million miles away from the war, from the minor differences and petty annoyances of every-day life in Russia, the city is blazing with Neon signs. There are swarms of cars and taxis. And the trains are comfortable and not overcrowded as they are in Moscow; and the shops have everything you wish for."

But hear what he adds: "Anyway, I miss Moscow, with its rough and tumble, with its touches of tragedy and comedy."

Moscow with all its discomforts holds the future, and Alexander Werth knew it.

But there was more to it than that. More than the sudden disillusionment. Koestler and other hostile critics reveal an understandable apprehension on suddenly discovering in Soviet Socialism an attack upon their personal irresponsibility, an irresponsibility clinging to a form of liberty little better than license to do precisely as they please.

Passing now from Koestler's self-revelation, we will select some of his specific charges*:

1. The average standard of living, rising in the period between the first year of the revolution up to 1929 by 54 per cent, had by 1937 dropped to a level 32 per cent lower than the pre-revolutionary stage.

Fantastic. Basic foodstuffs had increased from 800,000,000 quintals in 1913 to 1,200,000,000 in 1937. Other foodstuffs show similar increase. Russia was at the same time also exporting less abroad. Where did the surplus go to if not to raise the standard of living? Did the Soviets dump it into the sea? Outlay on social and cultural purposes also rose from 1,495,500 roubles in 1928 to 26,604,552,000 roubles in 1937.

2. Russia of all great countries publishes no standard of living index.

Neither do we. We publish a cost of living index chiefly to regulate civil service wages. Who indeed could estimate a standard of living index? No country undertakes a task which would present peculiar difficulties in Russia, where income is largely derived not from money at all but from social services, cost-free education, cost-free medical services, together with ample sick and pension benefits and an expanding round of cultural amenities.

3. The 1936 Constitution re-established inequality from birth by once more making inheritance legal, guaranteeing to each individual the right of unrestricted disposal of property through a Last Will.

I reiterate, Socialism never postulates complete equality. Socialist legal inheritance is an act of social justice. Furthermore, as none can invest his earnings in capitalist concerns, no man can live on the exploited labour of others, nor can any create or perpetuate oligarchies or exercise decisive political power thereby.

4. Inequality of education has been recreated by fixing tuition fees for secondary schools and universities, a law which has forced 600,000 students from poor families, who could not afford to pay the fee, to leave school, making higher education the prerogative of the children of parents who can afford it.

Absurd charges. The highest fees for university, 400 roubles a year, could be earned by any youth in a single month. Moscow or Georgian street shoeblacks earned 5 to 10 roubles in a few minutes

* *The Yogi and the Commissar.—Pt. III.*

polishing my boots. Furthermore, as I have explained elsewhere, special privileges for children of poor parents clear the road for any child who desires or could profit by higher education.

5. Russian civilians are forbidden to read and are refused access to foreign newspapers.

Foreign newspapers are not on sale in the Soviet Union. But we saw English journals covering a wide range of views in the reading room of the library of Moscow University. In Tashkent we met a Soviet citizen who regularly read *The Round Table*. In Moscow and Tbilisi we met Soviet citizens who listened regularly to the B.B.C.

6. All the great figures of Lenin's period excepting Stalin have been liquidated.

Did Mr. Koestler recollect who Mr. Kalinin was, and when and why he died?

7. In 1935 capital punishment was extended to children down to the age of twelve.

On 7th April, 1935, a decree to combat increase of juvenile crime, due to the maturing age of homeless children in the post civil-war years, laid it down that young people from twelve years of age found guilty of certain serious offences were to be punished "with all measures of the criminal code." Referring to the relevant sections of that code, they specifically state that "Notwithstanding any provisions contained herein, the death penalty shall not be applied to minors"—that is, in Soviet law, to persons under eighteen years of age. The death sentence has never been imposed on any child of twelve, fourteen or sixteen.

It is interesting and significant to note, in this connection, that by edict of the Supreme Soviet published 26th May, 1947, over the name of N. Shvernik, the Chairman, the death penalty in general is now abolished.

8. After the Stalin-Hitler pact, German anti-fascists were handed over to Nazi Germany. And yet the critics complain that three of them were in the Austrian Government. The critics can't have it both ways.

More crude than Koestler, and only important through wide publicity in the *Readers' Digest* and an English Sunday paper, was William L. White's story, openly repudiated by the majority of reputable correspondents in Moscow.

More damaging than these attacks, because more understandable and containing a considerable element of truth, are the stories of our own soldiers in Berlin and Austria. But neither can these stories, as our more balanced correspondents point out, be taken apart from their context and at their face value. British soldiers had received no pre-paration for meeting the Russians as they had for meeting the Americans. When they saw "scruffy," ill-clad, ill-equipped Russian soldiers they were readily inclined to believe German tales that the German armies were only "overborne by sheer numbers, by barbarian disregard of life and indifference to casualties." The German tale, of course, was nonsense, but the object of the Germans was to spread disunity between the allies. It was, indeed, doubly unfortunate that the allies, who could not converse because of the language difficulty, met on enemy soil, and that our men received so little help from authority in grasping the Russian situation. British soldiers were not told the reason for the use of horse carts instead of motor lorries in the Berlin streets, nor that the Russian line extended through thousands of miles, nor that transport was busier rehousing and re-establishing the 20,000,000 displaced Russians than parading Berlin streets, nor that the Red Army uniforms had travelled through fighting fronts for thousands of miles, nor that "hordes" are of small account against modern arms, nor that the Soviet population was 193,000,000, whilst Germany could, with allies and slaves, draw on 300,000,000 fighters and workers. Nor were British troops told that Russian first-line troops had largely gone, slain in heroic battles, which saved our land and our fighting men.

There has, indeed, been very general reluctance to let the British public know the full truth about our relative losses, a glaring case being the B.B.C. action in refusing to let Mr. Howard Smith, in his projected radio talk on the eve of the meeting of the Council of Foreign Ministers, use the statement, absolutely true in fact, that "in two world wars Russia lost fifteen times as many of her citizens, killed and starved, as America and Britain together in those two wars. She suffered a thousand times the material destruction to her industry and agriculture. A material loss which exceeds by nearly three times the annual national income of 167,000 of the U.S.A., rendering homeless nearly 25 million people, that is, more than half the population of Great Britain." *Picture Post* happily published the rejected MS. in full.

As to physique, many of the so-called "scruffy" men were possibly Asiatics or Mongolians, who are small in stature. My Georgian chauffeur might have looked scruffy to northern eyes: he was the salt of the earth. The Soviet Union embraces some 150 peoples and languages. A high English ecclesiastic told me of an alert-looking Red Army boy who could not read Russian and must be illiterate. Could he read Georgian or Armenian? I asked. He had never thought of that.

Of course, there is looting and loose living and raping in the Russian Army, as in all armies, alas. I deeply regret it. But what about the high percentage of venereal disease, for example, in the American Army? And judgment of men passing, as the Russians did, for three years, through a hell we happily never experienced, seeing their own country through a thousand miles ruined, and their people massacred, should, perhaps, be measured in the first flush of victory by another standard than ours. As to loot, we and America had, from all accounts, our spasm of that before we reached Berlin. Nor had German and Austrian houses been recipients of English loot. The tales of the German girls, who slept with Western troops without much hostile comment, had a fairly obvious motive behind them in accusing the Russians of rape.

The morale of the Russian troops happily improved after the early days and in the two autumn months of 1946 two cases of rape and five of looting in the British Zone in Berlin—and these may or may not have been Russian crimes—were the official figures shown to a British reporter who had been led to expect other and far more widespread troubles.

Stories of inefficiency and cruelty to "millions of exportees milling around" homeless and starved within the Russian Zone were exploded by Mr. N. Dodds, M.P., and then by the main body of reporters. Incidentally the bulk of these "exportees" were fleeing, not driven, but of their own accord; dreading to stay where the German name stank through such atrocities as Gdansk and Oswiecim. Stalin spoke to me of the evil influence of the press. Russian press and radio have attacked Britain and the U.S.A. But our own Alexander Werth and Eddie Gilmore of the American Associated Press both point out that our Western press vastly outweighs Russia's in bulk of bias, criticism, and attack.

On the positive side Werth points out that the press of no other country gave such a large proportion of its space to reports from U.N.O. with detailed accounts of the speeches of Bevin, Baker and others as well as Molotov and Vishinsky. Werth also denies the charge of Russian avoidance of foreign correspondents: "I have been," says he, "to more Russian homes in four years than inside French homes in ten years."

More serious, in one sense, because more specious, are the criticisms of the moral idealists, who, in the interest of absolute values, have launched a whole series of attacks on Soviet values as anti-liberal, anti-Western, anti-Christian. They charge the Soviet authorities with violating the sacred rights of personality, employing evil methods to attain their ends, doing wrong that good may come, and acting on the principle that the end justifies the means.

Take this last point first. To say that the end justifies the means need not imply that it is right to do wrong that good may come. That is to beg the question. It is to call an act wrong which may in particular circumstances be right. For what is wrong in one set of circumstances may well be right in another. To take a single instance, it is wrong to tell a lie. True, but is it always wrong? The absolute idealist will say yes. The orthodox moralist will say, "Let me hear of the circumstances before I pass judgment." Let us take a concrete example. In a lonely spot where two roads diverge through a wood you meet a child who takes one road. Shortly afterwards you meet a man who, you know, is bent on her destruction. He asks which road she took. To tell the truth delivers the child to her destroyer. To say the other road is to tell a lie. Must I then tell a lie that good may come? Must I do wrong that good may come?

The absolutist would say no: truth is an absolute value. I should say yes, and moral orthodoxy would approve, and so would the mass of all sane and moral people.

To the charge that I should be doing wrong that evil might come, I should retort: I am doing what in one set of circumstances would be wrong and in another is right because the rightness or wrongness of any act must be judged by its whole context, by its ultimate context, and not by any absolutist standard; it must be judged by its benefit, or otherwise, towards all human life, my own and others. This does not undermine the general rule that truthfulness is a duty. It does refuse to divorce truthfulness from its context and make it into an "absolute"; to make it a rule to be rigidly observed though the heavens fall.

Take another case. Violence is wrong. Must violence then never be used? If your sister is violated must you never use force against her assailant? The absolutists in theory would say no. The real absolutist of the East does say no and tries to practise his theory with a thoroughness from which his Western theoretical armchair absolutist would certainly shrink. The pacificism to which the absolutist doctrine of non-violence logically leads and which many such absolutists preached in times of peace—which indeed, incidentally, encouraged Hitler to think that he could attack us with impunity, and which prevented the presentation of a common front against him—broke down in time of totalitarian war: Did not Joad and Bertrand Russell and many more leave, for a time, the pacifist camp?

In the East men are more thorough, more logical. The principle of the sacredness of any and every form of life is exalted into a religious principle; its observance into an absolute law. Buddhism, which not only refuses a diet of animal flesh, or to brush away an insect from the face, will in its stricter sects command you to wear a veil over your mouth lest inadvertently you swallow a fly. They would leave insects in world possession as our less thoroughgoing pacifists would leave Hitler in possession.

Those who shrink from such lengths of the absolutist position still find in non-violence a Western and Christian virtue and use its non-observance in the stern events of Russia in the last quarter of a century as a stick with which to beat the Soviet Union, pointing to the violence of its early days: the death of the Tsar, the elimination of the Kulaks, the ruthlessness of the purges. Russia's answer to these charges would probably run as follows:

You, they would say, were determined at all costs, with violence if need be, to prevent Hitler from putting the shackles on your hands and your children's hands. You would sacrifice millions of lives to prevent it. Why, then, take a high moral platform and preach at us, who at the cost of a few thousand lives, and only by that cost, were enabled to shake off similar shackles which for centuries had crippled our ancestors and now us?

Then, the idealists would say, you justify the wrong?

By no means, they would reply. To call it wrong again is to beg the question. The rightness or wrongness of any act must be judged by its whole context and consequences. In the light of its context it would not be wrong.

And, indeed, no great moralist from Plato to Hegel has departed from this rule of judging by the whole context, least of all in its purity did Christian theory do so, though Protestant and Catholic practice, with its inflexible canon laws and puritan strictness, together with Hebrew practice, has sought to enforce absolute rules and laws.

The Founder of Christianity himself abjured the absolutist attitude. To take the case of the Sabbath, for example. Who shall deny that one day of rest in seven was good for men? Soviet Russia has returned to its observance. Jesus of Nazareth himself observed it: he went on the Sabbath day *as his custom was* into the synagogue. Yet he refused to make it into an "absolute." And did so precisely on the right lines— interest in the welfare of men: the Sabbath was made for man and not man for the Sabbath. Indeed, it was that over-riding concern for man's welfare, even to the cost of smashing conventions to secure it, and for his labour in this direction for the sick, the outcast, the poor, and against the traditions and wealthy privileges of his time, that compassed his death.

The welfare of man: that was, and is, the ultimate test of all goodness and morality. You can't be good apart from human welfare. Rulers are right only if they minister to human welfare.

Thus viewed the gulf between Lenin's action and Christ's shrinks. When Lenin wrote: "We say that our morality is wholly subordinated to the interests of the class struggle of the proletariat," he meant that everything must be subordinated to the release of the common man and the ending of exploitation of man by man. He meant that human need must take precedence of middle-class liberalism, or supernatural absolutes safeguarding sectional interests. Lenin, like Christ, made human welfare the supreme value.

The perfectionist standards which are applied to Soviet society are not applied elsewhere, frequently not even in the private lives and actions of those who employ them in this connexion, perhaps because they not only give a comfortable sense of superiority to the user, but also because they meet a warm welcome from the comfortable classes. They switch criticism from an existing order of society which is peculiarly pleasant to many, and which is endangered, not by the failure, but by the success of the U.S.S.R. Nor is this perfectionist form of attack hard: it is comparatively easy to criticise action in one set of circumstances from the standpoint of action in another and wholly different set.

The real danger, however, of this perfectionist criticism is that it becomes blind to positive achievement. Whilst dwelling perpetually on the absence of formal completeness of absolute ideals it fails to detect and welcome the real, even if imperfect, penetration of reality by the ideal. Because Soviet Russia does not yet possess in full, and even for the time being seems to ignore or underestimate what A. N. Whitehead calls the frills of freedom, it fails to do justice to the massive and positive present achievements of the Soviet Union. When Prometheus of the legend assailed heaven he returned, not with freedom of the press, but with fire to cook food and warm the body. And Russia, the modern Prometheus, in like manner brings back, not freedom of press and such-like valuable things, but the more elementary solid gifts—freedom from want and insecurity, free access to employment, to leisure, to health, to education. These achievements demand cordial welcome.

The perfectionist in effect ignores all these achievements, and concentrating on criticism is welcomed as an ally by those who start with a fundamental hatred of the Soviet order of life. The idealist finds himself in the camp of the reactionary. The transcendent ideal becomes the enemy of the possible ideal.

Russia has made mistakes and blunders and has done many wrong things. What country is innocent? In their place these faults may be noted with a view to their removal. There are many things in Russia which we wish would more quickly pass: the role of the police, for example, or the restrictions on foreign press correspondents. Some are already passing, as we saw recently in the removal of many press restrictions. Russia's growing strength will I am convinced, see Russia's enlarged liberties and Russia's strength will grow with peace and the peaceful activities which she seeks.

We must always remember, too, that a planned economy means restrictions which would be irksome to many of us. Russia is willing to sacrifice the lesser liberties for the sake of the higher liberties. Who can blame her for that. It is the whole picture that must be sought ere judgment is passed on the details.

BOOK XII

SUMMARY

GEORGE BERNARD SHAW describes an experience of his that took "a mob of appetites and organised them into an army of purposes and principles." The same phrase aptly describes the experience of the Soviet peoples. The same process produced the Soviet success. A mighty change from chaos to order in a brief space of time.

We live in a world of change. Geologists and zoologists reveal to us the line which progressive change has pursued throughout the ages, the line the human race would be wise to pursue in each age unless they wish to retrogress like the parasites or shunt themselves into a siding like the rock limpets.

Organisation is the keyword here. Organisation is the line of progressive evolution. The step to the organic from the inorganic, to life from lifelessness is a step in organisation. The step from single-cell to multi-cellular bodies is a step in organisation. The higher mammals mark the peak of the process, possessing a maximal number of parts and a maximal complexity of structure side by side with centralised control: the single brain directing the limbs through highly efficient, instantaneously operating nerve messengers. Mammals are flexible and versatile in action and to a large extent independent of their environment.

Precisely the same steps may likewise be observed in the development of human society, human history continuing the story which natural history began. Single human cells combine to form a social organism. Primitive farmers and industrialists learn to co-operate, relinquishing independence in one direction that they might, by combination, enjoy fuller freedom upon a higher plane; like roped Alpine climbers, who, pooling their powers, aptitudes and resources, rise as a close-knit team to otherwise inaccessible heights. Such steps in higher organisation have led to what we call "civilised living."

And the situation has constantly called for further organisation. Karl Marx, Lenin and Stalin looked out upon a world divided into sovereign states, restricted by no supreme moral law or unifying principle, a world where natural resources—land, mines, minerals, water power or great producing units—remained in private hands, with consequent disintegrating struggle amongst individuals or groups for ownership and control, making hard the practice of comradeship and friendship. Distribution of goods likewise not regulated by need, but by profit.

Against that background, akin to Bernard Shaw's "mob of appetites," examine the experience and present practice of the Soviet Union. In place of the lawless sovereignty of separate states, acknowledging no centre, the dominant one—should such arise—ruthless in its treatment of the culture of others, we see a multi-national state operative throughout a sixth of the world, where the ancient cultures of upwards of 150 nations or national groups are encouraged, cherished and developed, but all are linked together by a common economic bond or control.

In place of selfish unorganised ownership of natural resources and productive and distributive processes we find a highly organised pooling of resources and powers making possible astonishing practical results, and yielding a whole sheaf of rights, privileges and amenities for all: the right to work, the right to rest and leisure, the right to maintenance in old age, in sickness or in loss of capacity to work, the right to education; equality of rights for women with men in all spheres of economic, state, cultural, social and political life, equality of rights of the citizens of the U.S.S.R., irrespective of nationality or race, in all spheres of economic, state, cultural, social and political life; freedom of conscience; freedom of speech, press or assembly; inviolability of person . . . rights side by side with legal enactments on duties and services, such as are enshrined in no other national constitution.

These ample rights and privileges guaranteed to citizens in the U.S.S.R. may not yet be fully realised, Russia is at the beginning of a new civilisation: we at the end of an old one: it is much that they have been formulated and more that they are in process of realisation all along the line and even despite the terrible setback of the war, which sadly curtailed rights and liberties and amenities in all countries alike.

What is there in this Constitution or in general Soviet practice along these lines which does not accord with the standard of judgment declared in simple direct pictorial language by the Founder of Christianity when he said: "I was an hungred, and ye gave me meat: I was thirsty, and ye gave me drink: I was a stranger, and ye took me in: naked, and ye clothed me: I was sick, and ye visited me: I was in prison, and ye came unto me."

This collectivism thus formulated is precisely the collectivism science leads us to anticipate as the next stage in evolutionary advance. It is also precisely the collectivism which makes practical and positive the underlying Christian postulate of friendship and universal brotherhood.

If it is true as Professor John MacMurray suggests—and I believe it is true—that belief in God, whatever else it may involve, at least includes the capacity to live as part of the whole of things in a world that is unified, then there is something not other than religious about the myriad builders of the new Russia, for Soviet Communism seems to have captured the capacity to live as part of the whole of things.

Professor Hocking of Harvard reports the conversation of a member of his college: "A short time ago I was talking with a colleague, a psychiatrist. He said, 'Something has been occurring to me recently which seems to be important. . . . It is a way of taking the miscellany of events which make up the day's impressions of the world. One sees no trend in them. But suppose there were a trend which we cannot define, but can nevertheless have an inkling of. There is certainly some direction in evolution, why not in history? If there were such a trend, then we men could be either with it or against it. To be with it would give a certain peace and settlement, to be against it would involve a subtle inner restlessness. To have confidence in it would be a sort of commitment for better or for worse. I wonder if that is what you mean by religion?'

"'Yes,' I said, 'I think that is the substance of it. The great religious ones seem to have had a certainty that they were going along with the trend of the world. They have had a passion for right living which they conceived of as a cosmic demand.'"

These words might be an echo of Goethe's great saying: "The most singular and deepest themes in the history of the universe and mankind, to which all the rest are subordinate, are those in which there is a conflict between belief and unbelief, and all epochs wherein belief prevails, under which form it will, are splendid, heart-elevating and fruitful."

Precisely so, and it is because in Inna Koulakovskaya, in Karaganov, in Madame Mukhina and her son, in Kapitza—in the common man at one end and in Stalin at the other, with countless Soviet citizens in between—I see men and women inspired by belief, the belief that they are called upon to build and actually are building a new order which falls into line with the upward trend of the world, an order which has for its goal the highest, most intimate and most subtle integration of man with man as a real brotherhood, of mankind based upon equality of freedom, that I am conscious of something splendid, heart-elevating and fruitful in the Union of Soviet Socialist Republics and see there not an enemy but an ally of all that is best in the religions of the world.

THE END

For Product Safety Concerns and Information please contact our EU
representative GPSR@taylorandfrancis.com
Taylor & Francis Verlag GmbH, Kaufingerstraße 24, 80331 München, Germany